ISBN:
0-935180-79-6

AGGIE GREY: A SAMOAN SAGA

Also by Fay Calkins Alailima

MY SAMOAN CHIEF

AGGIE GREY
A Samoan Saga

by FAY ALAILIMA

MUTUAL PUBLISHING COMPANY
HONOLULU • HAWAII

Mutual Publishing
2055 N. King St. #201
Honolulu, Hawaii 96819
Tel. (808) 924-7732
Fax: (808) 943-1689

DEDICATED
To young Samoans
interested in their
lively heritage

TALOFA!

    A BIG WELCOME TO AGGIE GREY'S
HOTEL. WHILE YOU ARE OUR GUESTS,
IT IS OUR WISH THAT YOU COM-
PLETELY RELAX AND TAKE FULL
ADVANTAGE OF OUR WARM AND
FRIENDLY SAMOAN HOSPITALITY.
ANY LITTLE THING I CAN DO TO HELP
MAKE YOUR VISIT WITH US A HAPPY
AND PLEASANT TIME . . . PLEASE BE SO
KIND AS TO CONTACT.

                    YOURS VERY TRULY,

                    AGGIE GREY.

Postcard from Aggie Grey's Hotel.

FOREWORD

I REMEMBER AGGIE

by JAMES A. MICHENER

ANYONE who wants to read a biography that runs on like a novel should not overlook this authentic life story of a cross-cultural woman who spent ninety years demonstrating her ultimate unconquerable spirit in an exotic time and place.

Aggie Grey: A Samoan Saga, the life of the most celebrated hotelkeeper in the South Pacific, begins a hundred years ago when Willie Swann, roving son of a British colonialist, fell in love at first sight with Pele, fifteen-year-old daughter of a battling Samoan chieftain. The combination of romantic aspiration and sound business acumen inherited from these parents appeared in Agnes, usually called "Aggie," part of a robust, inter-ethnic clan that fought to survive all the challenges of modern history in the two Samoas—Western and American. They faced the tumults of internecine tribal wars; German and New Zealand occupation; two World Wars; epidemics; depression; the attainment of independence as a Pacific nation; and the maintaining of a constitutional democracy in a time when other Pacific groups are up in arms against the vestiges of colonialism.

For many years it has been argued that the twenty-first century will be the Century of the Pacific, during which history will record the confrontation or collaboration of the powerful nations that rim the Pacific Ocean. Between the Americas and Asia lie the island groups of Oceania. In many of these groups, a nativistic revolution is currently raging, a reaction against Western acculturation.

From the aborigine protests at the two-hundreth anniversary of the settlement of Australia and the Maori unrest in New Zealand, violent outbreaks have occurred northward in New Caledonia and in Vanuatu, where the people of the former New Hebrides have offered concessions to the Soviet Union. The tiny isle of Nauru has also opened diplomatic relations with Moscow. The Tahitians have for years protested the French nuclear tests on Moruoa, and the former crown colony of Fiji is an inter-ethnic shambles. The "Hawaiian Renaissance" is a more peaceful and laudatory expression of a yearning for the simplicities of the years before the arrival of Captain James Cook. Among all these rebellions, the proud people of the two Samoas have almost forgotten their legacies of civil strife, and the chiefly husband of the author of *Aggie Grey* is currently holding a seat in the national legislature from the district of Aiga-ile-Tai on the capital island of Upolu.

Fay Calkins Alailima, his American-born wife, published some years ago a chucklesome volume called *My Samoan Chief,* about her marriage and family in the islands. Now she has offered a well-researched life story of the most cele-brated resident of Western Samoa. Aggie Grey's fame and fortune, however, are recent fruits of a hard existence that overcame catastrophes of several kinds — bankruptcies, bereavements, and ill-starred love affairs. The biography is based on solid study and interviews with many leading characters in the story, and forms a refreshing review of Samoa's modern history. It is no wonder that a few years ago, the portrait of Aggie Grey, proprietress of Apia's foremost hostelry, appeared on Western Samoa's postage stamp.

I first became acquainted with Aggie's achievements when, during World War II, I was stationed on American Samoa and, like all other United States navy personnel, I connived at ways of traveling the short distance to what was then called British Samoa. The reason we longed to get to Apia was twofold: to get a taste of the excellent island food that Aggie Grey provided at her palm-thatched hotel, and to join her and the beautiful Samoan girls who appeared at night to dance the famous *siva-siva.* Often I sat along the edges of her lovely garden, leading the chorus of "Tofa, My Feleni" (Goodby My Friend) as the moon came up and the beer went down. They were among the finest nights I would spend in Polynesia, a wonderful respite from the battles farther west. In those wartorn years, Aggie made a multitude of friends who would return to Samoa in the decades ahead, whenever opportunity allowed.

After the war, I myself was able to observe, as a roving

travel writer, the amenities of the ever-expanding Aggie's Hotel on Apia's shore, and to share with most other Pacific wanderers the warm friendship of this elfin, steel-cored islander. I recall that a former guest, a disgruntled correspondent, spread the rumor that Aggie Grey was the "original" of my South Pacific character, Bloody Mary. How anyone could compare this charming *afakasi* lady of Apia with the Tonkinese plantation worker of New Caledonia, who sold shrunken human heads for fifty dollars, is still mystifying to me. During Aggie's final visit to New Zealand in 1985, which she made in spite of crippling ailments to meet once more with me, we sang Polynesian songs and chuckled again about the Bloody Mary slander.

Aggie Grey: A Samoan Saga, despite its scholarly underpinnings (it is accompanied by maps and four appendices), is a lively addition to the current literary landscape. It is truly a saga of a Pacific heroine whose like will probably never be seen again.

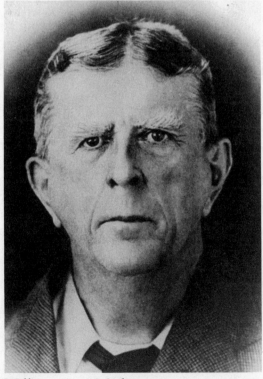

Willie — Aggie's father.

PREFACE

This is the story of Aggie Grey and her two communities in Western Samoa. Between the time Aggie's father arrived in Apia in 1888 and her own eightieth birthday ninety years later, the business community in Apia and the traditional community in the countryside witnessed some amazing events, often caused by the juxtaposition of their very different ways of life. Aggie had roots in both cultures and, like many *afakasi* (part-Samoans), felt these tensions and confusions within herself. She managed to blend her British grandfather's economic drive with her mother's Samoan manner of relating to people. But it was not an easy combination.

How much of this story is true? Historical events are as accurate as research in books and periodicals could make them. A bibliography and footnotes are given in Appendix A-1. The events of Aggie's life are taken from thirty hours of taped interviews with her and her sisters and friends. Dialogues, letters, dreams, and interpretations are the author's; only the footnoted quotations are exact.

Samoan words do not translate easily into English. *Fale* and *afakasi* translated as "house" and "half-caste" may give an erroneous impression. In Apia the term "European" includes Americans. To ease the problem without forcing the reader to master a new vocabulary, short translations of confusing terms are given in parenthesis. Careful readers will find a more detailed description of such words in the Glossary (Appendix B-1). Pronunciation of Samoan words is assisted by orthographic marks. As in Western Samoa, the marks are used sparingly in the text, primarily to prevent confusion between similar words. In the Glossary, however, they are entered in full as in Milner's dictionary.

Some concepts like *tamaaiga*, *pule* and *tumua*, and *tafaifa* cannot be defined at all without some explanation of Samoa's traditional political institutions. A simplified description of these is provided in Appendix B-2. It may help the reader understand the Samoan viewpoint on events of the last century, and also why tension is created in a person trying to get ahead in both worlds at once.

A book like this is not the work of one person. The author wishes to thank Aggie, Maggie, Mary, Allan, Marina, and their many friends. They generously shared the personal experiences which give the characters and events a human perspective. The author is also grateful to Samoa's departed champions who engineered the events, and to the libraries in which she found their stories: the Nelson Library in Apia, the Pacific Collection of the Hamilton Library at the University of Hawaii, and the Nelson Collection in the New Zealand Archives. She is especially grateful to her husband, Chief Leiataua Amituanai Vaiao Alailima, and his relatives for their patient efforts to acquaint her with the Samoan viewpoint and traditional political system.

This book would also never have materialized without facilities, advice, and sabbatical time provided by various divisions of the University of Hawaii, including: the Pacific Island Studies Program, the University Press, and Leeward Community College. John Mayer of the Department of Indo-European Languages provided his expertise with Samoan words and orthography. Especially forbearing have been the editors, proofreaders, and typists who helped shape up the tapes and manuscript: Louise Drollinger, Freda Hellinger, Sharon Sutter, Irene Hoebel, Terza Meller, Merrily Stover, Kit Glover, and A. Grove Day. Many thanks!

Fay Alailima

CONTENTS

PART VI. MATURITY

APPENDICES

List of Illustrations

PART I

ROOTS

Pele — Aggie's mother.

Chapter 1

The Warship and the Village

(January 22, 1888)

DARKNESS was sweeping over a restless South Pacific. In the engine room of the rusty warship *Mohican* a sweating sailor turned up the engine. In the chartroom above, Commander Day lit a swaying lantern, blew the soot from his log book, and slowly penned "January 22, 1888." He followed this with the dullest possible entry, only praying he could keep it that way for the next five months. Tomorrow at dawn they would enter Apia harbor, where they would relieve the U.S.S. *Adams.* This stupid little Samoan port had nearly cost him his commission two years ago and he had no intention of taking that risk again. But anything could happen in a place where three local "kings" and four European consuls vied for an island forty-eight miles long and twelve miles wide.

He sighed and sent for the new pharmacist-mate he had picked up in Fiji two days before. That scrawny little Britisher was now his only medic and he needed to know more about him in case the bullets started flying. Bum luck having to leave old Doc Sam back in Suva. It hadn't been the DT's this time but a high fever that had knocked him off his rocker.

"Meningitis," the port doctor had declared. "It's nip if he stays but tuck him under for sure if he goes on."

"But we are a warship, sir," Day had protested. "We sail at dawn and regulations call for a medic on board."

The doctor had shrugged. "All Suva can offer you at the moment, commander, is my young assistant here. Not a doctor, mind you, but a pretty fair chemist. Trained in England. He's picked up a bit of doctoring helping me give anesthetics the last six months."

Day had turned to look at the nondescript young man behind them. Even his leonine mustache and buttoned

1

waistcoat failed to give him a doctorly appearance, but there was a spark of eagerness in his eyes.

"The kid wants out for some reason," the commander thought, and indeed the young man agreed to a three-year tour without even asking where they were going. Day was so relieved to find a medic that he had made no further inquiries. But now they were approaching a sensitive duty station he needed to know more. What medical experience had the young man had? Why was he so anxious to leave home?

A few moments later two close-set gray eyes peered cautiously around the bulkhead. "Come in and sit down," the commander called to his new recruit. "Tell me something about yourself, son," he prompted as the little medic sat down uneasily on the edge of the bench twisting his hands.

"The name is Swann, sir. Willie Swann out of Suva."

"And how does a young Englishman like you find himself in Fiji?" the commander asked. His kindly tone loosed a flood from Willie.

"Well, sir, my father had a chemist shop in Staffordshire but times were hard. He heard about a settlement scheme in New Zealand and took our family down there. Tried setting up his chemist shop near Christchurch but times were hard there too. He read that long-staple cotton was doing well in Fiji, so we went over there in 1867, cleared a hundred acres of rainforest up the Rewa, and planted cotton."

"And made your fortune," Day concluded to speed the tale.

"Not exactly, sir," the boy replied honestly, "but he did make enough to buy a bottling machine. He moved us to Levuka and set up the first cordial factory in Fiji. Have you ever seen the sign on the wharf there: J.B. Swann—Cordials?"

Since the *Mohican* had never put into Levuka, Day shook his head and tried to get back to the point. "But how did you get into doctoring?"

"Mom had seven of us by that time," Willie went on, "and she had aristocratic tastes. She wanted a big house on a hill, so dad bought out old Ryley's Medical Hall and ran a chemist shop as well as the cordial factory. This time

2

he did very well. He was famous for fine fresh leeches. He built Mom a house with marble steps and bought a plantation on Koro island. He sent three of us boys back to England to apprentice in pharmacy. Now Frederick runs the Levuka chemist shop. Arthur and I were sent to Suva to open another. My brother Herbert manages Burns Philps in Levuka as well as the plantation on Koro and—"

"If Swanns are doing so well," the commander interrupted, to stem the tide, "why were you so keen to get away? Girl trouble?"

That did it! Willie stopped talking and a bright flush rose from his collar. He finally managed to stammer. "Oh, no, sir! It's not at all what you think. Cecilia St. Julian is a very fine girl, sir. She has promised to wait 'til I return."

The commander gave him a quizzical look, but Willie could not explain his desire to escape even to himself. It was just too ridiculous!

Marguerita, his mother, had greatly admired the St. Julian family ever since Sir Charles St. Julian had arrived in Levuka as chief justice for Cakabau's kingdom. His "Sir" title had brought culture to her bleak wilderness even though the distinction was of Hawaiian rather than British derivation. She had already destined her oldest daughter, Margaret, for the church, but she was determined to marry as many of the others as she could to St. Julians. Fortunately Sir Charles had nine children.

Fredrick had dutifully married a St. Julian girl, and Herbert St. Julian had married Willie's sister Mary and, when she died, his sister Agnes. Pretty little Cecilia St. Julian had been earmarked for Willie. She and Willie had played together since childhood. She was a nice girl and Willie knew what he was supposed to do. For five years now, Cecilia had been eagerly waiting, but for some reason he just could not pop the question. His mother was upset. All her other children had "jelled" nicely. They had married well and settled in business. But here was Willie, twenty-nine, and still "sloshing around." The trouble with him was that he was a hopeless romantic. He had run away from Arthur's chemist shop to tour the islands as interpreter for the Duke of Windsor. Then he had taken a job with the port doctor because he was curious about anesthetics. Such whimsical tendencies would never support a St.

3

Julian girl! Marguerita could not understand why Willie never grew up.

Neither could Willie. When he had kissed Cecilia goodbye last night, she had wept and promised to "wait for him forever." That was faithfulness any man should appreciate, but he had given her only a vague response. He longed to be crazily, hopelessly in love and somehow he just wasn't.

Noting that his medic's attention had wandered, Day sought to retrieve it by changing the subject. "Do you know where we are headed now, son?" he asked.

Willie shook his head as if to clear his mind.

"Samoa!" Day practically shouted at him. "You know what happened to me down there two years ago? Well, now it's my turn to tell *you* a story.

"There's a German on that island named Weber. He wants land, lots of land, so his Hamburg firm can supply Europe with coconuts. He and his German consul have found an easy way to get it, too. Samoans take kingship seriously. They now have three rivals for their 'crown' and Weber sells guns to them all. Since none of them have money, he is only too happy to take his pay in land. Why, he even got 'King' Malietoa to sell his capitol seat at Mulinuu and then threw him off for trespassing!

"Malietoa didn't take that lightly. He walked right over to our U.S. consul's office and asked him for help in getting his 'capitol' back. Our consul didn't like what the Germans were doing any better than the 'king,' but what could he do? There was a German squadron out in the harbor, and he didn't have a rowboat to his name!

"He told the 'king' to lie low for a couple of weeks, knowing that I was on my rounds with the *Mohican*. Meanwhile Weber and the German consul decided to install their own favorite 'king,' Tamasese, out at Mulinuu. They sent a German artillery officer named Brandeis out to train his warriors, and the German squadron left, assuming everything was now under control.

"You can imagine how upset Weber and his consul were when I sailed into the harbor on the *Mohican* and gave Malietoa a twenty-one-gun salute! The American consul told the 'king' to go right back out to his seat at Mulinuu while I held it in my cannon range. The Germans were now

4

the ones without the rowboat! All the German consul could do was ask us to sign a joint proclamation that neither country had the slightest interest in native politics. We agreed, providing he first haul down his German flag, over the Samoan council grounds.

"Now, wouldn't you say the U.S. consul and I deserved a medal for saving Samoa from the Germans without firing a shot?" The commander jabbed the question at Willie with his cigar.

"Of course, sir!" the medic replied wide-eyed, his attention fully restored.

"Then you're a damn sight smarter than Washington," the commander responded bitterly. "The State Department cited our consul for exceeding his authority, and I damn near lost my Navy commission. This time I'm carrying written orders not to interfere with anything ashore, and believe me I don't intend to mess around with Samoan 'kings' again. But just let me catch a German warship lurking around the harbor and I'll spread some bloody bodies on the waves!"

He settled back to enjoy the consternation on Willie's face as it dawned on the young man that he had inadvertently signed on a warship in his eagerness to seek romance. Even worse, he was its only medic. He would be the one responsible for any "bloody bodies on the waves." Willie finally collected his wits enough to ask, "What's happening in Samoa now, sir?"

"Who knows?" the commander laughed. "But there is one bit of advice we Americans always give to pharmacist-mates like you: keep your powder dry!"

The commander's guffaw followed Willie all the way back to his cabin.

A hundred miles to the north the same sunset was falling across the thatched roofs of Toamua village on Upolu island in the Samoa group. Chief Pepe Maiava sat at the edge of his stone platform, a strand of coconut fiber forgotten on his tattooed thigh. He had been braiding sennit twine for months to bind new thatches on his oval roof but that project was now irrelevant. He gazed around the circle of small thatched houses. Only a low stone pig fence and a grove of bushes separated Toamua from the sandy beach. Everything looked so peaceful in the fading light that it was hard to believe things could change. He could hear his wife Simativa in the cookhouse behind, telling twelve-year-old Misi to feed the chickens. He could catch the sound of the shell as fifteen-year-old Pele scraped a breadfruit. He recognized Cousin Kala's low grunt as she lifted an iron pot onto the open fire. Their evening meal was under way as usual, but tonight he treasured each familiar sound, his heart heavy with foreboding. Soon the family would gather for family prayers and he would have to tell them. Tomorrow they would be cast asunder like a broken canoe in heavy seas.

The crickets tuned up their evening song, only to be drowned out by the boom of a hollow log drum on the bluff in front of the church. It was the signal for evening prayers. Pepe watched as his neighbors scurried under their thatched domes. Then he turned to face his own family coming in from the rear. Simativa lifted down rolls of pandanus mats from the rafters and unrolled them across the pebble floor with a shake. Then she sat down beside him. There were nine in the family tonight: his wife, their son Misi and daughter Pele, a brother with his wife and child, Simativa's widowed mother, and cousin Kala, the perennial spinster.

Hymns began to sound across the grass, first from one house then another. A few moments later the shadows were filled with sonorous prayers. Pepe made his longest and loudest of all, to alert the family that something serious was to follow. After the final "Amene" they waited patiently in the gathering darkness. Pele lighted a kerosene lamp and the family circled around it. Finally Pepe began to talk in a low voice.

"No matter what may happen in the next few days, remember you have three families where you can always get food and protection. One is your mother's family under high chief Seumanutafa in Apia village. The others are my title groups: the Pepe's in this house, and the Maiavas on the stone platform up the road. Serve these three families well, for you will need them. Someday you may even hold their titles. Pele is already a *taupou* (ceremonial maiden)."

They nodded, wondering why he was reviewing this so carefully tonight.

6

"We live in Faleata district," Pepe continued. "Faleata has two *malae* (meeting grounds), where its villages meet to make important decisions: Lepea the *malae* of peace and Vaitagutu the *malae* of war. Tomorrow we meet on Vaitagutu!"

Simativa gasped. For as long as she could remember, Faleata chiefs had not gathered on their *malae* of war. What was happening? True, she had felt tension in the village the last two years, men slipping in and out at night with guns wrapped in tapa and rolled in sleeping mats. But she had never asked Pepe about it; politics was chiefly business. Nor had she discussed it with her neighbors. Who knew what side they might be on? Many of them, like Pepe Maiava, could trace their bloodlines to all three contenders for the "crowns" and carefully nurtured them all to be sure to emerge with a winner. But now something unusual was happening. The chiefs of Faleata were sufficiently united to declare themselves publicly behind one candidate and even go to war for him!

Pepe already knew they would support Mataafa Iosefo. He was not only a *tama aiga* eligible for the "crowns"; he was popular because he had no time for European ways. Samoa's traditional institutions were good enough for him. It took a crisis to unite Samoa's great extended family behind one royal contender, but interference by European consuls in Samoan politics had provided one. Several years ago the Germans had run Malietoa Laupepa out of Mulinuu, which had been his seat since 1867. They had tried to replace him with their own favorite "king," Tamasese. Malietoa had been restored briefly by the American warship *Mohican*. But as soon as it had left, the Germans had exiled him to the Marshall Islands and restored their Tamasese. Their own leader gone, Malietoa supporters turned to Mataafa. When the Germans ordered Tamasese to declare a head tax on every Samoan man, woman, and child on pain of forfeiting their land, Mataafa gained support from almost every angry village in Samoa. But the climax came when the Germans and a few supporters declared Tamasese *tafaifa* without consulting the *tumua* (ranking orators of Upolu), who were supposed to award this highest title. They too turned to Mataafa. Not since Vaiinupo (1830) had Samoa been so strongly united! All

7

over the island families were collecting fine mats, food, and warriors. They would soon show Tamasese and his Germans how "kings" are really made in Samoa!

At Vaitagutu tomorrow the chiefs of Faleata would show their support by addressing Mataafa by the four component titles of the *tafaifa*. After the meeting Pepe would lead a party of young men from Toamua to rendezvous with other village warriors at a cave in the hills above Apia. Though he was too old for the full rigors of bush warfare, Pepe tingled at the prospect.

But he was also concerned about his wife and children. Where would they be safe while he was away? Toamua lay only across a shallow bay from Mulinuu. A practical solution had occurred to him. In 1879 a British high commissioner from Fiji had negotiated with Malietoa Talavou for a protected area *(eleelesa)* for Europeans around Apia. The chiefs had agreed not to carry on Samoan warfare within those boundaries. The 350 Europeans in that area were to be governed by their three consuls and protected by their warships. Two traditional villages, however, Apia and Matafele, found themselves incorporated within the European refuge area. Seumanutafa, Simativa's adopted father, was high chief of the former village. What place could be safer for her and the children?

Pepe did not bother to explain all this to the family. He simply said, "War is coming and it may not be safe in Toamua. Until it is over I want you to stay with Seumanutafa in Apia village. Pack your things and walk over there at dawn tomorrow. I will come to visit you as often as I can."

He pushed his Bible and hymnal back to indicate that the family meeting was over and it was time to retire. Pele rose without a word to hang a tapa across the end of the house, pile her parents' sleeping mats, and lay out their bamboo headrests. After this she turned down the lamp and lay down with the others, scarcely able to grasp the fact that this might be her last night in this house.

Pepe lay on his back a long time, listening to the chirp of the crickets. The rest of the family might sleep but he could not. The events of the last few days had revived the old bitterness in him. He seldom talked about it any more. What God gives, God takes away! But tonight his lost

8

pride battered him like a storm. He was willing to use the European's protected area for his family, but he could never forgive them for what they had done to him.

Along with his two titles he had acquired a few small sections of the flat rich land stretching behind Toamua to the mountains. Planted with coconuts, bananas, and taro, these provided plenteously for his family. As a young chief he had gained considerable prominence by gambling this land on his fighting cocks. He smiled as he recalled his seven roosters, especially his champion cock *(toa)*, the terror of Faleata. Pepe had challenged every comer and eventually won a lot of land in Faleata. His, however, was a Samoan form of suzerainty. He would never think of driving a family off its land. How would they survive? Instead, he required the vanquished to address him as victor *(malo)* and send donations of food and fine mats to his ceremonies. As a result Pepe's sumptuous weddings, funerals, and dedications had brought his family and village great renown. Hundreds of people were invited and everyone was given a basket of food to take home. His own village gratefully renamed itself Toamua (leading cock) in honor of Pepe's champion bird.

British missionaries had finally forced Pepe to renounce this rewarding avocation. To them cockfighting was primitive, and a sin against God's creatures. But they compensated Pepe by making him a lay preacher.

Later, a German named Mr. Weber had appeared in Faleata looking for land for his "long-handle firm" (Deutsche Handels und Plantagen Gesellschaft). At first Pepe had ignored the squat little German who, like himself, enjoyed gambling for land. It was the fate of Vaitele village that finally made Pepe aware that Weber viewed ownership differently. Vaitele, like Toamua, had always used the flat, rich lands below the mountains for raising food. But one day a crew of "blackboys" (Solomon Islanders) appeared with an armed overseer and began to put a fence around Vaitele's coconuts.[3]

When High Chief Galumalemana ran out to object, he was informed that five hundred acres, including even the village *malae* (meeting ground), had been sold by his cousin Tamasese to DH&PG for fifty-one guns. Mr. Weber had both the deed to prove it and the guns to enforce it.

All the people of Vaitele could do was move in with relatives down the road and sneak back at night to steal their own coconuts. They were so skillful at the latter that Weber published endless warnings to "thieves" in his German newspaper, as if Samoans could read it. He even tried to fine Malietoa for "not controlling his people."

Thinking of this burning injustice, Pepe fell into an uneasy sleep. He dreamed he was a gambler again. His champion cock *(toa)* was in his arms, green-black tail feathers glistening, passionately eager for the fray. Across the pit Pepe caught sight of his opponent. It was Mr. Weber! On his wrist was an extraordinarily ugly bird, heavily beaked and battleship gray.

"My land against yours!" Pepe challenged proudly.

Mr. Weber nodded coldly.

Confident that *Toa* would be victorious, the Samoan crowd roared as the two birds met. A moment later their proud cock lay bleeding on the sand.

Pepe knelt and cradled the dying bird in his arms. Weber stood haughtily above him. Pepe glanced up at the bird with cruel eyes and powerful talons which had torn apart his treasure. It was a German eagle!

"You are victor *(malo)*!" he murmured humbly to Weber.

His tone was deferential; the man's eagle was indeed superior in strength. But Pepe's heart was full of anger and confusion. The German had changed the rules of the game. He played with land for keeps!

Chapter 2

Meeting

(January 23-25, 1888)

THE *MOHICAN* rounded Pilot Point at dawn and entered Apia harbor trailing smoke. The young pharmacist-mate stood at her bow peering anxiously through the rising mist. All he could see was a ramshackle line of wooden houses and three steeples along a shingle beach. They were separated from the mountains by a wide mangrove swamp. Everything was completely quiet except for the calls of the frigate birds; no shouting warriors, no gunfire, no cannon salutes. Off to his right a narrow spit of sand curved out to a desultory stand of coconuts. Could that possibly be Mulinuu, the "capitol" contended by Samoan "kings" and European empires? After the commander's description, Apia was a real let-down.

But the *Mohican* was not alone in the harbor that morning. She cast her line next to her sister warship, the U.S.S. *Adams.* And across the mirroring water a third huge iron hulk seemed to float in the brightening sky. Willie could make out a German flag and the name on her stern, *Adler.*

He stood and watched as the beachfront gradually wakened. Presently a dozen tiny canoes manned by lithe brown boys darted towards them from the shore. Their hollowed log craft rolled precariously as laughing paddlers stood up waving bunches of bananas and bottles of sea slugs.

An hour later a more sedate whaleboat detached itself from the wharf and Willie could make out six barebacked rowers with two Europeans in waistcoats waving orders in the stern. Apia's American and British consuls no doubt, coming out to tell Commander Day what's afoot in Samoa now. It was the following morning, however, before Willie got the news. His friend, a blond American officer, appeared at the pharmacy suffering from indul-

11

gence in a bottle of sea slugs. While Willie examined him, the officer described the meeting.

"The consuls told Day that after he left two years ago the Germans deported Malietoa and installed their favorite 'king,' Tamasese, at Mulinuu."

"Didn't the Samoans object?" Willie asked.

"I doubt it," the officer laughed. "They are simple, childlike people; all they do is make love. But the American and British merchants are sure hot as hell. They can't buy village copra anymore because the Germans are impounding it for taxes."

"Well, now the *Mohican* and *Adams* are both here, couldn't the German consul be persuaded to change his mind?" Willie asked. "He's only got the *Adler*."

"That's exactly what the consuls told Day," the officer smiled. "They want us to occupy Mulinuu just long enough to bring Malietoa back."

"And what did Day tell them?" Willie asked.

"That he wouldn't fire one shot," the officer laughed. "That man's not going to risk his career again, believe me! As far as he's concerned, all we're going to do 'til the *Adams* returns is sit here and look at the *Adler*. By June we'll both be dead of boredom!"

"Not if Samoan girls just live for love." Willie winked and they broke out laughing.

At noon Willie finally got permission to go ashore. The whaleboat was full of young American crewmen already boasting about their prowess with local "Marys." They traded stories about Bully Hayes, who brained his mate with a tiller, and Black Bill Henry of the Eagle Hotel, as if these long-departed heroes of Apia's waterfront had been their personal friends.

The wharf rolled under Willie's sea legs as he clambered up and its rancid butter smell flicked him back to trips from Koro astride the copra sacks with his best friend, John Bell. John was older than Willie. Some years ago he had married and set off for Samoa as a teacher. Willie intended to look him up first thing. He declined the invitation of the American crewmen to join them scouting bars, saying he was "off to find a friend."

"Send her our love," they leered. You could never tell about these close-mouthed little Englishmen.

Left alone in the noonday sun, Willie caught sight of an American flag across the road above a signboard reading "H.J. Moors. General Merchant." He crossed the dirt track and peered in the door. The store itself was empty but he caught sight of a white man in the back office. He was sound asleep with his feet on a desk.

"Sorry to disturb you, sir," Willie said politely, "but would you happen to know a family named Bell?"

The feet lowered slowly to the floor; the man opened his eyes and stared at Willie. "And who might you be?" he asked. When Willie introduced himself, the storekeeper scratched his head slowly as if searching for something, "Swann? Oh, of course! Swann's Cordials. Levuka."

Having discovered a connection, Moors treated Willie like a long-lost relative and invited him in for a cup of tea. Within a few minutes he was telling him the story of his life.[1]

"Ten years ago I fetched ashore here just like you. I was off a sailing ship, the *Ada Mae*. The cook had told me to stake my pay on a bag of potatoes and a bag of onions from the ship's store. Best advice I ever got. I traded them ashore the same day for a trunk of yard goods and a tin of kerosene and hopped aboard a longboat for Savaii. First village we pulled in at was so keen on tradin' they offered me two *fale* (Samoan houses) and all I could eat for two dollars a month. Three months later I was gettin' along in the lingo and sendin' back a boatload of copra to Apia every fortnight. Before the year was up I had saved enough to move back here myself.

"I bought into partnership with an old German named Grevsmuhl and two years later got this place of my own. Apia was great for business in those days, no customs, no taxes, no government—a man could be his own boss. We were all traders then. It was that German Weber and his Hamburg firm who started the idea of raising coconuts instead of just buyin' them. But that required land and roads, and a government to enforce claims and punish stealin'. But as soon as he started, of course we all had to get into the action. I must say I didn't do bad for myself.

"What was the result? Too damned much government. Consuls and courtrooms on every corner and Germans grabbin' the village copra for taxes. Now I'm losin' my shirt! What your *Mohican* should do is level one blast at Mulinuu. That's all it would take to stop the Germans and their 'king.' Otherwise they'll soon take over the island."

"Commander Day is under strict orders from Washington not to interfere with politics ashore," Willie told him.

"Do they think for one moment that the Kaiser would actually go to war for this God-forsaken rock?" the merchant asked. "That's just a bluff! Well, if Day won't stop them, I guess MacArthur and I will have to do it for him. We've got a royal contender of our own, you know, with enough warriors to send old Tamasese and his Germans packin'. If we stake *him* to a few guns, we'll soon get our copra back!"

Willie was profoundly shocked. "Should Europeans take advantage of simple, childlike people that way?" he asked, recalling the officer's description of Samoans.

Moors nearly fell of his chair laughing. "If you think Samoans are simple, you're the childlike one, my boy. They have a political system that makes ours look like a toy. And political savvy! When an orator says, 'Thank God you have come,' you're about to lose your shirt, my friend!"

Willie hastily repeated his inquiry about the Bells.

"Oh, so you know our school teachers!" Moors exclaimed. "But of course, they're also from Levuka. Just turn right at my front door and keep going down Beach Road 'til you reach the Vaisigano River. First house beyond the bridge."

Following these directions, Willie had no trouble locating a weathered, clapboard house with a wide veranda behind a hibiscus hedge. As he approached the steps he saw someone moving in the back and called out "Jane!"

A worn-looking woman in a long skirt and high-button shoes appeared in the doorway shading her eyes. As soon as she recognized Willie, she grabbed him into a hug, calling "John! John! Come see who's here!"

"School's just out," she explained to Willie as she motioned a girl to push back the heavy wooden forms and bring some chairs. John appeared at the doorway. The sight of Willie surprised him out of a yawn. They sat right down to exchange news. Willie explained how he hap-

14

pened to be on the warship and John described his school.

Most of his students, he explained, were *afakasi* (part Samoan). White women were so scarce that European traders and planters often took Samoan wives, who were better able to cope with the climate and house girls. Mixed blood carried no particular stigma and John felt his charges would someday be the elite of the European enclave. He offered to show Willie around it next day.

"Won't take long," he laughed.

Their tour began the following afternoon at the Vaisigano bridge.

"When Jane and I arrived," John said, "the only way to cross the river was to swim or ring a bell. An old Samoan would come over on a flatboat and pull you back along a cable for three pennies. The first bridge was built by an American named Williamson. It had to be replaced after every flood. That's his shack on the town side.[2] Samoans called him *ai polo* (eat-hot-peppers) because that's what he bought from them. He died four years ago but his daughter still lives there. The place seems to be falling down."

Williamson's shack was surrounded by marsh, but beyond that the shingle widened and a fashionable house of "slates"[3] was being built. John explained that it was for a well-known East Anglian settler named Westbrook, who had jumped ship some time ago and now owned a large store.

Next they came to Apia Protestant Church with a steep roof and short steeple. The Bells and many of their students belonged to its English-speaking congregation. Missionaries had originally started it for their own families. They had first met in a tiny "iron chapel" hauled in on the mission ship *John Williams*, but it had proved so stifling that they built this wooden structure.

Beyond the American consulate and Westbrook's store, they paused in the shade of an enormous *talie* tree and John pointed to a cluster of thatched houses in the rear.

"That's Apia village, which the harbor was named for," John explained to Willie. "It's one of two Samoan villages left inside our European protected area. About four hundred Samoans live there under a chief named Seumanutafa. That's their native church across the Siumu track."

Willie looked curiously at his first Samoan village, cramped between the European structures along the shoreline and the marsh. Carriages were apparently confined to Beach Road. The track John mentioned was only a path crisscrossed with pig fences.

Beyond the British consulate and MacArthur's store, they came to a second inland track called Leifiifi and John pointed to a crumbling European mansion on their left.[4]

"No one wants to live there," he whispered mysteriously. "It was built by a wealthy Frenchman named St. Foy, who was found murdered in his bed."

As they passed Moors' store, Willie described meeting the merchant the previous day and John laughed, "You should do well here. Five minutes ashore and you're closeted with our most energetic merchant — and politician."

The blistering sun had made them thirsty by the time they reached a sign reading "Family & Commercial Hotel." Through a swinging door Wille could hear the raucous laughter of his friends from the *Mohican*. He offered to buy John a beer.

"Might as well enjoy it while you can," his friend replied. "DH&PG just bought this old place and is going to turn it into a hostel for its workers."

Inside it was refreshingly dim. Willie caught sight of the blond American officer and they took their glasses to his table. After introductions the three of them tipped their chairs against the wall while John told them the story of its former owner, Emma Coe, a part-Samoan girl.

"Did you know her?" the officer asked.

"Unfortunately not," John said. "She's been gone for years but I did meet her once in Sydney, where they call her 'Queen of the South Seas.' Her dad still lives out near Pilot Point. At fifteen he was shipwrecked and floated into Savaii on a spar. The Malietoa family adopted him and he stayed until some missionary found him and sent him back to New York. He missed the islands and by '45 was back again. Just a roustabout, but he still had the lingo and connections. He married a real beaut from the Malietoa clan and had eight children by her, all of whom, thank God, took after their mother.

"Emma was her second and the pick of the crop — heavy hair, doe eyes, dusky skin, tall and slender-waisted.

That girl was smart as a whip and hot as a poker! Used to swim out to meet her seafaring lovers as they sailed into the harbor. Everyone loved Emma except missionary wives."

By his third beer, Willie had Emma's outlines firmly in mind and could well understand her problem with missionaries.

"Great head for business too," John continued. "Old Jonas never prospered until she began to run his store. But as she came into flower, he saw trouble coming and married her off quick to an old Scotch sea captain named Forsayth, who owned a store but spent most of his time at sea.

"Don't ask me how, but Emma had two children by the old man. She hated him with a passion from the moment he tried to send her to school in New Zealand. She wasn't a bit cut up when he sailed off one day and never returned. There she was, young, beautiful, footloose and fancy free!

"Her fancy ran to adventurers like a bright-eyed, black-mustached rascal named Steinberger, who popped up here about '73 saying he was sent by the American government. Before you know it she was not only his mistress but his liaison with the chiefs. She translated for him as he went around the villages and, thanks to her version, they soon viewed him as their savior. Malietoa made him prime minister and had him draw up a constitution forbidding the sale of Samoan land to foreigners.

"You can just imagine how our three consuls liked that! They had him deported on the next ship. When they went through his papers they found he was on the payroll not only of Malietoa and the American government but the German Goddefroy company as well—a man after Emma's own heart!

"She never heard from Steinberger again but didn't mind. She took up with an Irish sea captain named Tom Farrell. He owned a brig called the *Vision* as well as this hotel we're in. Emma loved this bar; dropped by every evening as soon as she closed her stores. Old Tom stood her to all the champagne she could drink and when she was mellow they would harmonize on old Irish ballads until your heart would break. People began calling this 'Emma Coe's Place.'

17

"She went with Tom to the Marshall Islands once to set up a trading station. They had a fight one night on Mili atoll and she got so mad she swam out and sailed off in his brig, leaving him stranded for two months. The project failed and poor Farrell went bankrupt. But Goddefroy offered him a job as manager of a small trading station in New Guinea and Emma went with him.

"It was Emma who became the millionaire. There was a fellow in France named the Marquis de Rays, who convinced hundreds of countrymen there was a paradise somewhere in the South Pacific. They filled four ships with fountains, lampposts, marble altars, crested stationery, and other essentials of paradise, and fetched up on the south coast of New Ireland in a place that is about as close as one can get to hell on earth — dense jungles, poisonous snakes, two hundred inches of rainfall, and every kind of fever. Without food, quinine or even bush knives they soon began to die. Two of the ships took off, leaving the captain of the *Marquis* and *Genil* anchored offshore. Unfortunately he was out of coal.

"Emma heard of his predicament and, ever the business woman, sailed over to strike a deal. She offered to fuel one ship in return for the other and all the accoutrements of paradise lying about. He hastily agreed. She used her loot to set up a trading company of her own at Ralum, buy 400,000 acres, and build a palace she calls Gunantambu. Her parties are famous and I hear she uses the marble altar as her liquor cabinet. Farrell died penniless in Sydney a few years ago. She's over forty herself now but still going strong. Her current lover is a dashing Dalmatian sailor in his twenties named Augustine Stalie."

By this time everyone in the bar was listening. "A toast to Emma!" someone shouted and they raised their glasses. "Here's to our Emma; beauty, brains, and a way with men. May Apia soon be blessed with another *afa-kasi* girl like her!" Willie drank to that.

The vision of her dark eyes and slender waist floated with him out the door as they started up Beach Road again. It cast a warm glow over the shabby stores and dusty road.

"You are about to enter Little Germany," John said as they crossed a short bridge over the Mulivai stream which drained the marsh. Indeed, many of the stores here

18

did bear German names and flags. They stopped in front of the two tall towers Willie had seen from the harbor. John told him that the Catholic Church had purchased most of this side of town from a Methodist missionary for sixpence an acre. It had recently erected this cathedral and was leasing the rest for stores. All the Methodists had left now was one small piece and a wooden chapel.

The German consulate at the next intersection was a beehive of activity. A deep-sea packet and a DH&PG merchantman had arrived and clerks were manning cashier cages. "That may be a Samoan 'king' out there at Mulinuu," John whispered, "but look who's collecting his customs!"

Just beyond stood still another church, this one with a slender pointed spire. John said it belonged to Matafele, the other Samoan village within the protected area. Sure enough, behind the stores another cluster of thatched roofs crowded into the marsh.

At the center of the town the coral strand widened and a short street ran back to the marsh. On its corner a two-story building with latticed porches bore the name "Conradt's Hotel."[5] Since it seemed to be Apia's finest hostelry, Willie suggested another toast to Emma. This bar was crowded with stout planters and *Adler* crewmen, all speaking German; but Willie did not hear. He was looking into his glass for Emma.

"Come on!" John shook him, "or we'll never make it out to Mulinuu."

They found the road outside in an uproar. A huge Samoan policeman with a pewter star was switching little boys aside to make room for two brown guards in resplendent uniforms. Behind them an even more impressive dark figure sailed down the center of the road with a small German bobbing at his elbow like a pilot craft.

"Tamasese and prime minister Brandeis on their way to the German consulate," John whispered. Willie's muscles registered respect as he beheld the chief. Such girth did not seem childish at all.

They passed only two more notable structures, Nelson's store on the left and the International Hotel on the right. After that the houses became sparser and smaller until they found themselves walking through an orange

19

grove belonging to the Sisters of Mary. They ran a school for girls on Convent Road just behind.

At the beginning of Mulinu'u peninsula, they came to the DH&PG area John called "Little Hamburg." Its two wharves were now hosting a fleet of square lighters plying out to the ships with bags of copra and back with "blackboys" and bales of supplies. Across the road a long warehouse with two courtyards housed stores, offices, and repair shops. Further along were barracks for clerks and residences for more important people.

Willie noted that in "Little Hamburg" no one slept with his feet on the desk or paused to pass the time of day. Weber and his sea captains prowled the upstairs offices and clerks scurried through the courtyards below. The hierarchy hummed like a clock from Weber to close-mouthed plantation managers, to weather-beaten over-seers and down to the youngest blond messenger boy. All were well fed, well housed, well paid, and career-minded. "Blackboys" were not counted in the hierarchy at all. They were, like its machinery and pack animals, used hard and replaced as necessary.

"DH&PG has about ten thousand acres in Samoa now," John said with awe. "Its plantations look like parks with cattle and horses browsing under perfect lines of coconuts. And it has taken them less time than it took our dads to develop that hundred acres on Koro."

"Do the Samoans mind losing their land?" Willie asked.

John sighed. "You know, sometimes I think they re-spect Germans more than us. Germans act like chiefs."

Beyond DH&PG's holdings, Beach Road narrowed to a footpath of coral rubble curving out a treeless strand caught between the ocean and the marsh. With no one in sight, it seemed like a bleak walk out to a few thatched roofs under the palms at the end. A cold wind suddenly breathed across the mangroves from the mountains.

"Rain coming," John said. "We'd better start back." They turned and trotted towards town shoulder to shoulder. Just as the torrent caught up with them, they jumped, laughing and panting, onto the porch of the International Hotel.

"Time to toast Emma again," Willie said, pushing towards the door. When he returned to the crowded porch they stood silently at the railing nursing their glasses. Willie gazed deeply into his again, hoping to find Emma.

Suddenly he raised his eyes and—there she was, standing on the lowest step almost in front of him! He stiffened in surprise and looked again. She was unmistakable: tall, slender-waisted, dusky-skinned, and doe-eyed. Her abundant black hair was caught on top of her head by a large comb, the raindrops on it glistening like jewels. She was so close he could have touched her, but he dared not move for fear she would vanish. He riveted her with his eyes instead.

A short girl laughed and talked beside her, but "Emma" was not listening. She just stood there calmly looking out into the rain. Presently the short girl turned and, catching Willie's gaze, shook a saucy finger in his direction. That broke the spell, Willie pulled at John's sleeve but by the time his friend turned, "Emma" had vanished.

Willie did not say a word all the way back to the wharf. That fleeting vision was too precious to share. John might laugh at him. Willie was in agony. How could he ever find her again?

Finally, as they stood waiting for the whaleboat, he asked in desperation, "John, where do young Samoan girls live?" His friend gave him a quizzical glance.

"That depends upon what kind of girl you're thinking of," he said. "If you want a local 'Mary,' ask at a bar. If you want a housegirl ask a European family. If it's a village girl you're looking for, be careful. They have brothers. What's on your mind, old boy?"

Willie wasn't sure.

Chapter 3

Wooing

(1888-1891)

PEPE MAIAVA tossed restlessly on a mat in Seumanutafa's thatched house. It was a warm quiet April afternoon and Simativa sat at the back of the platform weaving a fine mat. Her right hand deftly picked up alternate strands while her left laid the diagonals. When her husband mumbled in his sleep, she glanced at him anxiously, her fingers still flying. He had seemed feverish when he arrived from the bush this morning. What if he had the "flying fever" (*mumu lele*), which runs up the body from the toes to head and must be caught at the neck before it reaches the brain? What a time for the healer to be away! Simativa only wished Pepe would stay home. He was too old for war.

As for herself, she felt like a girl again, living here in Apia with her family. When Pepe visited he talked deferentially like a son-in-law, but Seumanutafa always treated him with the dignity due a great chief. This time Pepe had brought word that Mataafa was now living in a cave at Afiomalu, right above Apia. Hundreds of warriors had joined him, not only from Faleata but all the districts. Lauati, the silver-tongued *pule* (ranking orator of Savaii) had arrived with a contingent from his island. Even the rival Laupepa and Talavou relatives of Malietoa had sent representatives. For the first time in fifty years they agreed on something. Now that their own titleholder was in exile, they would all support Mataafa.

With such unanimity the *tumua* (ranking orators of Upolu) would normally give him the four titles of the Tupua "crown," and with Malietoa's support as well, Samoa should have a single "king" like Vaiinupo.

But the great traditional game was different now, thanks to Europeans. The Germans were arming Tamasese; the British and Americans were trying to reinstate Malietoa Laupepe. It was as if the consuls were trying to replace the ranking orators as kingmakers, using guns and warships instead of fine mats and warriors to make their point. Despite his overwhelming Samoan support, Mata-afa would be at a disadvantage unless his warriors too could find European guns. But he already knew where he could get them. That is why he had sent Pepe to town this morning with a message for H.J. Moors.

After delivering it, Pepe had stopped to see his family. He felt tired and sick but the Apia village chiefs had immediately gathered at Seumanutafa's house to greet him and ask for news. They brought kava roots in his honor and Pele had squeezed the ceremonial drink, sitting cross-legged in front of Seumanutafa's great wooden bowl. With her black hair loose over her shoulders she no longer looked like a child, Pepe noted with some surprise.

After the chiefs had gone, Pepe had fallen into a feverish sleep, so that Simativa had not been able to tell him of her concern about Pele and her cousin Eliza. Simativa's sister had married a German named Freuan and their daughter Eliza was also living in Seumanutafa's household. Simativa feared that this lively little part-European (afakasi) cousin might lead a traditional village girl like Pele into trouble. They two were always together. The problem with Eliza was that she was an incurable romantic. She had already presented the family with a fair-skinned baby girl eight months after the departure of a British warship. She was fluent in English and German as well as Samoan, and used these skills not only as family interpreter but in pursuing affairs of her own. Simativa did not want Pele exposed to such temptations. Any such diversions would shame Pepe as an LMS pastor; even worse, they could disgrace his family and village. Pele was, after all, Toamua's taupou (ceremonial virgin).

Simativa looked up from her fine mat and glanced out across the grass. Suddenly her fingers froze and her eyes narrowed as they focused on two figures half-hidden behind the church hedge. The shorter definitely belonged to Eliza. She was having an animated conversation with a sandy-mustached palagi (Caucasian) sailor.

Every sense in Simativa's body alerted. Not again! This

23

young marine with the skinny legs had been poking around the village for several weeks—no doubt looking for Eliza. Simativa was about to call Misi to go over and chase him away, as was a brother's duty, but she did not have to. Eliza suddenly turned and tripped back to the cookhouse. The girl was obviously up to mischief again but fortunately Pele was not involved this time. Simativa could see her daughter in the cookhouse dutifully peeling green bananas with a little stick. Relieved, she returned to her weaving.

If she had continued her observation a few moments longer, she might not have felt so sure. Eliza sprang lightly over the low railing across the cookhouse door and crouched next to Pele, whispering excitedly into her ear. Pele blushed, threw something out on the grass, and continued her work without looking at her cousin.

Like Simativa, Pele had been under the impression that the sandy-haired sailor had been hanging around the village looking for Eliza. As a matter of fact, Eliza herself had been under that impression until a few days ago, when she had offered to show him the back way to the Vaisigano bridge. By the time they returned she was aware of the truth. The young man was completely smitten with Pele, whom he unaccountably referred to as "Emma." He had quizzed Eliza on every detail of "Emma's" existence, even down to how she brushed her hair.

Far from being jealous, Eliza instantly decided to act as go-between. It would be as exciting as an affair of her own, without the risks. She began by asking him why he called his beloved "Emma."

"It's not a good name for her," Eliza explained. "She is not a bold *afakasi* (part European) girl like me. She is more like the shy *iao* bird which hides in the deep forest. You should call her 'Pele' instead. That means 'beloved.'"

The young man was enchanted with that name and all the other vital information Eliza had passed on. According to Eliza, the thing Pele wanted most in all the world was a European hairbrush with a mirror on the back, just like the one now on display in Grevsmuhl's window.

When Willie had met Eliza by the church this morning he was carrying a package. He explained that an inspiration had befallen him while passing Grevsmuhl's store. All he

24

asked was that she pass the package to her cousin Pele along with the message that if she looked in the back she would see his "beloved."

Eliza was torn briefly between her own desire for a brush and her duties as a "go-between," but family loyalty prevailed and she followed his directions as she crouched by Pele in the cookhouse. Heaven immediately rewarded her. When Pele opened the package and heard the message, she blushed and threw the brush out onto the grass, saying she was much too young for such nonsense.

Eliza immediately retrieved the brush and next day transmitted Pele's thanks to the young man, together with the message that Pele would be strolling on the Vaisigano bridge the following evening at five. Eliza then asked Pele to carry an urgent letter for her to a white man who would be waiting on the bridge at that time. At first Pele demurred. Simativa had warned her against getting involved in Eliza's affairs. But family loyalty prevailed and she finally agreed.

Pele was dumbfounded when she found the same skinny sailor on the bridge. She handed him the note and would have taken off at full speed were it not for the look on his face. He was even more frightened than she was! It was intriguing to discover that she was the one in control of this situation. So she walked away casually instead, just to see what he would do. He followed at a respectful distance.

At the end of the bridge she turned off by Williamson's shack to take the way back home to the village. He turned too, shortening the distance a little as if to protect her. Half-way home, they found themselves walking in silence side by side, but he never touched her except once when she tripped on a root. All he did then was point to himself and say "Willie" and point at her and say "Pele." That apparently exhausted his vocabulary and he continued walking in silence, glancing sidewise at her now and then with something like reverence. By the time they reached the cookhouse her apprehensions had completely subsided. This sailor wasn't dangerous.

A few weeks went by with only casual meetings at which Willie seemed unable to communicate. Inside, however, he was desperate. He couldn't eat and he couldn't sleep. When he tried to forget his shy wild bird by looking for Emma in the bottom of a glass, he found Pele's face smiling up at him instead.

At the end of April, there was another flap between the consuls and it looked as if the *Mohican* might see action. Brandeis proclaimed that not only taxes but all village copra must henceforth be turned in at the German firm. To MacArthur, who had a long-standing contract with Fasitoo village, this was the last straw. The American and British consuls again implored Day to intervene, but he steadfastly refused.

One day, however, the *Adler* pulled anchor and started down the coast. Immediately the American commander took action. He ordered his crew and medic back on the *Mohican* and followed the German vessel. Nothing happened. They simply watched each other.

By the time the two warships returned to Apia in May, Willie was in panic, realizing that the *Adams* would soon return to relieve his ship. He would have to take some positive step or this idyll with Pele would end forever when he left in June. Bracelets and candy did not seem to move her and usually ended up with Eliza. He couldn't think what to do next. Finally he confided his turmoil to John Bell as they sat on the porch one evening.

John knew that Willie had been seeing someone. His visits to their house had been less frequent. He assumed it must be some "local Mary" at Emma Coe's place. Sailors will be sailors. When he learned that it was not a "local Mary" but a *taupou* living in Seumanutafa's household, he leaped out of his chair in consternation.

"Willie! Have you lost your mind? Didn't I tell you that a *taupou* is a special ceremonial maiden whose virginity is guarded not only by her brothers but every young man in the village? You could get yourself killed fooling around with a girl like that!"

Willie tried to explain. Far from fooling around, he proposed to marry Pele. He just didn't know how to go about asking for her hand. John stared at him, incredulous. Willie was hopelessly, crazily, in love!

"It's probably none of my business, Willie, but aren't you already engaged to that St. Julian girl in Fiji? I can't imagine what your mother would say if she heard of something like this."

26

That hurt! Willie stared in agony at his fingernails. The last few months he had felt in charge of his own life; now he realized he was still tied to his family. Love was not something you did on purpose; when it grabbed you there was nothing you could do. Its effect was giddier than a good stiff drink but its hangover was excruciating.

John sensed Willie's pain and felt sorry for him. "Don't worry, old boy. You'll be sailing soon and after three years you won't even remember her name."

Willie was incensed that John should so grossly underestimate his feeling, but his friend continued ruthlessly. "I've seen her, Willie, and she's only a child. She can't speak a word of English and she's never been inside a European house. What kind of a wife do you think she'd make for you? You might as well forget it anyway. By the time you get back her father will have her married to a big chief who won't want to see you hanging around."

The thought that she might be gone by the time he returned was too painful to bear. Willie blurted out the plan that had been developing in his mind.

"I have already thought of all that, John, and I have a solution if you and Jane will help me. I intend to declare my intentions to her father next time he comes to town and explain that I can't marry her right away. I will offer to send her to your school instead and pay for everything. All I want you and Jane to do is treat her like a daughter. Teach her to cook and sew and speak English. It's the most important thing you could ever do for me! I would be grateful the rest of my life."

The plea was so genuine that John could think of nothing more to say. He only sat there blinking, trying to put things in perspective. When he discussed it with Jane that evening he was amazed at her very practical reaction.

"Don't try to reason with him, John. Love is not reasonable and he will just think you are making light of it. You know he doesn't have a chance in the world of convincing a chief like Pepe Maiava. That man hates Europeans. Even the girl herself doesn't seem interested. She's only playing him along. All you need to do is keep her brothers and cousins from chopping Willie to bits with a bush knife before he sails."

The only person that Jane underestimated was Eliza.

Unlike everyone else, she allied herself with Willie and planned his strategy with care. One April evening beside the church she informed him that the time for action had arrived. Pepe had come from the bush that morning, suffering again with fever. He would have to rest for several days.

Now that Willie was faced with his last chance he suddenly lost his nerve. "Let's wait until he gets better," he quavered in a panic.

But Eliza would have none of that. "It's now or never," she said firmly. "As soon as he gets better he'll be off." She proceeded to give Willie detailed instructions. First he was to go to Moors' store and buy a keg of salt beef. "It's as good as a big fat pig on important occasions," she explained. He was to send it to Pepe Maiava that very afternoon, together with a note offering to attend his sickness the following morning.

"Be sure to bring that blond American officer with you," she directed. "He can act as your spokesman."

"But he doesn't speak a word of Samoan!" Willie protested.

Eliza looked at him scornfully. Such a naive young man would never catch a wife on his own! "Who do you think will be translating for him?" she asked rhetorically. "What's the matter? Don't you trust me?"

Willie realized that he was no longer in control of the situation. With Eliza at the helm there was now no turning back. "When you come tomorrow morning," she continued, "be sure to bring a big bottle of hard candies and a white coat—the kind you wear in parades. Carry your black bag too and be sure it is full of bottles."

She flicked him away with her finger and tripped off. Willie stood behind the hedge for several minutes, shaking his head to steady his heart. Then he straightened his shoulders bravely and set off towards Moors' store.

Eliza ran to the cookhouse and whispered the momentous news to Pele. The distinguished doctor was coming to visit Pepe Maiava tomorrow. He would cure her father's fever and ask for her hand in marriage!

The final decision, of course, would be up to Pepe Maiava. It affected the future of the family. But in Pele's eyes Willie was suddenly elevated from a silly sailor with skinny legs to a distinguished doctor able to cure her father. Even more intriguing, it elevated her from a child to a young woman desired by men of distinction. How exciting!

Eliza had no idea how Pepe might react to a request for Pele's hand. Europeans usually slipped off with girls in the night. A formal proposal like this was, to say the least, unusual.

By nightfall everyone in the village knew that a European doctor was coming to cure Pepe Maiava. They were buzzing even more about the other motive behind his call. In honor of the event, the keg of beef was multiplied by ten as word spread. Next morning almost everyone stayed home, sitting discreetly behind a house post, eyes on the road.

Fortunately Willie and the officer were unaware of the hundred eyes that followed their progress across the grass. Most identified the blond American as the "distinguished doctor" because he was taller and carried a large package. It was in fact his own dress coat, donated to a cause that was breaking the monotony of his life on an idle warship. He had international experience with romance himself, but nothing compared to this thing of Willie's. He had taken due note of their position between the American and British consulates in case a sudden evacuation became necessary.

As they mounted the steps to Seumanutafa's thatched house, Willie's eyes searched desperately for Eliza. They would have to take to their heels immediately without her. To his relief, he saw her giggling with some other girls behind the house. Scarcely glancing in their direction, she indicated that they should shake hands with Pepe Maiava sitting at one end of the house and then seat themselves at the other end.

As soon as they had their backs to these posts, Pepe began a welcome speech in Samoan, referring to Willie as the "distinguished doctor" and his friend as the "commander of the American fleet". Unaware of their elevation in rank, Willie and the officer smiled and nodded. Curious villagers crowding around the platform didn't take the titles literally anyway; they simply concluded that Pepe held his guests in high regard.

When the host had concluded his welcome, all eyes turned towards the guests for a reply. There was a prolonged silence, during which the two marines grinned and waved. Willie's eyes frantically sought Eliza, but she was nowhere to be seen.

Sensing their discomfort, Pepe called for a translator and someone located Eliza in the cookhouse scraping taro. She modestly seated herself beside the guests and greeted Pepe on their behalf with the necessary polite phrases.

When she had finished, Willie tried to add something in English, but Eliza shook her head and nudged the officer, whispering, "Just say anything. I'll take care of it."

He coughed and went straight to the point like a true American. "My good friend Willie here is greatly taken with your daughter, Mr. Chief—"

Eliza broke in with her translation, "May God bless the household of Seumanutafa, highest chief of Apia village, and his distinguished guest Pepe Maiava, high chief of Toamua. We are delighted that Pepe has come to bring us good news from the mountain. But the doctor is distressed to hear that he is ill. He would be happy to provide any assistance within his humble power. As a token of his esteem and concern, the doctor wishes to present Pastor Pepe with a gift, a white coat like those worn by all great missionaries of the gospel."

Willie nodded politely and Eliza nudged the officer to lay his package on the mat in front of him. A little boy jumped up and transmitted it to Pepe Maiava. Pepe was under no illusions about Eliza's translation, but his pleasure in the gift was genuine. He had always wanted a white missionary coat for Sunday. It would lend impressiveness to his sermons. But it also showed him something else. Pele's suitor must be a God-fearing man and a Protestant because Catholic priests wore black on Sunday. He held it above his head with a bow to Willie saying, *"Fa'afetai tele le alofa"* (Thank you so much for your kindness).

Eliza nudged the American to continue with his speech. Encouraged by his deferential audience, the blond officer warmed to the task. "My friend Willie here is not just the ordinary sailor you find around these ports. No indeed! When he sees a girl he likes, it's not 'here today and gone tomorrow.' He—"

Eliza broke in hastily with her translation.

"The distinguished doctor also wishes to transmit to the honored mother of this great family a humble token of his respect for the beauty and industry she has so ably transmitted to her daughter."

She beckoned the officer to push forward the gallon jar of colored candies and the little boy, eyes bulging, carried it carefully to Simativa. Her delight was as genuine as Pepe's. The jar held enough for every woman in the church. What a considerate young man! She lifted the bottle and thanked him.

"Well now, Mr. Chief, let's come right to the point," the officer concluded abruptly. "My friend Willie here wants to marry your daughter. Will you have him?"

"The distinguished doctor," said Eliza, "has some powerful European medicines that might help Pepe's illness if the high chief would like to be treated."

Pepe nodded his agreement, grateful that the young doctor had noted his discomfort and was willing to help him. He was tired—too tired to make important decisions today. Simativa had massaged his limbs and pressed a cool ti leaf to his brow, but he still felt hot. His head pounded. Even if this doctor's treatment did no good, it would at least give him an excuse to lie down. He motioned to Pele to unroll his sleeping mats. She piled them in front of him.

"My God!" the officer breathed to Willie, unaware of Eliza's translation. "Do you think that's the bridal bed?" They had both heard tales of public virginity tests.

"Has Pepe agreed?" Willie whispered to Eliza in panic.

"How could I even ask him?" she retorted loftily. "You haven't cured him yet! I have told him you would treat him and he has agreed. You must go over and help him now."

Profoundly relieved to find himself on familiar ground, Willie went over and sat down beside his patient. Opening his black bag, he laid out his bottles and instruments carefully on a towel. Their familiar gleam helped restore his confidence.

He spoke reassuringly to Pepe in tones that required no translation, laying a hand on his forehead, listening to his breathing, and counting his pulse. The old man did have a high fever. He was also very thin. Life in the bush was apparently not easy. Willie peered down his throat—

31

fine teeth, smooth tonsils, no problem there. He wasn't sure whether the island harbored malaria, but he had seen plenty of swollen arms and legs that bespoke filariasis. Finally he decided upon a multiple approach. With a great shaking of bottles, he produced a concoction of quinine, epsom salts, and cochin powder. It might taste noxious but it had a gorgeous color. The old chief swallowed it without wincing, gave one sigh, and fell sleep.

Willie returned to check on his progress next day and every day after that. Usually he brought a gift. The village children always spotted him first and trouped after him across the grass calling "Suani! Suani! *palagi! palagi!*" (Swann, Swann, white man, white man) so that the whole village knew he had arrived.

He always headed for Seumanutafa's house. Pepe did not need an interpreter to ascertain, quite correctly, that this young doctor was an earnest, friendly, but very naive young man, hopelessly in love with his daughter.

By the end of the week, whether due to Willie's powders or his patient's Samoan constitution, Pepe felt better. He sat up and chatted with the village matrons with sick children, who now crowded his platform every afternoon waiting to see "the distinguished doctor." Willie's favorite prescription was "salts." He liked children and was appalled to discover he was the first European doctor most of them had ever seen.

His visits were never complete without a prayer by Pepe Maiava and food presented on a woven leaf tray: yam, pigeon, boiled bananas, a leaf packet filled with coconut cream, or some other Samoan delicacy. What Willie enjoyed most was that Pele served it herself, sitting across from him on the mat to fan away the flies. He could then smile at her without offending and even touch her hand as she arranged his food. Here with her family she did not seem shy at all. Her movements were relaxed, and graceful as a bird's.

He could see that Pele's opinion of him had changed. She now respected him as a healer, consulted by her father and the matrons of the village. Even more important, his opinion of himself was changing. He was no longer the son of James or the brother of Arthur; he was a distinguished doctor in his own right. Because he felt like one he acted like one. Because he acted like one, people respected him. Because he felt respected, his self-confidence began to grow. He now knew whom he wanted to marry and where he wanted to live. He had found himself!

For several weeks a formal marriage proposal never surmounted the language barrier, though the village buzzed with rumors. Simativa fueled these with tempting morsels about Willie's extraordinary talents, generosity, and infatuation with Pele. Her neighbors embroidered on that. The only thing that unnerved them was Pepe's complete silence on the subject. A chief who had lost his land to a European might not want to lose his daughter as well!

Actually, Pepe was taking time to rethink his position. These were troublous times. War was a certainty now and here within his grasp was an unusual resource, a doctor who could set bones, mend heads, and mix fever potions. Such skills could prove useful not only to the family and village but also to Mataafa. This doctor was both rich and generous. His contributions might even help replace the tribute Pepe had lost to Weber. At least it would enable him to put on a wedding everyone would remember.

On the other hand, Pepe really loved his only daughter. He did not want to lose her to some far-off land. In addition, Willie's bloodlines would not augment the titled families open to Pele's children. She would soon have Samoan suitors able to provide her offspring with connections to their own titles as well as Pepe's. He decided to ascertain Pele's feelings on the matter. It was his decision but her happiness was relevant too.

One evening after prayers, he asked her to sit beside him and said, "Suani is deeply in love with you, my child. Do you want to marry him and go to his home in Fiji?"

Pele had spent sleepless nights considering marriage, but the second part of his question took her by surprise. Living on some other island had never occurred to her.

"Oh no, father!" she cried in real distress. "I would never be happy to leave our family and move to a strange place. Please tell him I am too young to marry; I can't speak English or cook for him."

That settled the matter. When Willie finally did make a formal proposal, Pepe simply told him what Pele had said. To his astonishment, Willie was prepared for it. With

Eliza's help, he explained that all he proposed was an "engagement" while he was away on the *Mohican*. During this period he would send Pele to the Bell's school, where she could learn English, cooking, and sewing, as well as the "three Rs." He would not only pay her way but send her pretty dresses from abroad. Furthermore, he had no intention of ever taking her to Fiji. He intended to settle in Apia anyway. If she felt comfortable with him and his way of life three years from now, they would marry. If not, she would be under no obligation.

This proposal surprised Pepe Maiava so much that he called for evening prayers an hour early, to give him time to think it over. The only formal education his children ever had was at Toamua pastor's school, where they had learned to sing hymns, read the Bible in Samoan, and give recitations on Children's Sunday *(Aso Sa o Tamaiti)*. An education at Bell's school was unheard of for a village girl. It would expose Pele to the white man's knowledge, for which Pepe had considerable respect. He consulted Pele again.

She was now torn between fear and curiosity. Since her former excuses no longer held and she didn't know what to say, she fell back on filial obedience. "Father, if you want me to attend this school, I will become engaged."

If this reply seemed less than enthusiastic to Willie, at least it gave him an opportunity to know his fiancee better. They were allowed to go walking, and one afternoon he took her over to meet the Bells. She made a good impression. John and Jane agreed she was one of the most beautiful Samoan girls they had ever seen. On the back path to the village that evening, Willie kissed her. This too was a new experience to Pele, who was used to rubbing noses. She accepted the gesture with a self-conscious smile but did not kiss him back. Willie began to wonder if he had staked his future on a Samoan Mona Lisa and was desperate for a more positive response.

Eliza tried to explain. "You see why I wouldn't let you call her Emma. She's just not an assertive kind of girl."

Willie nodded. Maybe what intrigued him about Pele was the allure of the shy iao bird, which had to be lured, netted, and nourished gently lest it die in captivity.

It was not until the afternoon the *Mohican* was sailing

that he could be sure he had touched her heart at all. He and Pele were standing with Eliza on the noisy wharf. A crowd had gathered to bid farewell to the Americans. Willie was about to jump down into the longboat when Pele said something in Samoan and Eliza shouted the translation into Willie's ear.

"She wants to know what you would do if you came back and found her already married."

Willie turned and looked at his "beloved" with such pain that her dazed heart suddenly shattered. She threw her arms around his neck, sobbing, "No! No, Suani! I wait, I wait!"

Bell's School
Apia, Samoan Islands
December 15, 1888

Dear Willie,

Thank you for Pele's tuition, which was forwarded to me through the American consul. Pele sends her thanks also for the beautiful flowered frock. I intended to save it for Christmas but she insisted on opening it immediately. She looks like a grown-up lady in her new finery, bustle and all!

You would be happy with her progress this year. She hesitates to speak in English but she understands directions. She can count and sum single numbers. Unfortunately school has been disrupted this year.

Shortly after you left, the German consul sent an ultimatum to Mataafa to disband his forces. When he got no response, he sent German marines up the hill to Tanugamanono, where they encountered an outpost of armed Mataafa warriors and were forced to retreat.

The following night hundreds of Mataafa warriors in red turbans slipped down and surrounded our protected area. Brandeis barricaded himself and Tamasese out at Mulinuu, under the guns of the Adler. The rest of us on Beach Road were sitting ducks. If Mataafa chose to ignore the refuge, all we could do was abandon everything and run for the Adams.

On September 11th we woke and found not a single Samoan

in town, so we knew an attack was coming. Tamasese warriors in white turbans were guarding Matautu Point, so I figured Mataafa's warriors would come down the Vaisigano right beside our house. Sure enough, at dawn we saw red turbans and blackened faces slipping through the trees. Their women and children began to dig a shallow trench with bush knives and coconut shells in front of our house. Tamasese's warriors ignored them and our family as if we were invisible. Apparently they were not after women, children, or foreigners! That was a relief, but I took my family to the mission compound anyway and went down Beach Road to look around.

The Europeans had barricaded themselves upstairs. Only Moors' store was open. I followed some women up the Siumu Track and came upon a large group of warriors sitting on the grass while Mataafa himself directed the battle from a nearby porch. They waved at me. When I got home I found shooting going on across the trench. Samoans are terrible marksmen, but if someone did get hit, his opponent would jump over and cut off his head. Actually the excitement exceeded the casualties, which I hear numbered about forty as the white turbans were pushed back to Pilot Point.[1]

That night it poured! Mataafa warriors dragged up an old thatch to sleep under and their opponents soon joined them. Next morning they appeared in red turbans too! Mataafa now held not only the point but Beach Road as far as the Mulivai. The German consul hastily warned him that he was violating the refuge. Lo and behold, he obediently moved his warriors back behind the marsh, leaving us greatly relieved. Thank God for Samoan beliefs! The three consuls are in charge again.

With best regards from all of us,
John

Bell's School
Apia, Samoan Islands
December, 1889

Dear Willie,

Thank you again this year for Pele's tuition. She loved the high-button shoes. When she wears them with her flowered dress *you would swear she was an* afakasi *lady!*

Her progress has been good this year. Her English though ungrammatical is usable for everyday affairs, thanks not so much to us as to our daughters, who treat her like a sister. We are all benefitting from her stews and she can even sew an apron. She's not yet good in writing but school has been interrupted again this year.

Last January Tamasese's forces moved from Mulinuu and camped behind Luatanu'u east of Apia. Mataafa followed and dug in across the gorge at Lauli'i. When the Richmond *arrived with 28,000 cartridges for Mataafa, Brandeis realized the game was up and wanted to come to terms with the British and American consuls. But unfortunately a new German consul had just arrived. He called for more German warships instead. So we were at it again!*

In February the Eber *and* Olga *joined the* Adler. *America sent in the* Nipsic, Trenton, *and* Vandalia *and Britain the* Caliope. *It was an unusually stormy month. All seven warships had to steam at anchor in the harbor to hold their moorings.*

On March 15th the barometer fell to an unheard-of 29 inches! Any reasonable ships would have put to sea to weather the hurricane. But these warships had to stay to watch each other!

The winds that night were the worst I have ever seen. We lost the roof off our shed and spent the night under the dining table. Rain drove clear across the room. I dared not think of the men in the harbor! At daybreak I crept to the window and found our house surrounded by water. The bridge had gone and the Vaisigano was such a torrent we were cut off from Apia. Out in the harbor three warships had collided. The Eber *had sunk but the* Nipsic *had managed to beach on our side, and the* Adler *had been tossed up on the reef.*

Further out the Vandalia *and* Olga *were out of control and threatening to smash our British* Caliope. *I was so proud of her! She was the only warship with her engines still going, struggling to beat it out of the harbor in the teeth of that incredible gale! In four hours she gained only four cables. We prayed for her as she finally came abreast of the* Trenton, *stranded in the harbor mouth. She squeezed by so close that her foreyard swept the* Trenton's *deck and sailed on into open sea, the only war-*

ship of the seven to survive the holocaust. Jane and I cried with relief. We knew so many of those boys!

Impossible wind and surf continued the next night. The following day Seumanutafa and the men of Apia village made it through the surf with a line to the Adler and Trenton on the reef, and began bringing in survivors. It was hard to believe that three days before these men had been their enemies.

The injured were taken to Seumanutafa's house. Simativa and Pele helped with the nursing. "If only the distinguished doctor was here," they kept saying, and indeed they could have used your skills. German crewmen were evacuated shortly to their side of town, but the Americans stayed on for several months awaiting a ship home. At their farewell feast they composed a catchy tune, "Tofa my Feleni" ("Goodby My Friend") in a mixture of Samoan and English.

When word of the disaster reached world newspapers, all three powers as usual disavowed any interest in Samoa, and the Kaiser ordered his bellicose consul home in disgrace. The three powers called a conference in Berlin to settle the Samoan kingship question once and for all. The "king" they refused to accept was Mataafa, the one to whom the Samoans had given all their "crowns" and who was still strong enough to hold Beach Road hostage. Instead, they decided to bring Malietoa Laupepa back from exile. He seemed more compliant.

This posed a problem, however, since Mataafa had already been given the Malietoa title by the Samoans and had taken over the native government at Mulinuu. To my astonishment, when the two old rivals met on the wharf, they declared themselves "cousins" and politely offered each other the "crowns"! For a month Mataafa was "king" and Malietoa "vice-king" with the blessing of the consuls. When news recently arrived that Mataafa was not acceptable to Berlin the two chiefs obligingly reversed positions! I guess they're just tired of fighting.

Things in the protected area have not changed much. We still have three consuls but now have four courts! The Conference added a chief justice to settle disputes among the consuls. A courthouse is being built for him where St. Foy's mansion used to be. We also have a municipal council for the town with a German president. For all intents and purposes, he and the chief justice are the government.

Jane, the children, and I send our best regards. I'll let Pele speak for herself.

Your true friend,
John

Dear Doktor Suani,

May the almighty Three-in-One bless you and bring you back to this island. I work hard for our future life. I serve Mr. and Mrs. Bell with my true heart. They is my parents. We are blessed, thanks to God, but I wish you is here to help the hurted sailors in the hurricane.

Thank you for the dress and shoes. I now is a lady. I wait for you with my love,

Pele

The wreck of the Adler — 1889.

Chapter 4

Winning and Trapped

(1891-1897)

TOWARDS THE end of January, 1891, a small packet from Fiji entered Apia harbor. Its passenger list included a William J. Swann, who was now standing at its bow squinting at the wharf. Would Pele be there to meet him as he had suggested in his letter? The gravel strand looked as peaceful as ever except that now two twisted iron hulks lay on their sides in the shallow water like huge dead whales. The name on one rusting stern read *Adler*. That shocked Willie into an uneasy feeling about his own future as well. What was this mania that still held him in its grip? During the last month he had irrevocably smashed his life in Fiji. His mother had disowned him and poor sweet Cecilia St. Julian was on her way to join his sister Margaret's convent in Australia. All this because of a timid, doe-eyed, Samoan girl half his age whom he had not seen for three years! Was she real or just a ridiculous fantasy, as his mother had claimed?

He hardly knew himself any more but her vision still haunted him. He stepped into the tender and was soon close enough to see the wharf clearly. His heart sank. No one was in sight except a boy waiting to catch the rope. He clambered ashore and paused for a moment to still his pounding heart and decide what to do next. Again the pervasive copra smell flashed him back to Levuka. Resolutely he buried an unbidden twinge of homesickness. Apia was now his home for good regardless of Pele. There was no turning back.

Ten minutes later he arrived at the hedge in front of the Bell's house. School was still in session and he could hear the murmur of young voices from the porch. Crouching behind the hibiscus hedge, he desperately scanned each face.

Suddenly he saw her! She was sitting on a back bench idly gazing out to sea at his packet. She was even more beautiful than he remembered. Her breasts had filled out and her slenderness was accentuated by the nip-waist frock he had sent with its high neck and long skirt. Her feet were hidden in high-button shoes and her heavy black hair was twisted into a neat bun at the back of her neck. She must still be waiting for him or she would not be sitting there!

Just then Jane Bell called on Pele to stand and describe a sheep farm in Australia. She rose slowly and Willie held his breath to catch his first word of her English.

"The farms in Australia is big," Pele recited as if she had memorized each word, "and it has sheeps. There is no river so they drink tanks. Australians is rich from sheeps. Samoa needs sheeps for its future life."

Tears of joy welled up in Willie's eyes. Even these few ungrammatical sentences unlocked her to him as a person. Now they could do more than look at each other. They could talk! He watched without moving until school was over and the children ran shouting into the yard. In the commotion he bounded up the steps as if he had just arrived. Jane caught sight of him first and grabbed him with a cry of surprise. John pumped his hand. Then they introduced him to Pele as formally as if she were a stranger. She stood transfixed as Willie embraced her but he saw tears in her eyes again and knew that all was well. She did not utter a word as she laid the table, served the biscuits and poured the tea, but her eyes followed Willie's every move until Jane burst out laughing.

"Too bad she didn't get down to the wharf to meet you, Willie. See, she is dressed up for the occasion. We understood that the packet was disembarking at noon. Finding you so suddenly has scared away her words. But don't worry; when they come back you won't be able to stop her!"

That evening, as Willie and Pele strolled across the bridge, he slipped an arm around her narrow waist. She did not jump; apparently she felt more confident with him now. She was trying to explain something in English and he finally gathered that she was taking him to see Eliza, who had a new overseas friend now, a solicitor named Skeen. He intended to marry her and adopt her child. They

41

were only waiting until Willie arrived to make it a double wedding.

As soon as greetings were over, Willie realized that Eliza was as resourceful as ever. She had the double wedding planned down to the last detail. It was to be a grand affair at the Apia village church. The brides would wear white gowns and the grooms dress suits. Skeen would pay for everything, she assured Willie. He was very rich.

A few days later Willie began to wonder. No sooner had the grooms agreed to go fifty-fifty on expenses than Skeen asked him for a loan of £100. That put the wedding in a different light, since Willie had only £69 to his name, carefully saved from his severance pay. He could see that if he wanted to get married, that sum would have to cover everything.

A second complication was the church. Although Willie's father was Anglican and he himself seldom attended church, his mother had instilled in him a firm belief that lasting marriages required a Catholic blessing. Willie needed all the divine help he could get with this one. He went to a priest at the cathedral for advice. The priest assured him that his mother was indeed correct. Divorce was impossible in the Catholic church. It was only unfortunate, he said, that Pele was a Protestant, for they could not be married at the altar. However, if they both agreed to raise their children in the Catholic faith, he would marry them in the vestry without charge. That seemed a small price to pay for the solution to the problem. They all agreed. All they needed now was legal permission from Trood, the British consul. He was happy to oblige and both couples were quietly united the next day in the Catholic vestry, with only the Bells as witnesses.

If Pele had any qualms about these arrangements, they were completely overridden by her faith in Willie. He could solve anything, just like her father. The happy couples walked out of the quiet vestry and into the sunlight of Beach Road in blissful conviction that their troubles were over. They had only to "live happily ever after."

This assumption lasted as long as the walk back to Apia village. It was Pepe Maiava's reaction to their announcement that first made them realize they might have difficulty splicing their two worlds. He promptly disowned Pele.

After the hurricane had brought peace to Samoa, Pepe had returned to Toamua and was preaching all over Faleata. He had assumed that Willie was Protestant and sufficiently affluent to marry his daughter in traditional style. He had carefully planned the occasion. Toamua would serve as the bride's village since she was its *taupou* (ceremonial maiden), and Apia village would act as Willie's village since he was its distinguished doctor. Pepe knew he could collect at least two hundred fine mats from his families. All his relatives and neighbors would be eager for a hand in the ceremonial exchange. The groom's side would have to count heavily on Willie to defend its honor. At least £1,000 would be needed to match Pele's two hundred fine mats. If the groom's side could present more than that they would feel victorious. If they couldn't they would suffer great humiliation.

It was like a contest. On the day before the wedding, members of each side would gather to collect their presentations. As chiefs in charge, Pepe and Seumanutafa would recognize each titled contributor with a *sua* (ceremonial food presentation). Relatives and neighbors would spend the rest of the day feasting and enjoying each other's company. The wedding itself would take place next day at Toamua. The church on the bluff was far too small to hold both villages, but when the couple emerged everyone would dance. This performance would be followed by a great feast spread on banana leaves under a coconut frond arbor extending all around the village square. Gifts of money would be presented to every pastor and orator and everyone would have a basket of food to take home.

The final day would begin with oratory, and a great exchange of fine mats, food, and money would follow. After another feast, guests would meet as separate sides again for redivision of the gifts they had obtained. Hurt and angry feelings were almost inevitable, but both villages had orators skilled at distribution. Everyone would at least emerge knowing the rank and relationship of everyone else. What better way to build the ties that bind Samoa's great extended families?

As chief instigator of the celebration, Pepe would gain even if it took every mat and pig he had. The lavish event would be widely discussed when the guests got home. The district would realize that his prize-winning rooster had now been replaced with an equally wondrous *palagi* doctor. Pepe's title and his family would gain prominence again.

When Pepe learned that Pele had forfeited all this for a few words in the Catholic vestry, he could not be consoled. To make matters worse, Pele's Catholic wedding, especially her promise to raise Catholic children, affected Pepe's credibility as a Protestant preacher. How could he bring sheep to a fold his own daughter had deserted! In bitter humiliation he vowed never to preach again; and he never did!

Disownment was a terrible shock to Pele, though Seumanutafa immediately took the couple in. He allotted them a small thatched hut in the banana patch beside the Vaisigano and a piece of land on the mountain. With pigeons in the bush and fish in the harbor, they certainly would not starve.

It was bad enough to lose a father, but Pele began to realize something was also happening to Willie. It began about a week after the wedding, when the last of his severance pay was gone. Money did not bother Pele. She had never had any and did not need it now. In addition to what nature and Seumanutafa provided, mothers came to consult Willie about their children, leaving a chicken, a basket of taro, or a word of respect. Pele felt secure.

Not Willie! Pele's pandanus mats and black cooking pot made him feel as if he were living in abject poverty and without capital, he saw no hope of ever improving this deplorable condition. He and Pele would live and die in this miserable hut. He was trapped!

When Pele noticed his deepening depression, she consulted Eliza, who had moved into Skeen's small wooden house up the hill at Papaloa. "Let me tell you about white men," her cousin confided. "They can't perform like males on sleeping mats and that depresses them. What they need is beds with mattresses."

Pele was delighted to understand the source of Willie's difficulty. But where would she find a European bed? Next day a boy appeared at the hut with a heavy hand-carved bedstead on his back. Eliza had sent them her own!

In the next few weeks Pele painstakingly sewed eight copra sacks together to form a huge bag and collected hundreds of kapok pods from the trees along the river. A group of grateful mothers helped pick out the hard black seeds amid endless chatter about how it would feel to lie on such a thing with a white man. They stuffed the bag so full it was almost round. Nothing was too good for their distinguished doctor.

After the mattress was presented, Willie flatly refused to sleep on it. Every time he looked at the clumsy thing his despair deepened. It seemed to epitomize his problem. What if his mother came to visit and found him sleeping on an overstuffed copra sack? Was this all he could offer his beautiful Samoan bride? He was as humiliated by the mattress as Pepe Maiava had been by the wedding. He sat listlessly on the platform all day long gazing at the river. His future had collapsed just when he was finally ready to show everyone he could make it on his own.

Pele had no idea of the forces that move a white man's heart or what can happen when these are thwarted. But she could see that the bed had only speeded Willie's decline. She consulted her mother.

Simativa told her that an evil spirit was haunting Willie, possibly an old sweetheart who had died of a broken heart. She generously offered to drive the dreadful demon out of him. As a pastor's wife, Simativa was not a novice at exorcism, Christian or traditional. She proposed to ask the missionary God to inspire her hands and then massage the ugly demon out of Willie's head, down his neck, body and legs, and out his big toe. He flatly refused to even let her try. Such superstitions were insulting to a doctor!

"What does Skeen do all day?" Pele asked, turning again to Eliza. "He seems to be happy."

"He goes to his office every morning and makes money," Eliza declared, forbearing to describe the grubby little room and dubious transactions that went on there.

"That's exactly what Willie needs," Pele agreed; "an office where he can make money."

Eliza nodded sagely. The white men she knew never actually made much but they certainly kept busy trying.

"But what would Willie do in an office all day long?" Eliza wondered out loud. "He's not a solicitor."

"He's a distinguished doctor!" Pele retorted defensively. "He could keep his medicines there."

45

"But he's only got a black bag and six empty bottles!" Eliza pointed out unkindly.

Pele could not gainsay that but it set her thinking. As soon as she got home she lifted a corner of the copra sack mattress and picked up her only treasure. It was a strangely soft fine mat with strands so slender they resembled threads. The bottom edge had a long fringe and was decorated with the red feathers of the sea bird. Simativa had spent a year weaving it for her own wedding to Pepe. When it was swept around the village square, his relatives appraised its size and evenness, and exclaimed *"Sa o faalalelei!"* (how beautiful!). It was conclusive evidence that he was marrying into a worthy family.

Simativa had preserved it carefully for her own daughter's wedding, but unfortunately the mat had been another casualty of that calamitous event. Not a single fine mat had changed hands! A week later however, Simativa had slipped it secretly to Pele.

Willie had not been impressed. "What use is it?" he asked. Fine mats are not to be laid on floors, hung on walls, or slept under, so Pele could not answer him. But to her it was infinitely precious. She had folded it lovingly and placed it under the copra sack mattress for safekeeping. Someday she would sweep it across a village square at her own daughter's wedding. Meanwhile it would lie beneath her mattress every night, a reminder that she was still in her mother's heart.

What worried her now was that she might never have a daughter at all the way things were going. She must do something to revive Willie's spirits. She had no alternative. She gave her treasure a final caress with her cheek, wrapped it lovingly in an old tapa, and took it to the Grevsmuhl, the shopkeeper. He peered at it over his spectacles, felt its texture, and handed her one gold coin.

Running back to the hut, she laid the gold piece in Willie's inert hand. When he finally noticed it, he frowned and dark suspicions crossed his mind. "Pele," he asked severely, "where did you get this?"

"For your bottles," was all she would say.

All afternoon Willie sat morosely turning the gold coin in his palm. If penury had forced Pele into prostitution, he decided, he would treat the boys at Emma Coe's to a last wild party, then blow his brains out to avenge her honor. When his emotions settled, he suddenly realized that such an exploit would have been impossible for Pele. She was far too shy. She must have sold something else instead. But what did she have to sell? Suddenly he leaped up and pulled the kapok mattress off the bed. Pele's cherished fine mat was gone. She had sold her treasure for him!

He threw himself on the sack in a paroxysm of tears. His "beloved!" How could he ever have suspected her? Exhausted with shame and guilt he fell asleep. In his dream he saw bottles — rows and rows of bottles — and in the center the biggest bottle of them all filled with moving, varicolored liquids. Above them hung a bright new sign: "William J. Swann, Chemist."

He awoke refreshed thinking of chemist shops. For some reason the thought no longer revolted him. He strode round and round the platform, ideas pounding through his mind. One gold coin would not buy a chemist shop. That would go for a large jar of colored waters like the one in his father's window. He knew where to get the rest. It meant swallowing his pride, but Pele had sacrificed her treasure for him.

That evening he carefully composed a letter to his father. It was not a personal letter; there was too much between them now. It was simply the kind of letter one businessman writes to another for a loan.

When James received it he rejoiced and Marguerita lit a votive candle to the Virgin Mary. Their errant son had finally returned to his senses! James and Arthur caught the next packet to Apia. As soon as they had ensconced themselves at the International Hotel, they dispatched an equally formal note to Willie inviting him to a business meeting.

For several days the three men discussed terms. Willie agreed to repay a loan from his father with interest and purchase supplies from his brother Arthur. No one mentioned Pele or the hut by the river. Willie's personal life, if he still had one, was his own concern. The important thing was his renewed interest in the family business.

Together they scoured Beach Road for a suitable site. A German firm had just completed a new building on Catholic land at the corner of Salelufi Street right across from the International Hotel. It was a modern two-story structure with living quarters above and commercial space below. On an island as unstable as this one, James felt a businessman should sleep above his inventory. He discussed terms with the firm and they found his credit impeccable. Before Willie knew it, he was discussing shelving with a carpenter and preparing an order for Arthur. Now his feet were on the ground—and his own ground— Willie's energy returned in a flood. He found he could work sixteen hours a day and still have time for his "beloved" at night. He could even joke about sleeping on a copra sack, now that he saw it as the beginning rather than the end of his career. Soon, he assured Pele, he would buy her a "real" mattress. She didn't care; she was just glad to have a "real" husband to sleep with.

Within a few months they were able to move into their new apartment. Beach Road was notified of their presence by a bright new sign, "William J. Swann, Chemist."

Their new living quarters were a far cry from a thatched hut in the banana patch. A switchback flight of steps outside the building led to an upstairs veranda and four rooms. The sitting room in front faced Beach Road, with a dining room behind it and two bedrooms in the back. The water tank and kitchen were down in the back yard under a mango tree. Behind the tree was the fence of a holding pen for a butcher shop facing Convent Road.

All this personal property made Pele uneasy. Everything had to be dusted, scoured, or polished all the time. In the hut by the river she had been able to chat and play cards with her neighbors all afternoon. Here she was running up and down the stairs from dawn to dark, fetching water, serving food, and taking laundry to the Mulivai. In Toamua she would have had sisters and cousins to help her. Here everything had to be done alone. European food was so complicated. Every day she had to make her rounds of the bakery, the butcher shop, and Volkner's grocery. By bedtime she was exhausted.

Willie informed her sternly that there would be no Samoan customs in this house. He was a businessman from now on, not a chief. That meant saving every penny to buy supplies and repay loans. Respect in the commercial world, he carefully explained, came from making money, not holding ceremonies. He would no longer be able to let her relatives and friends live with them. He could not contribute to weddings, funerals, and church dedications. After this everyone who came to him for medical help would have to pay. How else could he pay for his office and supplies?

These new rules were a terrible embarrassment to Pele. Whenever she visited Toamua or Apia village she was urged to stay and was given baskets of food to take home. How could she possibly refuse to do the same? They would call her selfish as a European and that would be unbearable.

She tried to live up to the new rules because she loved Willie and wanted his "office" to succeed, but her own life ceased to have meaning. What was the use of all these new things unless she could show them off, pass them around, or give them away? Selfishness had serious implications. If her relatives and friends cut her off, to whom would she turn if something happened to Willie? She felt so lonely and insecure that Willie often found her weeping. She would have fallen into a depression as deep as his had been except for one thing. She got pregnant.

Babies were something they agreed on. Willie loved children and the prospect of one of his own filled him with joy and spurred his efforts. If it were a boy, he would train him as a chemist and this shop would be his some day. If it were a girl, Pele would have someone to help her wash clothes, fetch water, clean the house, and serve guests. She would never feel lonely or tired again.

In deference to her condition, Willie relented enough to allow her to bring two girls from Toamua to help her with the housework. She looked radiant as her form filled out. The big bottle of swirling colored waters, purchased with Pele's gold coin, arrived from England. They unpacked it together and set it in the shop window. Pele spent hours watching the red, yellow, and green liquids, forever entwining, never mixing. How much like herself and Willie, she thought, trapped in the same jar but unable to dissolve the colors of their birth.

"Samoan girls usually go home to their mothers to give birth," Jane advised Willie. Actually he was relieved to hear it. He had never delivered a baby in his life, but as a pastor's wife Simativa had successfully introduced hundreds of new souls into the world.

All went well, and Pele returned from a happy month at Toamua with a fine baby girl in her arms. Simativa had already given the child a long Samoan name, but Willie could not pronounce it. He had the baby christened "Margaret" at the font in the Catholic cathedral in honor of his older sister in the Australian convent, who was now studying for the mission field and had agreed to act as the baby's godmother. Pele found it equally difficult to say "Margaret." Everyone finally settled on "Maggie" or "Meki" as befitted his tongue.

Pele regained her strength slowly and Willie allowed the Toamua girls to stay and help her. His business was prospering and he needed someone to wash bottles. He particularly enjoyed inventing new concoctions. The glorious red color of his cochin and epsom-salt mixture had made it famous for stomach aches. He developed plasters to draw boils and quinine remedies to cool fevers. He even began selling Samoan medicines: the dried and pounded bark of the milo for eyes that had slipped in their sockets; viscous liquid from a waxy flower for tonic; and yellow lega powder for sores and rashes. Babies were still his specialty.

Distraught mothers came to him even from the outer islands and rowers speeded the journey by composing a rowing song:[1]

Aue si pepe, ua fa'alau tagitagi.
Si'i lou ma'i, ave ia Suani.
Fesili mai Suani, "Po'o le a lona ma'i?"
Ua tupu le pasai talu lou fa'avai.
Ua tupu le pato talu lou ta'apo.

(Alas, the baby is piteously crying.
If his sickness gets worse take him to Swann.
Swann asks, "What are his symptoms?"
His throat is swollen from sitting in the water.
His glands are enlarged from being out at night.)

Though his sign read chemist, Willie was expected to act as doctor. In the small room behind the shop he lanced boils, pulled teeth, and set broken bones. No matter what service or prescription he provided, he charged the same fee — two shillings. If the patient did not have money, a brace of pigeons, or a giant taro would suffice. So many customers opted for payment in kind that it was often difficult to repay Arthur for supplies. But the pot on Pele's stove was always full.

One of Willie's cash customers was a gaunt, bright-eyed storyteller by the name of Robert Louis Stevenson. He had his own doctor, but once a week he rode his horse down the Siumu Track from his mansion at Vailima to pick up his prescriptions. Willie had read his book *Treasure Island* and often invited Stevenson to stay for lunch. He discovered the author had just completed a book on Samoa describing the conflict of the three powers and the hurricane.[2] He seemed fascinated with Samoan politics and kept Willie up to date.

Mataafa had not been content with the position of vice-king for long. In 1891 he had left Mulinuu for Malie, where he tried to set up an opposition government. He had the support of the Talavou faction of the Malietoa family, half of Tuamasaga district, plus Manono and the southern side of Savaii. That made the Europeans nervous, and the consuls and chief justice had him deported to the Marshalls in 1893. Stevenson admired Mataafa and helped get his followers released from jail. In gratitude they were now clearing the Siumu Trail from his house at Vailima to town, so that he could drive down in his carriage.

The municipal council mandated for Apia by the Conference in Berlin had not been able to do much to improve the town budget. Apia still had no public school, hospital, water supply, sewage facility, or garbage collection. Each family took care of its own. Public revenue in 1894 amounted to $27,000, the duty on less than six thousand tons of copra,[3] and most of that was spent on the new courthouse. According to Stevenson, the only real advance since the hurricane was an international commission under Chief Justice Cedercrantz, which reviewed four thousand scrambled European land claims totaling more than the entire islands. DH&PG claims stood their scrutiny but many others were disallowed and the land returned to the villages.

One morning Willie caught Stevenson coughing blood. TB was a terrible scourge in Samoa and there was no remedy for it in any of his bottles. He offered the only advice he could think of. "Stop writing, my friend. Just rest."

Stephenson smiled. Time was too short for that. A few weeks later he died, leaving Willie as a legacy a standing mirror to pass on to little Maggie. Together with hundreds of others, the Swanns followed his casket to the top of Mount Vaea on a second trail cleared by his Samoan admirers. They named it the Path of the Loving Heart (*Ala o le Alofa*).

After that Willie got his news from the gossip of traders, planters, and traveling salesmen at H.J. Moors' new bar. His merchant friend continued to prosper. He had built the Tivoli Hotel at the corner of the widened Siumu Track (now called Falealili Road). This was the largest and most modern hostelry in town, equipped with amazing acetylene lamps, a windmill for pumping water, and a wharf of its own.

As Willie's world widened, Pele's closed in. There was more housework than ever, with a baby to tend and Willie's new friends to feed. When she could stand it no longer, she took Maggie in her arms and walked the six miles to Toamua. Willie let her go, hoping she would come back refreshed, but often she returned more distressed than ever. Her father's problems were mounting. Pele's brother Misi had grown into a good-looking lad. The daughter of the American consul, Churchward, wanted him, but he himself had succumbed to Elena Passi, a part Portuguese girl and a Catholic. Pepe adamantly refused to lose his last child to that church, but when Elena became pregnant there was another quiet wedding in the Catholic vestry. Pepe died a few weeks later, feeling he had lost his land, his favorite "king," and his children.

Fortunately, Samoans have another way to measure a man's worth, the number of fine mats he receives at his funeral. By that test Pepe's life was a great success. Hundreds of people came with fine mats, food, and palm fronds. Vanquished cockfighters recalled their obligations and sent their biggest pigs. Warriors who had followed him to the bush came to honor him wearing their turbans.

52

Churches from all over the district sent choirs to sing at his wake, and pastors of Faleata pronounced him one of "Samoa's greatest preachers." Even Willie forgot his creditors long enough to send five kegs of beef and ten tins of biscuits. It was a ceremony that would have rejoiced Pepe.

But Pele's heart was troubled by another concern. It was four years now since Maggie's birth and she had not conceived again. Despairing of Willie's tonics, she finally decided to go to Toamua and consult her mother.

She left the chemist shop in mid-afternoon, but it was twilight before she walked into the village. The families were having evening prayers. She sat down beside Pepe's grave outside the house to wait, fingering her rosary. The hymns came to an end, followed by the low murmur of prayers. In the quietness she suddenly heard a strange sound. It was as if the stones on top of Pepe's grave were sliding down! A cold fear clutched her heart. What was happening? Suddenly she felt something grab her. Her mind began to spin, her muscles went out of control. Writhing and kicking, she fell down on the grass.

Her family cut short their prayers and rushed out of the house. Simativa took one look at her daughter shaking with convulsions, and called the boys to carry her inside the house. Cousin Kala ran to find the old healer who lived nearby. Pele obviously needed an expert.

By the time that respected lady with the scraggly hair arrived, most of the village had gathered. It took five strong young men to hold Pele down. The slender girl had suddenly become amazingly strong. They could only hold her still by sitting on her. The old lady had seen this sort of thing before. Pele was possessed by a devil! The healer sat down beside her delirious patient, massaging her head and limbs, searching for the evil creature within her.

Suddenly she found it in Pele's armpit! The old lady could feel that demon wildly thrashing around. She grabbed the flesh of Pele's shoulder in her strong brown hands and squeezed it as hard as she could.

"Let go! Let me go! You're hurting me!" an angry male voice suddenly shouted. Everyone gazed in horror. The voice was coming from Pele's lips!

That did not deter the healer. She squeezed harder.

"Who are you?" she shouted. "Tell us who you are!"

"Ouch!" the voice replied as the old lady dug in with her thumb. "I'll tell you! I'm Pepe and I have every right to punish this girl."

"Why?" the old lady demanded. "What has she done to you?"

"She disgraced me before my LMS congregation by marrying in the cathedral. Even worse, she promised that my grandchildren would be raised as Catholics. And she was actually reciting her rosary on my grave. Now let me go! I want to take her with me!" Pepe's spirit was so angry that it bit one of the boys with Pele's teeth and in the ensuing commotion almost got away.

But the old healer held on firmly. When the boys held Pele's body secure again, she reminded the demon, "Pepe, you were a man of God. The Bible tells us to forgive not just seven times but seventy times seven. You should be able to forgive your daughter!"

There was a pause as the demon considered these words, and the healer pressed her advantage. "I know how much you love your daughter. You would not want to kill her. She is troubled because she is barren. If you released her from this suffering, she will always think of you with gratitude. If you promise to forgive her and leave her body, I will let go."

The devil could see the healer had the upper hand. He gave a sigh of resignation and said, "All right, but give me something to drink first. I am very thirsty."

"Get a basin of water!" the healer called and Cousin Kala ran outside. She returned with water in Simativa's best enamel basin. The old lady held it to Pele's lips. The onlookers gasped with amazement as the demon drank it all.

"Goodby," the devil said. "I am leaving now." Pele's body suddenly relaxed in a deep sleep. Simativa covered her and sat beside her all night long, caressing her daughter's brow.

Next morning Pele awoke completely refreshed. She had no recollection of the night before. Her body and spirit felt unaccountably light. She skipped and ran practically all the way back to Apia, she was so anxious to see Willie.

Nine months later to the day, on October 10, 1897, she presented her husband with a second daughter. Willie was delighted that his tonics had finally proved efficacious. He wrote to his cloistered sister Margaret, who had recently been rechristened Sister Joseph, that he planned to name the baby Agnes after their second sister.

A few months later he received a letter from Australia, but it was not in his sister's hand. Its message moved him strangely.

December 1897

Dear William,

I was delighted to learn from Sister Joseph that you now have a second daughter and that she is to be named after your dear sister Agnes. Please extend my congratulations to your wife.

It would please me greatly if you would allow me to serve as godmother to this child as Sister Joseph does for little Margaret. I would be happy to contribute to her upbringing and supervise her education and training in the Church. Sister Joseph and I feel a special affection for your children, since we will have none of our own.

Our years of training for the mission field will be concluded shortly. We do not yet know where we will be assigned but pray that someday we will be able to meet our godchildren.

Yours in Christ,
Sister Genevieve
(nee Cecilia St. Julian)

At the font in the cathedral the priest took the baby in his arms. How tiny she was to carry blood from two such diverse cultures! He had seen the Samoan and settlers living in two different worlds on the same island. He had noted the pain of Pele and Willie, trying to live two kinds of lives in the same house. But what about a baby trying to nourish two bloodlines in a single body? He raised his eyes in silent supplication: "God give this child a stout heart!" Then he touched her forehead and christened her: Agnes Genevieve Swann. He was the last one to use that name. Everyone else called her "Aggie."

Government Building—Courthouse and Central Office; Apia.

Battleships five months after the One Day War. Porpoise (British) at right, with flag; Falke *(German), left;* Philadelphia *(U.S.), second left.*

PART II

CHILD

Mataafa Iosefo and his thirteen advisors during 1899 January to March Provisional Government.

Chapter 5

The One-Day War

(1898-1900)

DOWNSTAIRS, Willie was examining a sick baby. Upstairs, Pele was trying to keep Aggie off the veranda rail while fixing lunch for Willie's oldest friend. She could never have managed without Maggie. The grave little six-year-old was already an expert at baby-tending, bottle washing, taro scraping, and fixing dishes.

Promptly at noon Willie came upstairs with H.J. Moors. It was the last day of December, 1898, and the merchant had dropped by for his annual tonic. This year he certainly looked as if he needed one. His face was so tired and drawn that Willie had invited him up for a "nip and a bite."

Willie was not particularly interested in politics. All he knew was that Malietoa Laupepa had been unable to collect taxes from his factionalized country, and since 1896 there had been virtually no government at Mulinuu. Laupepe had died in August, 1898, and a month later Mataafa, now seventy-two, had been returned from exile. The "crowns" were up for grabs again. Tamasese Lealofi and Laupepa's nineteen-year-old son, Tanu, still at a mission school in Fiji, were contending the matter with the elderly Mataafa.

Willie was therefore taken by surprise when Moors downed his drink in one gulp and advised, "You had better board your shop, Willie, and lock your family upstairs tonight. This is going to be a New Year's Eve to remember!"

"For God's sake, what's happening now?" Willie asked. Moors brought him up to date. The traditional *tumua* (ranking orators of Upolu) had declared themselves for Mataafa at a meeting in Lelulumoega on November 12. Tamasese had retired in favor of Tanu. Lauati, the great *pule* (ranking orator from Savaii) had again proposed unanimous support for Mataafa at Mulinuu, but Tanu supporters had refused to give their consent. As a result the decision was now up to the chief justice at the courthouse, a newly arrived American named Chambers. He had held several tumultuous sessions on the subject. At the hearing on December 19, Lauati, speaking for Mataafa, had pointed out that the "crowns" had already been formally bestowed on him by Samoa's official traditional kingmakers, the *tumua*. Tanu's spokesman did not argue that. He simply reminded the judge that Mataafa had been made ineligible for the kingship by Europeans at the 1889 conference in Berlin. As Moors pointed out to Willie, this was more than a question of who would be "king"; the real issue was who would be Samoa's "kingmakers."

The merchant snorted with derision. "Samoa is supposedly an independent country! Can you imagine an American with no experience on this island being asked to decide on an issue like that?"

"Well, it's better to make the decision in a courtroom than out in the harbor with warships or up in the mountains with bush knives like before," Willie maintained.

Moors was surprised at his naivete. "Since when have Samoans agreed to abide by someone else's courts? If Chambers doesn't have enough sense to look where the power lies, Mataafa's warriors are sure to take the matter into their own hands. Don't think for a moment that chief is too old to care! I saw several thousand red turbans at Mulinuu this morning and even more at Vaimoso. Tomorrow we will see who really determines Samoa's kings!"

Willie was shocked, but pointed out that there was another interested power to consider. "If Chambers does decide for Tanu, won't the British marines on the H.M.S. *Porpoise* out there in the harbor stand behind him?"

"Who cares about Tanu?" the merchant answered in his practical manner. "What I'm worried about is you and me and our property here on Beach Road. The consuls have now abolished the idea of a European protected area, so we don't even have Samoan superstition going for us anymore. And don't count on a few marines out there, my friend. Apia's surrounded by angry Samoans on three sides out of four. Westbrook says there are at least a thousand Tanu warriors over at Matautu. Tamasese is up at Malifa ready to march down and join him. With Mataafa and his warriors out at Vaimoso and Mulinuu, just where do you think this battle is going to take place?"

Willie asked no more questions. He ran for his hammer and spent the afternoon nailing on shutters and barricading the outside stairs. Pele carried the jar of swirling waters upstairs for safekeeping and cooked extra food.

At two o'clock that afternoon, Chief Justice Chambers appeared in his judicial robes just long enough to nail his pronouncement on the courthouse door. Then he too barricaded himself upstairs to await the holocaust.

Samoans quickly gathered at the courthouse door, trying to decipher Chambers' legal jargon. During the conference in Berlin ten years ago, it read, the German Kaiser had declared both Mataafa and Tamasese ineligible for Samoan "crowns." That left young Tanu the winner.

Angry mutters spread through the crowd. Who gave either the Kaiser or this American newcomer the right to determine Samoa's "crowns"? Such decisions were for *tumua* or the battlefield!

Mataafa certainly did not consider himself ineligible because of Chambers' piece of paper. By three o'clock he was explaining strategy to his warriors in Vaimoso. Young Tanu was in the British consul's office, nervously requesting help from marines on the *Porpoise*.

Both the British and American consuls cast a wary look at the German warship *Falke* also at anchor in the harbor, and hastily informed Tanu that unfortunately their governments forbade them to "interfere in Samoan politics." But they did feel a clear mandate to protect their own citizens. By nightfall the British marines had set up a gun emplacement by the talie tree in front of the LMS Mission compound and made the *Porpoise* ready for evacuees. The German consul and the admiral on the *Falke* piously declared their neutrality. The Catholic Mission favored Mataafa this time. Since he was apt to win, they made no evacuation preparations. All along Beach Road New Year's parties were hastily cancelled and settlers' families huddled in their upstairs rooms, praying that Samoan warriors would concentrate on each other and leave them alone.

Maggie helped her father bolt the upstairs door and then lighted the lamp so that he could clean and load his three guns. Guns had fascinated her ever since Willie had taken her hunting for pigeons. She hung the loaded guns back on the wall except for her favorite, the choke-bore. This she slung over her shoulder and dragged to her bedroom. It was thrilling to imagine herself protecting her baby sister. Two-year-old Aggie was already asleep, her dark curls touseled against the pillow. "Dont' wake her," Pele called as she packed their clothes in a basket. "Lie down beside her and call me if she cries. Just don't go near the window no matter what you hear. You might get shot!"

Maggie struggled out of the gun strap and curled up next to Aggie, but she couldn't fall asleep. Beach Road was deathly quiet, but the crickets in the marsh behind seemed to be shrilling unusually loud tonight. Perhaps they were warning of dugout canoes slipping through the mangroves from Vaimoso to Mulinuu, and brown bodies with blackened faces darting between the palms to encircle the town. The night seemed alive with movement. She put her arms around Aggie, pressed her back against the choke-bore gun, and lay rigid for hours before she finally dozed off.

A single gunshot sent her bolt upright! It had come from close by, a house in Matafele village perhaps. This was followed by a scream, hoarse shouts, and the pounding of bare feet. Then silence. Despite her mother's warning, curiosity got the better of Maggie and she crept to the window.

A hint of light tinged the eastern sky but she could still make out nothing in the eerie gloom. Her scalp tingled as if a thousand other eyes, like hers, were watching for the dawn.

Sure enough, just as the butcher shop became visible, a fusillade of shots rang out from Mulinuu. The warriors were coming! Aggie woke and began to cry. Pele ran in and dragged both children into the center room, where she sat crosslegged on a mat in the middle of the floor with Aggie on her lap. Maggie crouched behind her and Willie knelt beside the front window with a rifle in his hand.

The four of them listened in terror to the growing uproar in the street below. Hundreds of warriors with black lines on their cheeks and turbans of cloth or leaves raced by. Stones hit Willie's shutters from time to time but no one tried to come upstairs. Willie felt a surge of relief.

Again the warriors only seemed to have eyes for each other. Europeans were bystanders even though it was their judge who had made the decision.

By ten o'clock the center of action had moved past their shop. The shouting and shooting were now centered beyond Vaea Road. Willie went downstairs to look for a safer place for his family. He was particularly concerned about Pele, who was now pregnant for the third time. Who knew what excited warriors might do at a victory celebration?

Half an hour after he had gone, Pele told Maggie to slip down to the kitchen and bring up a basket of food that was hanging on the wall. Going downstairs alone frightened the little girl. What if one of those huge warriors was hungry and came after her basket waving his bush knife? Suddenly she remembered the choke-bore in the bedroom. That would scare him! Without telling Pele she crept downstairs cradling the gun in both arms. Fortunately, no one was in sight. She found the basket and, unable to carry both, left the gun on the table in the kitchen shed.

Meanwhile Willie was standing behind a barricade of timber and old boxes in front of the cathedral. Two Samoan preachers in white coats were just crossing the Mulivai bridge from the Tanu side. As men of God they were allowed to walk freely between the lines. Willie ran over to talk to them. They told him that a group of Mataafa warriors had slipped down the path by the Vaisigano and now held Matautu as well as Mulinuu. Tanu was trapped between the Vaisigano and the Mulivai. They also said that the Reverend Mr. Hacket had set up a refuge for British and American women and children in the LMS compound behind the talie tree. A gun and thirty marines had been detailed to guard them and, if necessary, evacuate them out to the *Porpoise*.

That satisfied Willie. He returned to the shop for Pele and the children and their baskets of food and clothing. Huddling together, they slipped down the steps and up Beach Road. The front at the Mulivai was quiet and they crossed the bridge into Tanu territory unchallenged. As they passed Apia village, Pele noticed that the church was packed with Samoan women and children. She longed to join them but she had to depend on Willie's people now.

Across the street at Moors' Tivoli Hotel, the guests had just finished New Year's dinner and were clustered on the porch, discussing the merits of the British gun emplacement under the talie tree. Willie waved at Moors as they passed and turned into the mission compound.

The Bells and their children were already there with several boxes. John told Willie he had decided to send Jane and the girls back to Fiji on the *Taveuni* packet, which had just put in. That would be better than an indefinite stay on the crowded *Porpoise*. Willie agreed the warship was no place for a pregnant woman and promptly decided to send Pele and the children to his parents in Levuka until the danger was over. Passage would be no problem. His cousin was engineer on the *Taveuni*.

Shortly after the Swanns had passed over the Mulivai bridge, fighting erupted again. With wild shouts and volleys of gunfire, Mataafa's men drove Tanu's warriors back towards the Moors store. They would then have been forced to surrender forthwith, except that a Tamasese war group came marching down Ifiifi Street at that moment to reinforce them. Chief Justice Chambers watched the turbulence from his rooms above the courthouse. Something had gone wrong with legal recourse. It was easy to see that Tamasese had brought Tanu's forces only a temporary reprieve and that Mataafa would emerge victorious. As soon as it was dark the nervous judge himself slipped over to the mission compound. Tanu and Tamasese were already there, and the three of them rowed quietly out to the *Porpoise*. Defeated warriors followed in dugout canoes, clustering around the warship like ducklings around a mother.

Pastor Hackett then woke the women and children in his compound, telling them it was time to go. Pele handed Maggie a basket and boosted sleeping Aggie to her shoulder. Soon they found themselves huddling on the Tivoli wharf in pitch darkness. Maggie heard frightened murmurs and splashing paddles but could see nothing. After what seemed like hours, she heard the creak of oarlocks. Strong arms lifted them into a whaleboat and rowed them silently across the dark water. They clambered onto the crowded deck of the *Porpoise* and stumbled over recumbent bodies until they finally found a place to sit down. Pele lowered herself gratefully to the deck with Aggie on her lap and Maggie fell asleep against her shoulder.

John and Willie spent the night at the chemist shop to guard against looting, but nothing happened. Early next morning John went out to the *Taveuni* to arrange passage to Fiji for both families while Willie opened the back door of his shop and tended wounded from both camps. Sporadic shooting continued during the morning as victorious warriors looted and set fire to the empty thatched houses of their erstwhile rivals, but European homes and shops were left untouched.

At noon Willie went upstairs to eat and rest. Just as he was about to sit down, he heard shouting from Convent Road and ran out on the porch to see what was happening. To his consternation, he saw Pele's brother Misi and his friend Iosefa closely pursued by two angry warriors with bush knives. They leaped over the fence and hid in Pele's wood pile. Their pursuers dashed by and into the kitchen shed, emerging a moment later with Willie's choke-bore gun. They tested it by firing shots at the woodpile and then ran gleefully down Beach Road, waving their new-found treasure.

Wondering how in the world his gun got out there, Willie raced downstairs and kicked away the logs. Misi and Iosefa lay inert, bleeding profusely, but both still alive. Willie dragged them up the steps, leaving a trail of blood. Realizing the warriors might soon return for heads, he tried to think of some place to hide the boys. His rooms were far too open. He set up a ladder and hoisted the bleeding bodies into the space above the ceiling, laying them gently between Pele's storage boxes.

Just as he removed the ladder the warriors returned. They soon caught sight of blood in the scattered woodpile and followed the trail upstairs. Willie found himself staring into the wrong end of his own choke-bore gun. When they asked for the wounded men he shook his head helplessly, trying to swallow the lump of fear in his throat. They pushed by and searched the apartment.

Returning empty-handed, they were about to leave when one of them gave a shout and pointed at a growing red pool behind Willie. Blood was dripping from the ceiling!

While one of them tried to jump for the trapdoor, the other aimed the choke-bore gun at Willie's head. Willie didn't dare move but his eyes traveled slowly down the barrel to the dark eyes at the other end.

Suddenly the lump in his throat dissolved. That eye looked familiar despite the black paint. It did not belong to a savage after all; it belonged to Iosua, whose baby he had treated for colic. That rascal had never paid him. Transformed suddenly from victim to doctor, Willie found his voice again. "How's the baby, Iosua?" he asked. "Is he eating again?"

The gun barrel slowly lowered. Iosua seemed relieved to be a father rather than a warrior, but also recalled his debt. "No bring money," he said plaintively. "Mother sick. Big toothache."

"Well, bring her by tomorrow and I'll pull it," Willie said. "But be sure to bring four shillings this time."

"I bring right now," Iosua proposed, thinking he would like to sleep tonight without a groaning mother.

"No, Iosua." Willie replied firmly. "I have to take care of my wife's brother up there in the attic first. Someone has wounded him in the chest."

"Talofa e ia Misi!" (poor Misi!) Iosua sounded deeply concerned. "Mother send him soup when she come well."

"That would be nice of her," Willie said. "Now let me have my gun. I can't imagine how it got downstairs."

Iosua obediently handed him the choke-bore and ran down the steps with his friend, explaining that he carried considerable influence with the distinguished doctor.

Out in the harbor, the *Porpoise* was a scene of utter chaos. Women, children, and missionaries were fainting on the blistering deck. Chiefs, consuls, and captains were conferring in the hold. Hundreds of Tanu warriors shouted to each other across their bobbing canoes, wondering what was happening to their families ashore.

Aggie was hot and fretful. Pele bathed her in a ship's bucket filled with seawater, but drinking water was unobtainable. She tried to move under the sail-cover the marines were rigging up and then got sick herself. By nightfall, however, John had completed arrangements. Pele, Jane, and their children were rowed across to the *Taveuni*. Here too they had to sleep on deck, but at least there was room to lie down.

Maggie woke next morning in a shower of soot. Pele had spread their mats next to the smokestack and the packet was building up steam for departure. A whistle blasted their ears as the little ship started moving and puffed slowly out of the tumult in the harbor.

Maggie found the trip exciting. She trundled Aggie around the deck, washed the soot off her face, and fetched bowls of stew from the galley. But Pele seldom moved from the smokestack. She had never seen her island disappear over the horizon before and was not sure she would ever see it again. Soon she would be completely dependent on Willie's family, rich white people who had never approved of her or the marriage. Seasickness, morning sickness, and homesickness all swept over her at once and she could not eat. She spent the hours weeping into her lava-lava.

Three days later, her dark eyes larger than ever, Pele stepped onto the wharf at Levuka with Aggie in her arms and Maggie clinging to her skirt. Herbert, Frederick, their wives, and numerous children crowded around her, eager to see the refugees from Samoa. Only Willie's mother was missing. They were handed into an elegant carriage. It swept by signs reading "Swann's Cordials", "Swann's Chemist shop", and "Burns Philip—Herbert Swann, Mgr.", and halted at a flight of marble steps leading to Uncle Herbert's house on a terrace high above. It looked like some kind of palace up there with wide white veranda, and tall roofs. Servants had tea waiting for them: dainty cakes and little sandwiches surrounded a shining silver urn. All this made Pele very uneasy. She longed for a small thatched hut where she could relax.

Maggie, on the other hand, was thrilled with her new relatives and their lives. Never had she dreamed of such magnificence! After tea Herbert's wife showed them to a large room upstairs with a canopied bed for Pele, a crib for Aggie, and a cot for Maggie. A servant bathed her with warm water from a pitcher as she stood in a crockery basin. She felt wonderfully clean and secure as she slipped between the white sheets. A deep sleep soon wiped away her terrors.

Pele's recovery was slower. Frederick and James consulted and prescribed a tonic for pregnant females and ten days of bed rest. Actually the latter was a blessing to Pele. As long as she stayed in bed she didn't have to worry about her grammar and her table manners. Herbert's wife declared her a model patient. She never demanded or complained. In fact she seldom spoke. She just followed visitors with large dark eyes which never wept. Every tear had already been shed on the *Taveuni*.

After two weeks she dressed, came downstairs to meals and spent most of her time in the garden playing with Aggie and arranging flowers. She plucked bright hibiscus, threaded them on coconut midribs, and stuck them into green breadfruit. That reminded her of home. Herbert's wife was enchanted with the huge flower balls and hung them around the veranda.

On her third Sunday in Levuka, Pele donned a long white dress, pulled cream-colored gloves over her brown fingers, and anchored a wide-brimmed hat to her bun. Herbert's wife lent her a parasol and they drove to mass together in the open carriage. As soon as they were seated in the family pew, curious eyes turned discreetly to stare at the tall dark Samoan girl among the Swanns. The most piercing of these eyes belonged to mother Marguerita seated just in front of her. This elegant elderly lady took advantage of every genuflection to peek back at her strange daughter-in-law, so different from dear Cecilia St. Julian, now known as Sister Genevieve.

Actually, the old lady was not entirely dissatisfied with what she saw. The girl was indeed beautiful and carried herself with a quiet dignity that bordered on royalty. Hadn't Willie said she was the daughter of a chief? Marguerita was a proud woman but she was also pragmatic. After the mass she asked Herbert's wife to introduce them and ended up by giving her half-Samoan grandchildren a kiss and inviting Pele for tea the following day.

The tea for two turned out to be a great success, not because they unburdened their hearts to each other but because they did not. Marguerita was greatly impressed that her new daughter-in-law poured tea and served cakes in deferential silence without taking a bite for herself. There was no hint of servility, only respect. Pele was equally relieved that, unlike the others, Marquerita neither inquired about her flight nor extended her sympathies. Like Simativa she confined herself to giving instructions. Here at last was someone who would tell her what to do without asking how she felt. The old lady acted like an authoritative elder and that put Pele at ease. Pele's natural deference made Maguerita feel like the matriarch she had always longed to be. It was an excellent relationship and the old lady immediately took over Willie's family. She had Maggie enrolled in the Convent School forthwith, assuring the sister superior that this new little Margaret would someday be "her second gift to the church."

Maggie loved school. Nuns fascinated her with their flowing habits, swinging beads, and mysterious relationship to God. They were relentless disciplinarians but she never felt their rulers on her palm because she never had the slightest inclination to disobey them. Reading and writing came easily to her and the good sisters were pleased with her progress. She was learning a lot at home as well. Beautiful things had always caught her eye and here she saw them every day. She loved to feel her aunt's long beaded dresses, peek into her jewelry box, and gaze at her own reflection in the silver tea urn. Would she own things like that someday?

Uncle Herbert told her such wonders were a reward for paying attention to business. He himself managed a big store and several plantations. Uncle Fred ran the cordial factory and the chemist shop. Uncle Arthur's enterprise in Suva was now so large he was training an Indian to help him. Grandfather, even though retired, still monitored accounts.

Swann women were equally enterprising in their own way. Aunt Agnes married the postmaster general of Fiji and Herbert's wife had nine children, including two sets of twins. But they all referred with greatest deference to an aunt Maggie had never seen. Grandmother especially kept telling her about Margaret, the godmother she had been named for, whose religious name was Sister Joseph. This exceptional lady had renounced all earthly wealth to "marry Christ" and become a "teacher to the heathen." Maggie could see that the future lay in becoming either the wife of a businessman or a nun.

Romping with Pele in the garden and watching grown-up revels in the parlor, Aggie acquired a somewhat different perspective on success. Personality seemed as relevant as industry in reaping worldly rewards. She tested hers out on her grandfather. When she spied him toiling up the marble steps after tedious hours at his account books, she ran to the door and threw herself into his arms, laughing and shouting "Kempa!" at the top of her lungs. He found that irresistible. This child was as vivacious and naughty as her sister was grave and obedient. She revived a tired man's heart. He rewarded her with a piece of candy and a toss in the air and she responded by clowning outrageously. That didn't bring down his wrath, just gales of laughter. Obedience and hard work were not the only road to success.

By June and her sixth month of pregnancy, Pele was increasingly anxious to get home. She dreamed of Toamua even more than the chemist shop. Marguerita noticed her homesickness and sent Willie a note on the *Taveuni*. His letter came with its return.

Swann's Chemist Shop
Apia, Samoa
June 26, 1900

My dear Mother and Father:
I am indeed indebted to you and Herbert for sheltering my wife and daughters during this trying period.
It is a custom in Samoa for wives to return to their mothers for delivery and I realize that Pele's time is near. Also her brother Misi is seriously ill. I have not told her but he was shot in the chest the day she left. I was unable to remove the lead from his lungs. No one here is capable of such a delicate operation. Don't tell Pele but I fear for his life. For these reasons I have arranged passage for her and the children on the next Taveuni *and would be grateful if you would see them aboard.*
You asked if things were now safe in Samoa. The consuls arranged a ceasefire after the January battle and Tanu's side surrendered its weapons. As victor, Mataafa refused to disarm and set up a provisional government of thirteen chiefs out at Mulinuu, awaiting a trilateral commission from Europe. The German con-

sul supported his provisional government but not the British and Americans. In March when Admiral Krantz came in on the U.S.S. Philadelphia with six hundred marines, they declared Mataafa's government illegal and restored Tanu "for the safety of Apia!" Mataafa withdrew beyond the marshes and it looked like war again.

On May 13 [1900], the trilateral commission finally arrived. It first disarmed all factions. Even at this, Mataafa was dramatic. He came into Apia harbor standing on a double canoe and dressed in a long white robe with a rosary around his neck. Behind him stood thirteen warriors in loincloths, bare-chested, tattooed, and each over six feet tall.

The commission then abolished the troublesome "kingship" entirely. Young Tanu formally abdicated and was sent back to school. Now there is no Samoan government at all. Mulinuu is deserted and a German administrator named Solf is running the town. We are awaiting another conference in Berlin to determine a permanent solution. I rather hope it will abolish the three consuls too and put one European power in charge of everyone. Then we might have some peace for a change.

Your grateful son,
William

Beach and Vaea roads. The original Matafale Church, and the Burns Philp store and the Huch house can be seen in the rear.

Chapter 6

Flight of the Wild Bird

(1900-1903)

THE SUDDEN transition from the great white house with marble steps back to the small thatched platform in Toamua did not bother Aggie in the slightest. She had doting relatives in both places. Instead of a satin-lined crib she now shared a pile of mats with Cousin Kala, who lugged her around on her hip all day, mashed her food with her own teeth, and scrubbed her along with the clothes in a stream. There were chickens to chase, no furniture to damage, and guardians in every house across the grass. As a result, Aggie was free to explore. But she saw very little of her mother. Simativa had Pele secreted behind a tapa at one end of the house. When Aggie tried to peek in, she found herself being trundled away on a friendly shoulder. It was confusing but not alarming. Her mother had stayed in bed before.

A few weeks later Aggie woke late after a noisy night. The tapa had been removed and she saw Pele sitting up on her mat with a strange baby in her lap. In consternation, Aggie rushed over to claim her rightful place but Pele only smiled and introduced her to Mary, her new sister. Aggie was relegated to Maggie's old place at her mother's back. It was Mary who now got the breast.

After Pele had regained some strength, Willie told her of Misi's illness and she insisted on visiting her brother immediately. She was not at all prepared for the feverish skeleton she found lying on the mat. This was not the handsome man she had left eight months before. He was a living corpse, wracked with coughs and too weak to sit up. She moved in to nurse him, leaving Aggie with cousin Kala.

Willie was not happy about this arrangement. Misi now had consumption as well as lead in his lungs, and Pele had barely recovered from childbirth. But his pleadings, warnings, and orders failed to move her. She refused to leave her brother's side.

Misi died just before Christmas and was buried from the Catholic cathedral. Willie donated five kegs of beef to the funeral, not so much for Misi as for Pele, who was in a state of collapse. He brought her back to the chemist shop and put her to bed.

After a year of disruption, family life resumed. But it was a slow start. Since Pele was too weak to take charge of the household, Willie sent for the Toamua girls again; but often enough it was seven-year-old Maggie who made the soup, fed little Aggie, and washed the clothes. She made her voice harsh and strident but the older girls just burst out laughing when she tried to give them orders.

Desperately anxious to have his enterprise respected in the European business community, Willie worked around the clock. Since financial stability rather than noble descent was Apia's criteria, he sacrificed everything to pay his debts and then reinvested every penny. Like his fellow merchants he was delighted when the second conference in Berlin abolished the three consuls and left Western Samoa in the hands of one power, even though the hands were German.[1] Governor Solf was an excellent administrator. He enforced laws, settled disputes, collected taxes, and built public works with careful impartiality. The "Pax Kaiserlika" was great for business. German planters and British merchants began to prosper. So did Willie.

As governor of Samoans as well as settlers, Solf took time to examine their unusual political system more carefully. Unlike the consuls, he learned to fluently speak chiefly Samoan, and spent weeks touring the villages talking with Samoan orators like the powerful *pule* Lauati, a ranking orator of Savai'i. The six-foot German governor with the dueling scar was under no illusion about "childlike natives." He was amazed to find a society in which everyone was related to a title and whose language could elevate friends and devastate enemies with the subtle change of a verb. His loyalty to the Kaiser, however, never wavered. Like any good orator he studied Samoan traditional methods in order to advance the interests of his own chief at home.

73

Instead of deporting Mataafa, he encouraged Samoa's political families to collect fine mats and present their hero to the tumua (ranking orators of Upolu) for long overdue installation as highest chief. He required only two changes. Mataafa was to be called Samoa's paramount chief *(ali'i sili)* rather than its "four crown king" *(tafaifa)* and he was to send fine mats to the Kaiser's weddings and funerals through the governors. Every Samoan immediately got the message. The Samoan hierarchy would remain intact, but now the Kaiser was at its pinnacle with Solf as his high orator. Lesser chiefs could run their districts and villages as they always had, provided they showed proper deference. Some might grumble, but at least there was no more confusion.

Moors had lived in Samoa too long to think that Solf's solution would last. "He's smart enough to back the same candidate as the *pule* and *tumua*," the merchant told Willie. "But just wait until he and those ranking orators disagree. Then the real issue will have to be decided, not who is 'king' but who is 'kingmaker!' In a face-off like that you and I would soon be hostages again!"[1]

But Willie was convinced that the problem was settled. As far as he could see, the Europeans were now clearly in control. Germany expected its colonies to subsidize the fatherland, not vice versa, and Solf soon discovered creative methods of financing public works while encouraging European immigration. In 1901 a German millionaire named Kunst bought ten thousand acres and parceled them out to taxable German settlers. From his profits he also refurbished Stevenson's mansion for himself, built a European hospital at Motootua, and erected Market Hall[2] on Beach Road for community entertainments. The rising revenues were used for roads, bridges, research stations, and a public school for settlers' children[3] — German, British, and American alike.

The expanding little European town blossomed culturally as well as economically: social clubs, concerts, a bandstand across from the post office, well-built homes for German administrators at Motootua, and even a merry-go-round for children next to the Tivoli Hotel. Willie helped found a Sports Club and racetrack at Vaiala and purchased sixteen acres with a rambling house at

Lotopa to stable his horses.

Maggie continued her education at Sisters' School on Convent Road, but four-year-old Aggie still trundled after her mother on daily rounds of Saleufi bakery, Verniliker's grocery, and Walter's butcher shop. She enjoyed peeking through the slats of Walter's holding pen in their back yard. Once he even let her ride a huge turtle brought in from Rose Island on Moors' kerosene boat.

Pele undertook a laundry contract for the International Hotel and Aggie followed her mother to the stream every day. The new proprietor, a man named Easthope, had installed a carom room, billiard parlor, bagatelle table, and fresh and salt water baths, and was rewarded by a host of salesmen with clothing to wash.

Aggie loved the bustle and excitement of the hotel and wandered over as often as she could. One day an American noticed the pretty curly-haired little girl playing on the veranda and snapped her picture. Almost a year later, Aggie received a package in the mail. Inside was a cut-glass cake stand with a note explaining that her picture had won a baby contest in the U.S.A.

Mary was as naughty as Aggie. Willie had to put wire netting around the upstairs porch to keep her in. On one occasion she set fire to the curtains and was astonished at the sound whipping she got from her gentle mother. Pele's greatest tribulation, however, was the laundry. Faleola and Kemeli were supposed to collect it every day, wash it in the stream at the end of post-office road, and return it ironed. Dirty clothes appeared regularly but not the girls, and Pele and Maggie often had to do the big bundles themselves.

In June, 1901, Willie got word that his father had died in Levuka. Soon thereafter Pele's mother, Simativa, passed away. Pele spent a week at Toamua for the funeral and after that seldom asked to go home. When she became pregnant for the fourth time, she agreed to have this baby at the chemist shop.

After the funeral Willie became stricter than ever about Samoan custom. One afternoon an old friend of Pele's father came to visit. Seating himself on the floor of the front room, he presented Pele with a basket of fish Samoan fashion. Touched that he still remembered her, she sat down on the floor across from him to acknowledge the gift, slipping her luncheon roast in his basket in return.

Tired after a busy morning, Willie opened the door just in time to see his lunch disappearing into the old man's basket. That was too much for a hungry man.

"Get up off the floor!" he shouted at Pele. "You are the wife of a chemist, not a chief. Haven't I forbidden you to carry on your *faa Samoa* in this house?"

The old man disappeared hastily down the steps with the basket while Pele struggled heavily to her feet. "Don't be angry with me, Willie," she sobbed. "I can't help it. I'm a Samoan."

They had argued about such things before, but this time something in Pele's face touched Willie. He scooped her up in his arms. Despite her pregnancy she had gained very little weight. She looked more beautiful than ever with her large dark eyes and a blush on her cheeks. He kissed her and suddenly started. Could that rosy complexion be due to fever? That night he noticed she was coughing. His heart stood still. Did she too have tuberculosis?

On October 16, 1902, Pele gave birth to her first son and named him William after his father. Baby Bill was perfectly healthy but Pele realized that this time she would not recover. So did Willie. He took Maggie out of school and taught her to strain the jelly of an immature coconut and a piece of pounded sugar cane through muslin to make food for the baby. Pele was too sick to nurse him. Aggie and Mary were sent to live with Cousin Kala at Toamua.

Pele lay in the large bed day after day, worrying about the future of her family. She had already seen what could happen to Willie when he fell into despair. One day she called Maggie to her bedside and whispered, "If anything happens to me, my child, and your father begins drinking, promise me you will take the children and go live with Cousin Kala." Maggie nodded, cold with fright.

European as well as Samoan friends sent food, but all of them knew full well that chicken soup could not cure this scourge of the islands. Why did God have to visit this terrible affliction on a quiet, beautiful thirty-year-old woman with four children to raise? It seemed so cruel!

Unaware of the event so soon to change her life, Aggie

returned home for Christmas. To divert them both, Willie took her to Apia's first toy auction in the display room at the International Hotel. Neither of them had ever seen a German Christmas with fragrant pine boughs, twinkling candles, anise cakes, gingerbread men, tiny fruits of almond paste, and toys of every kind from manger scenes to rocking horses. Aggie was enchanted. The wealth of the world seemed to collect in hotels. Even Willie forgot his pain for the moment in the pleasure of his five-year-old.

At home in bed, Pele picked up the weekly paper and read about a burglary at Dean's house up the street.[4] The thief had slipped upstairs while the family was eating and stolen a gold watch and a purse containing their entire savings, thirty-eight British pounds. That troubled Pele.

On January 10, 1903, Maggie fixed breakfast for Willie and ran downstairs for a game of marbles with her friend Sarah. Suddenly her mother called, "Maggie, come up here!"

Pele was lying in bed too weak to sit up, her hollow eyes bright with fever. "Get the key from my chest," she told the child, "and open the tall cupboard in the corner."

Maggie did as she was told and Pele continued, "Now look on the top shelf."

Maggie had to get a chair, but by stretching she could catch sight of three heavy bags pushed into a corner. "Get them down," Pele ordered.

Maggie's nine-year-old arms were too short to reach the bags but she finally pushed one forward with a stick. It fell to the floor with a heavy clank. Pele told her to untie the bag and Maggie was amazed to find it full of Bolivian gold coins. So this is where Pele hid her laundry money! Merchants had their office safes but, with no bank in town, women had to find secret places of their own. "That bag is for you children," Pele told Maggie between coughs. "Tie it up again and hide it among your dresses but don't tell anyone. This town is full of thieves. Leave the other two bags for Willie. He can put them in his safe."

Pele closed her eyes, exhausted, while Maggie hid the bag. When she returned Pele whispered softly, "Now bring my rosary and wind it around my fingers. I am going away."

Maggie did as she was told, whispering desperately,

"Mother! Mother! Where are you going?" But Pele only gave a mysterious smile and closed her eyes.

A few minutes later Willie came upstairs and ordered Maggie outside. She crouched at the bedroom door.

Suddenly she heard her mother saying, "Willie, please don't marry a village girl. It wouldn't be good for the children. Find an educated *afakasi* (part European) lady from a good family. I want them to get ahead in this town."

She heard her father reply in a shaking voice, "Pele, I don't intend to marry anyone, at least until the children are grown. They are yours and I couldn't bear to give them to another woman. I will raise them myself."

"One more thing," Pele finished weakly. "If there are any fine mats at my funeral, save the three best, one for each of my daughters. Someday they may want to marry chiefs. His family must know she too has good Samoan connections."

Maggie couldn't bear to listen any more. She ran downstairs and sat numbly on the bottom step until she fell asleep with her head against the post.

She wakened to the sound of her father's sobbing and rushed upstairs again. He was kneeling beside the bed still holding Pele's hand. "My 'beloved' has flown," he said brokenly.

Death was not new to Willie, but Pele's was different. He could not think what to do next. It was Maggie who ran for the priest and carried baby Bill to the convent for the night. After performing the last rites, the priest arranged for a funeral mass next day. Willie wanted his wife to be buried at the end of Saleufi Street close to the shop.

As dusk fell, Willie still knelt motionless beside Pele's bed with his head on the coverlet. His sobs had died but a great numbness pervaded him. How could he possibly live through this, their last night together?

As darkness lowered, soft murmurs slipped in around him and unseen hands bore Pele's body to a thick pile of Samoan mats in the front room. Twinkling candles flickered to life around it, revealing a silken fine mat bordered with soft red feathers covering her feet. Her lips were now relaxed in a peaceful smile. She was home again.

The candlelit stillness suddenly swelled with the opening chord of an LMS hymn. Someone seemed to have touched the keys of a great human organ, men's voices resonant and deep, women's soaring above. Utterly astonished, Willie looked up.

The furniture had been pushed back and pandanus mats laid over the carpet. Motionless brown bodies sat shoulder to shoulder filling the entire room — Toamua's choir!

Without thinking, Willie dropped crosslegged to the floor himself. He closed his eyes, leaned his aching head against the wall, and let the deep chords wash over him. Absorbing the music, his twisted heart relaxed. The unbearable emptiness faded. He was no longer alone; he was suddenly part of Pele's great Samoan family. It was bearing him too on its strong shoulders during his hour of need. In his urgency to establish himself in his European community, how could he ever have denied Pele the security of her own? Now, here it was reaching out to him!

All night long choirs from all over Faleata came and went around him. Fine mats swept over his head and piled up beside Pele's bier. How did they know she had flown? Why were they there? Willie would never understand but he knew that Pele must be pleased. This was her heritage from the endless contributions her parents had made to the rites of others. And for once her home was filled with people of her own.

Moor's Wharf and Beach Road, 1905. The Apia Protestant Church, Westbrook house and Vasigano are on the far left.

Chapter 7

Rebels

(1904-1909)

PELE'S BODY may have been buried at the end of the street, but her spirit still haunted the chemist shop. Willie lost all interest in doctoring. It had proved useless to the person he loved most. Sometimes, as he sat listlessly among his bottles, he could hear her moving around upstairs and waited for her to call him to lunch. But she never did.

He found relief only when he closed the shop, packed the four children in his buggy, and spent the day on his sixteen acres at Lotopa. Exercising horses and chasing children kept his mind in the present. As the months went by, he spent less and less time in the shop, and his customers drifted over to Sabiel's new apothecary. When he could no longer afford to pay the lease, he turned the shop back to Krauss and Preuss and moved out to the plantation for good. If evenings at Lotopa proved lonely, he hitched up the buggy and headed to town with two convivial neighbors, Harrington and Danielson. The three of them returned past midnight, their arms around each other, singing at the top of their lungs—to keep Pele's memory at bay.

Aggie was delighted with their new surroundings. This clearing in the forest was far more exciting than an upstairs apartment in town, and she now had a fun-loving father instead of a preoccupied chemist to explore it with. She ran around after Willie all day in her little black bloomers, helping him curry horses, weed vegetables, and chase ducks. He taught her how to snatch gangling prawns from under ledges in the stream and shuck off their tails to make delicious curries. Her vocabulary exploded with his earthy phrases and the stories he brought home from the bar. That made him laugh. She knew how to snap him out of his blues.

"Aggie," he said, tousling the curls of his jolly little companion, "you should have been a boy."

Harrington and Danielson did not agree. "Ten years and old Willie'll have an Emma Coe on his hands," they nodded sagely over their mugs. "That li'l tyke already cheers a man's heart. Seems to cum' to her jes' natural."

Willie hired a Chinese named Kuka to help with the meals and the garden, but it was Maggie who bathed and dressed the children and tried to teach them manners. She blustered and fumed, but it was an uphill battle, especially with Aggie. Willie was no help. He just kept egging Aggie on.

Mary was the venturesome one. She enjoyed visiting. Willie often found her at Toamua with Cousin Kala, who kept her for weeks on the excuse that she was treating her for ringworm. Mr. Garrick, the well-to-do manager of Tanumapua plantation, wanted to adopt the lively little girl who was always coming to see him. Willie flatly refused. "Thank you, sir, but I promised to raise the children myself."

Heaven seemed determined, however, to provide a mother for his little brood. The two godmothers who had studied so assiduously for the mission field finally found themselves appointed not to darkest Africa but to the Samoan Islands. Sister Joseph was made mother superior of the convent school in Leone, American Samoa; and Sister Genevieve was assigned to teach at Sisters' School in Apia. It did not take them long to locate their godchildren at Lotopa.

"Maggie looks tired and underfed," Sister Joseph declared after examining her godchild. "I am taking her back to Leone with me to prepare for confirmation."

Maggie was ecstatic. Willie had reservations but had to let her go. He did not want his strong-minded sister to lure Maggie into his mother's trap for oldest daughters. He was no believer in celibacy, especially for women.

Sister Genevieve could hardly proclaim her godchild either overworked or underfed. Aggie was robust and very happy where she was. She felt no need for a mother. But Sister Genevieve did have need of a child. It was finally agreed that Aggie would live at Lotopa but attend Sisters' School in Apia every day, where her godmother could monitor her progress. Mary would also be enrolled there the following year.

Shorn of his children, Willie might have become depressed again. But Sister Joseph insisted that, while there was a time for grief, two years of it amounted to self-indulgence. She urged Willie to reopen his shop in new surroundings where Pele's ghost could not find him. Their brother Arthur was quite willing to help him start again.

With his sister's firm finger in his back, Willie browsed around Beach Road and found that Wilkes was leaving a small one-story shop near the Mulivai, right next to the spot where he had drunk his first toast to Emma. The Family and Commercial Hotel had long since been replaced by a hostelry full of DH&PG clerks, so that customers would be close at hand.

Willie opened his second shop in May, 1905, setting the big jar of swirling waters in the window to attract business from Sabiel's apothecary down the road. Now he hitched up the buggy early every morning and drove to work, dropping Aggie at Sisters' School. Two Solomon Islanders took care of his horses and old Kuka minded Mary and baby Bill.

Aggie assessed her new situation for two days. Sisters' School was an attractive cement structure with arched porches along the front and a chapel at one end. The sisters lived upstairs. In front stood a statue of the Virgin Mary surrounded by a spacious flower garden. A low wall separated it from Convent Road.

Most of the pupils were part-Samoan like herself, daughters of merchants and planters. They ranged in age from six to twenty. For some reason there were far more boys than girls in this little colonial town, and since the Sisters hoped to produce enough good Catholic wives to go around, they were happy to enroll any female not already married.

The first thing Aggie proposed to check out was Convent Road, but the nuns had organized themselves to forestall such inclinations. Every moment of the day they were strategically located with tinkling bells and long switches to herd the girls into line and march them to their three R's, needlework, or chapel.

By the end of the second day Aggie knew she hated this

place. Black bloomers were more comfortable than blue pleated jumpers and starched middy blouses. Shrimping was far more fun than sitting on a hard plank in an airless classroom. If there was anything of interest in what Sister Aloysia pointed to on the blackboard, it was lost on Aggie anyway because it was in German. She sat as far back as possible so that the teacher would not call on her. Perhaps she would not even notice if the seat were vacant.

Unfortunately, one nun always noticed. At recess time, when the other children were finally released to run around the yard, Sister Genevieve took Aggie by the hand and led her upstairs to her own room for a glass of milk and a few motherly admonitions.

At first Aggie was embarrassed by this special attention. What would the other girls think? Why was this woman so partial to her anyway? Did she feel she could replace Pele? But before long Aggie realized that the relationship might have some advantages. When she claimed to be sick, Sister Genevieve let her sleep on the bed. When she got in trouble, Sister Genevieve came to her rescue.

Maggie's education in American Samoa lasted only three months, not because she was a poor pupil but because she was such an ardent one. Her admiration for her godmother was unbounded. When Sister Joseph commanded, everyone obeyed. She didn't have to shout. Maggie studied diligently for confirmation, praying she would someday be just like her godmother. On confirmation day she wrote Willie that she had found her vocation —the holy church.

Willie's response was an irate letter to Sister Joseph, demanding that his daughter be returned immediately. When she did not appear on the next boat, he threatened to come get her himself.

Maggie sighed and resigned herself to her fate. Heaven must have destined her to be a mother. Otherwise why would it have given her so much practice? She returned home to mind her small brother and help Willie in his new shop. Doctoring appealed to her and she tried operating on her own finger when her sewing needle became embedded near the bone. It never did heal properly. Having headed Maggie towards motherhood, Willie allowed her to go to dances. Aggie watched her older sister with envy. Why couldn't she also quit school and go to balls?

Mary entered Sisters' School the following year and Aggie's attitude was not improved by the discovery that Mary was an excellent pupil. She sat up front, volunteered answers, and did her homework. It did not take her long to outstrip Aggie in the three R's. Both were natural actresses, but Mary took these gifts seriously. She studied German songs and poetry. Aggie preferred to "play the fool."

Annual prize-giving was the greatest event of the school year. Marist Brothers and Sisters of Mary vied in displaying the talents of their boys and girls to doting parents. In 1908 the festivities were held in the Vorbildungs Verein, a German social club in Saleufi. According to the local paper[1] Mary Swann, a student in the first class, was hilarious as lead actress in "Eine Schulmeisterein aus Zopfzeit" and also appeared in "Das Locke in der Tischdecke" and an English sketch, "The Duchess." Miss Aggie Swann of the second class got rave reviews as "Impudent Topsy."

"Aggie just happened to be perfectly cast," grouched Sister Aloysia, disappointed that far better students like Freuan, Stowers, and Hellesoe girls had been mentioned only as "others."

Aggie considered Mary's enthusiasm for school a betrayal. Caught between a "dedicated student" and a "little mother," the only possible role left for her was "black sheep." She played that with flair and was rewarded with anxious attention from Sister Genevieve, chuckles from her father, and secret admiration from classmates who wished they dared do the same.

She and Mary now rode to school on bicycles, but Aggie's bike was prone to problems. Mary often arrived to find no one pedalling behind her. Sister Genevieve finally settled that problem by driving to Lotopa each morning in a buggy to bring her godchild to school. Walking home in the afternoon, Aggie liked to take detours, exploring alleys, climbing trees, and arriving home bedraggled, too late for tea.

"Just look at you!" Maggie fumed. "What happened?"

"Fell out of a tree," Aggie shrugged.

"Well you can just stay home tomorrow and wash your

84

own uniform this time!" Maggied snapped. Aggie gave a sly smile and so did Willie.

Sister Genevieve began to wonder if heaven itself opposed an education for this child. One morning as she turned the buggy into the school yard, Aggie jumped out unexpectedly. Her blue jumper caught on a nail and the frightened horse dragged her twenty feet before someone could stop him. The children bent over her inert body, sure that she was dead. Sister Genevieve's heart stood still. She laid the limp form on her bed and sent for a doctor. He pronounced the victim scratched but by no means dead and prescribed a week's vacation. Aggie enjoyed every minute of it.

A few months later, when Sister Genevieve parked the buggy in the driveway, Aggie refused to get out. Her godmother finally left her there and she fell asleep. Presently a coconut dropped from a palm, deflected on a branch, and glanced off Aggie's head. Again Sister Genevieve laid the unconscious body on her bed and called the doctor. That required two more weeks of rest.

"What if her brain has been damaged?" worried Sister Genevieve at the refectory table.

"What brain?" Sister Aloysia harrumphed unkindly. "If she ever had one, it wilted on the vine. You've spoiled that child rotten, Sister Genevieve."

Aggie was not alone in suffering inner stress. In August, 1905, Mauga Mu crater on Savaii blew up, sending streams of red-hot lava down the mountainside, destroying forests and plantations before splashing into the ocean in a cloud of steam. Sister Aloysia took pains to explain to Aggie that such an eruption might happen to sinners whose conduct did not recommend them to heaven. But patient Sister Genevieve never lost hope. When Aggie was eleven she arranged to have her godchild sleep at the convent for a week to prepare for her first communion.

It was an exciting week for Aggie. Girls in the communion class were regarded with awe by younger pupils. Something mysterious was happening to them. They were excused from class for special prayers in the chapel, followed by lectures on proper conduct for young Catholic women. There was something faintly sexual about the whole thing, but Aggie wasn't quite sure what it was. They ate in the refectory and their table manners were carefully scrutinized. In the evenings they sewed themselves pure white gowns.

On confirmation Sunday they marched down the aisle of the cathedral wearing flowered crowns on their hair and knelt in front of the altar. It felt like getting married! Afterwards everyone congratulated them on their new lives. It was a great let-down to Aggie to return to school on Monday and discover she was still "Blacksheep Aggie."

But she and *Mauga Mu* (Burning Mountain) on Savaii were not the only ones in the mood for rebellion. Governor Solf was experiencing even more serious problems than Sister Genevieve. Lauati Namulauulu, the great *pule* from Savaii, had always been the chief he respected the most. The orator was quick-witted and knew his people well. He had also learned enough English and German to mix freely with Europeans. Those were just the qualities Solf needed in a right-hand man to handle his dealings with Samoan society.

But Lauati had one serious disqualification for the job. Instead of believing what Solf told him, he had a distressing tendency to draw his own conclusions. Solf told him that Germany had made Samoa a "protectorate" to preserve and advance its unique way of life. Lauati concluded that the governor was more concerned with protecting and advancing DH&PG than the *faa Samoa*. In fact, he suspected with good reason[2] that the governor intended to abolish the *pule* and *tumua* and make himself sole "king-maker." Lauati concluded that it was high time to abolish the governor instead.

That was not easy. He could no longer stir up a rival consul. But Lauati did not lack political ingenuity. First he encouraged the small incoming German planters to protest to the Kaiser that the governor was favoring large corporations like DH&PG. Perhaps that would get him removed. It did not. Next he talked Mataafa into starting a Samoan corporation to buy up copra. Perhaps that would bankrupt Solf's administration. Unfortunately, Samoans lacked sufficient experience to run a corporation and it soon foundered.

Solf did not feel seriously threatened until Lauati declared in a speech to the high chiefs' council at Mulinuu that "the *pule* and *tumua* are the only rightful rulers of Samoa."[3] Solf could not afford that kind of competition. He immediately declared an end to the *pule* and *tumua* and had those ranking orators, including Lauati, expelled from Mulinuu. That should show Samoa who was picking "kings"!

Nothing could have helped Lauati more. The traditional hierarchy coalesced behind him as it had for Mataafa. No overseas governor with all his warships could abolish a Samoan institution from the hearts of its people! Lauati lost no opportunity to honor Samoa's traditional figures. He toured the villages with great ceremony. *Tamaaiga, tumua* and political families, demoralized by exclusion from the governor's hand-picked council of chiefs at Mulinuu, took heart once again.

"The *faa Samoa* is stirring!" Moors warned Willie. "If Lauati can convince all the *tumua* and *tama aiga* to join his rebellion, their warriors could have us running for cover again! Samoans still control their villages."

Willie realized that this time he could not barricade his family upstairs on Beach Road. They were now living out in the country at Lotopa. He decided to move back to town. What place could be safer than Moto'otua, just up Falealili Road where Solf and his administrators had built substantial homes? Willie settled his brood in a house at Malifa.

Eleven-year-old Aggie was delighted to discover that her new backyard ran down to a stream. The Vaisigano was beautiful, bordered with trees and babbling over smooth gray stones. Not far below was *Loto Samasoni* (Sampson's Pool), where she could leap into deep water from a high rock. The river was lined with mossy ledges where shrimps could hide.

A few weeks later, as she started to school with Mary, she realized that it was a perfect shrimping day. A fragrant breeze wafted through the air, flickering the leaves so that they sent shafts of sunlight across the road. She could imagine how the stream looked now. The shrimp would be out chasing sunbeams across the ripples. Her feet slowed and she turned aside, pretending to examine a ginger blossom until Mary's sturdy form disappeared around the bend. Then she turned and ran through the backyards to their laundry shed. Here she stopped just long enough to don her little black bloomers and grab a hand net on two sticks. Tying a lavalava around her waist, she ran down to the river.

As soon as the water caressed her ankles, she knew she was right. It *was* a perfect shrimping day. She felt along under a mossy ledge and shrimp fled in all directions. She snatched at one with her net and held it up to examine its gangling legs, beady eyes, and curled-up tail. Then she rolled the lavalava around her waist and tucked the wiggling creature into the folds at her back. By the time she reached the bridge upstream, six of them were tickling her ribs, and by late afternoon her pouch was so full she could not bend at the middle. She felt at peace with the world and only hoped it would remain like that when Willie came home.

Kuka was hanging laundry in the back yard. Aggie dipped some water over herself in the shed and put on dry clothes. Then she slipped into the kitchen and dropped her treasures into Kuka's pot of boiling water. When they turned pink she snapped off their legs and shells and stirred up a fragrant curry. Hopefully that would remind Willie of the fun that they had together at Lotopa and he would forgive her.

Even before he started home from work, Willie knew that Aggie had played hooky. Sister Genevieve had sent him a note asking if she were sick. He was also aware that Maggie and Mary would demand justice. On the other hand, he understood Aggie's temptation. He only wished he could play hooky from his chemist shop.

When he opened the door and smelled shrimp curry, he couldn't help but smile. "Anyone home?" he called.

Maggie, Mary, and young Bill responded from the dining room, but Aggie's chair was still empty as they sat down.

"Aggie!" Willie called. "Come eat! We have nice shrimp curry for tea."

"Yes, dad," responded a tiny voice from the kitchen. Aggie slipped into her seat but could not eat a mouthful. Apprehensively she sat watching Willie's fork go up and down. Finally he wiped his mouth with a flourish and called, "Kuka, that was a delicious curry! Where did you get the shrimps? I didn't give you any money."

Kuka did not answer.

"Kuka!" he asked sternly, "Did you steal them?"

"Oh, no, Doctor Suani, sir!" Kuka replied hastily, appearing at the door. "Aggie catch them."

Willie turned slowly and glowered at Aggie's bowed head. "Aggie! Didn't you go to school with Mary today?"

"No, dad," she responded in a whisper. "I dodged back. I wanted to make you something special for tea."

"Aggie, you are a very naughty girl and deserve to be punished!" he said, standing up. They all waited breathless as he unbuckled his belt. Justice was finally at hand.

"But you sure make a damned good curry!" he suddenly concluded, and collapsed into his chair, laughing.

Sister Aloysia heard this outcome with disgust and poor Sister Genevieve began her escort service again. Willie instructed Kuka that, as punishment, Aggie was to report home at three o'clock every day for a month to help with the housework. Aggie complied. At least she had one perfect day to remember.

Actually she got more holidays than she expected that year (1909) thanks to another rebellious spirit, Lauati. In November, Solf returned from Germany with a new bride and found the "bush wireless" crackling. Lauati was on his way to Apia from Savaii with a fleet of canoes and hundreds of warriors. He was going to stop at Leulumoega on the way and ask the *tumua* of Aana to join him in a return to Mulinuu. With no warship in the harbor, the only obstacles to reestablishing a Samoan "king" at Mulinuu were twelve German administrators and a defenseless little town.

Solf may have been an autocrat but he was no coward. Before dawn the following morning he called for his two-seater, kissed his new wife goodby, and trotted through the deserted streets to Mataafa's residence at Mulinuu. He knew his paramount chief (Alii Sili) was bitter about the lack of power and deference accorded him under the new regime, but he also knew the old hero was aging and needed the house and stipend he was now enjoying.

After greetings had been exchanged, Solf said, "You have served your people long and well, my friend. They regard you quite rightly as their hero. That is why I have come to ask you to save them once again. Only your influence can protect them now from disaster. Will you come with me to Leulumoega and explain to the *tumua* that if they join Lauati they will face the wrath of the Kaiser?"

The old warrior hesitated, torn. He had already complained to Lauati that he was being treated "lower than the youngest German clerk." The *pule* was leading this rebellion for him.

Solf then tried a more Samoan approach. "Remember, my friend, that you were installed by the *tumua* of Aana and Atua, not by the *pule* of Savaii. Since when have the proud *tumua* yielded leadership to a *pule*? You and the *tumua* must show this upstart Lauati who has the last word."

That did it. Mataafa got into Solf's carriage and the two men set off at a trot for Leulumoega. Anxious faces watched them from the windows along Beach Road. What could two men do against that angry Samoan horde?

Next morning Germany's ablest administrator faced Samoa's greatest orator across the *malae* (meeting ground) at Leulumoega. Behind Solf stood his *alii sili*, Mataafa. Behind Lauati crouched the warriors of Savaii. On the slope above them the *tumua* of Aana listened from their open council house. Which side would they choose?

Lauati spoke first, planting his orator's staff in the ground between his first two toes and swinging his orator's switch *(fue)* from shoulder to shoulder. In the tradition of great orators, he began in a whisper and raised his voice gradually in grand crescendo. His tongue was smooth as silver, his words were music to Samoan ears. The gist of his message was that the *tumua* were indeed the "fathers of Samoa's kings." As such they must never allow themselves to be "seduced by a foreign mistress." His metaphor was clear to everyone.

Solf rose to reply. His Samoan was as good as Lauati's but he did not carry an orator's switch. Instead he unfurled his own symbol: a huge German flag emblazoned by an enormous bird with outstretched wings. "Take good note of your Kaiser's eagle!" he thundered. "Its wings are wide enough to protect his loyal subjects all over the world. But," and his voice fell to a menacing whisper, "look also at its talons and its beak. They are long and sharp enough to tear his enemies limb from limb!"

Mataafa followed with a plea for peace.

Out of deference to their *alii sili* and the talons of the German eagle, the *tumua* of Aana did not join Lauati's rebellion. Bitterly disappointed, the *pule* returned to Savaii with his warriors. His rebellion became known as the *Mau a Pule* (belief of the *Pule*).

Solf trotted back to Apia with Mataafa. To the great relief of the good burghers, no warriors pursued him. Opinion at the Tivoli bar favored deportation of Lauati on the first warship. But Solf had respect for the daring Samoan. He even went to Savaii in person to offer the silver-tongued orator not only forgiveness but a position in his government as Samoan judge *(faa masino)*. Lauati proudly rejected the offer, declaring it would be like "committing adultery!"

Regretfully, Solf ordered his opponent to appear before him at Mulinuu. This time the governor took the precaution of having a warship at hand. The great *pule* arrived with Savaii's fleet and war canoes from the Aiga-ile-Tai and Tuamasaga districts as well. The warriors camped on the bluff at Vaiusu across the bay from Mulinuu, and Beach Road panicked again at the sight of blackened faces. But Solf knew he had won. So did Lauati. The German eagle now inspired more fear than the *pule* and *tumua*. The denouement had only to be played to its inevitable conclusion. The missionaries pleaded with Lauati to recant in the name of peace. He refused, and was deported to Saipan on the warship, together with his wife and a few loyal supporters. He never saw Samoa again.[4]

The European community sighed with relief and settled back to enjoy its prosperity and conviviality once more. Maggie, now sixteen, attended weekly balls at Market Hall. Once when a German warship was in port she made herself an especially beautiful muslin frock, as soft as silk. Willie drove the whole family to town that evening. He jumped off at the Tivoli bar, instructing Aggie and Mary to continue on to Market Hall with Maggie and wait outside until the ball was over. They were still too young for dances.

Two hours later, Maggie was waltzing with a young clerk form Kneubuhl's store when she noticed people looking at a tall, handsome German officer. He was danc-

91

ing with a schoolgirl in a blue jumper, socks, and white middy. Maggie froze with horror. There was Aggie, oblivious of her age and attire, chatting and flirting with the officer as if she had attended dances all her life!

Overcome with embarrassment, Maggie grabbed her twelve-year-old sister by the arm and blurted in her ear: "What do you think you are doing? In your socks, too! Just wait until Dad hears about this!" She was so angry she drove them straight home, completely forgetting to pick up Willie.

Next morning at breakfast, Aggie decided to take the initiative this time. "Guess why Maggie forgot to pick you up last night, Dad," she began.

Willie already knew. "She was probably just jealous!" he laughed. Maggie was so furious she stamped out of the room. Why did her father always side with Aggie instead of helping her put reins on this unregenerate little hedonist?

Sister Aloysia rose to the challenge this time. In her classes a student's state of grace was made visible in the seating arrangement. Desks were assigned according to plus and minus points for behavior. According to current calculation, Mary had a plus seven and was sitting in the front row. Aggie with a minus seven was in the last.

Actually Aggie took pains to keep this position because it put her beside her best friend, Louisa Sase. Louisa's father ran a bakery and every morning sent her to school with two cinnamon buns — the soft, sticky, delicious kind. One for herself, the other for Aggie. Instead of finishing it outside, Aggie slipped her bun into her desk to make it last as long as possible. She lifted the desk top to shield herself from view whenever she took a nibble.

One morning she was so hungry she forgot to check the teacher's position before lifting the top. As she lowered it with a delicious morsel in her mouth, she found herself face to face with irate Sister Aloysia.

"Aggie! What have you got in your mouth?" the nun asked in such a stentorian voice that everyone turned around.

"Nothing, Sister," Aggie lied, tucking the morsel back into her cheek to make room for the words.

"Let me see inside your desk!" Sister Aloysia ordered

angrily, jerking the top from her hand.

In an agony of fright the culprit hastily recanted. "Sorry, Sister. I told you a fib. I do have something! I'm sorry! I'm sorry!"

But Sister Aloysia was beyond forgiveness. She strode to the corner and returned with her switch. "Stand up!" she ordered.

Aggie rose slowly to her feet. Every eye in the room was on her. "You are the naughtiest girl in this school!" The German words were cold as steel. "And for once you're going to get what you deserve. Put out your hand!"

Aggie extended her fingers gingerly but retracted them quickly as the stick whistled down. That made Sister Aloysia angrier than ever. "Put out your hand and keep it there!" she ordered harshly.

Again the stick whistled down and spent itself uselessly in the nun's habit. Someone tittered. Sister Aloysia was now beside herself with rage. Next time the switch found its mark right across Aggie's cheek. "That will teach you to disobey!" she thundered. "Now go to the corner, kneel down facing the class, and stay there until I tell you to get up."

Aggie obeyed like a robot. The welt across her cheek throbbed and puffed until her right eye was only a slit. She closed both eyes to hold back tears, not of repentance but anger. When she finally did peek out, she saw a first grader in the front row was mimicking her by squinting one eye. That was the last straw!

When the bell rang Sister Aloysia swept by her, saying in a normal voice, "You can get up now, Aggie. Just don't let me catch you doing such silly things again!"

It might be over for the nun, but not for Aggie. By the time she had her stiff knees straightened out, the classroom was empty except for Louisa, who sat sobbing in the back row. Aggie went back to her desk without a word and began to take out her books. "What are you going to do?" Louisa asked in a choked voice.

"I'm going to work for my Dad," Aggie replied loftily. "I'm never coming back here!"

The brave words made her feel better. She strode over to the chemist shop. Willie did not mention her swollen eye. She must have got the better of someone. He just set her to washing bottles.

Next morning Aggie got up and made her father's breakfast. "Aren't you going to school today?" he asked.

"No," she replied firmly. "I'm going to help in the shop from now on and study at night. I'll learn more that way."

That was quite possible. She certainly couldn't learn less than she had in school. Here she was twelve and still in the third grade! So Willie did not insist. He just bought an exercise book and a pen and hoped for the best.

To his astonishment, Aggie suddenly became an avid reader. Even in the daytime he sometimes caught her with a book and she wrote down words to check with him at night. Unfortunately he could never brag about this to Sister Genevieve. Aggie's literary interests were confined to cowboys, Indians, and romances.

Lauati, the silver-tongued orator, 1909.

Chapter 8

Tifitifi

(1910-1912)

WITH SOLF'S HELP, the European plantations were able to solve the major problems of raising and marketing copra, cocoa, and rubber on a commercial scale. Only one ingredient held them back—cheap and docile labor. In the Solomons the British had put an end to "blackbirding" (kidnapping laborers) and Samoans had never proved satisfactory as plantation hands. They had land of their own. Solf finally found the solution in south China, where illiterate Swatow farm boys were so oppressed by warlords that three shillings a month for six ten-hour days a week sounded like a bounty. The governor arranged eight transports of "coolies" between 1903 and 1914. He outlawed whippings but saw to it that the workers remained affordable and uncompetitive. They were strictly forbidden to start businesses of their own and were repatriated after three years unless they had married Samoans.

Once the labor problem was solved and land made available for forty-year leases convertible to freehold, European enterprise flourished. DH&PG expanded its holdings and was joined by the Deutsche Samoa Gesellschaft (DSG), Safata Samoa Gesellschaft (SSG), and Samoa Kautschuh (rubber). A Herr Langen purchased twelve thousand acres, including Faleula plantation and the Cornwall estates, to sell off in small parcels. Solf did not confine development to German enterprises. A British venture, Upolu Rubber and Cacao, leased six thousand acres and old settlers were allowed to improve their holdings. Cobcroft purchased seventeen thousand acres and a Dane named Nelson started a string of bush stores. H.J. Moors did better than ever. By 1913 he owned not only the Tivoli Hotel but fourteen stores, Papaloa and Palauli plantations, and Rose and Sofia islands. Per capita production reached heights unknown before (or since).

Social clubs in Apia also proliferated. When the German Concorda Verein erected a building at the west end of Beach Road, English-speaking settlers decided to build theirs at the east end. Heatherington-Carruthers rescued some kauri timbers from the International Hotel when it burned in 1911 and hauled them up to a piece of land he had purchased by the Vaisigano bridge. He erected a fine two-story building on it which he entitled the British Club.

Cultural groups flourished as well: a Littarische Verein, operatic society, symphony, and town band. There were sports clubs like the Turf Club, Tennis Association, and Hockey Society; philanthropic societies like the Red Cross; and all sorts of church groups. Seldom has a community of less than two thousand souls had more options to fill its spare time. The same faces met each other morning, afternoon, and evening — only the activity varied.

Origin did not determine who "belonged" to this buzzing human hive. Newcomers arrived from everywhere. Ah Sue, the Chinese bandmaster, was "in" as well as any *afakasi* who managed to succeed in business. What counted was money or a government position. This custom resulted in a ladder with the governor and wealthy merchants or planters at the top, managers and small businessmen in the middle, and clerks at the bottom. Traditional Samoans were not included; they had their own hierarchy. Also excluded were Chinese "coolies" and "fallen" Europeans. The latter were white men who had failed in business, "gone native," or otherwise disgraced themselves. "Coolies" had their way paid home, but "fallen" Europeans were in limbo. Most of these unfortunates slept on crowded thatched platforms in the marshes, courtesy of Samoan friends, and spent their waking hours looking for a bottle.

As long as Willie had a chemist shop, the Swanns were half-way up the ladder. What chance did his three lively daughters have to raise their status? They couldn't very well get rich on their own. The only enterprises owned by women were brothels and boarding houses, which gave no status. But Sisters' School provided a very acceptable route up the ladder. With training in two languages, good manners, and housewifely skills, their girls could usually benefit from the oversupply of males by marrying "up."

96

Once "there," they could engage in an endless round of parties and club meetings without having to work at all. It was an enviable position. After seeing the "good life" in Fiji, the Swann sisters wholeheartedly subscribed to this route. Given their vivacity and good looks, success was almost certain.

With the Swann girls, it was now clear that upward mobility would depend on a husband rather than their father. After Pele's death, Willie had a difficult time holding onto a rung at all. Sick babies, luminous eyes, screaming horse races, and curly-haired daughters brought out uneconomic impulses in him. His children found these traits rather loveable and adjusted to them in various ways: Maggie as "little mother," Mary as "high achiever," and Aggie as "co-conspirator." It never occurred to them that these selfsame traits might cause them all to "fall"!

Sitting alone in his hot dusty shop one morning, Willie glanced up to see two large dark eyes staring in his front window at the jar of swirling waters. The eyes were brimming with tears! The sight startled him. Had Pele's ghost returned? No. It was not Pele but Lui's pretty young wife, Faafete. She came from the Tuiletufuga family, which lived in Apia village right behind his shop. He recalled treating her baby the month before, surprised that so young a girl already had two children.

Seeing her in tears upset him strangely. He opened the door and she came inside, baby Denny in her arms. He offered her a cordial and after she had regained her composure she explained that Lui had decamped with Pela "because she was rich" and that her in-laws had turned her out. She was afraid to return to her relatives because her own family chief, Tuiletufuga had disapproved of Lui in the first place. Now she had nowhere to go.

Deeply distressed at the inhumanity of it all, Willie offered to rent a room for her and the baby nearby. He brought them a basket of food each day when he came to work. Faafete was so grateful to the generous gentleman old enough to be her father that she massaged his back when he was tired, pressed ti leaves to his forehead when he was sick and made love to him when he felt lonesome.

Love had a wonderful effect on Willie. After eight years of deprivation, his heart blossomed and his eyes sparkled again. Faafete believed him inexhaustibly rich and he tried never to disillusion her. His generosity provided her not only with a livelihood but a chance to show "that bastard Lui" she could do better without him. It also offered her a chance to get back into the good graces of the Tuiletufugas.

It reminded Willie of old times again, requests for kegs of beef, tins of biscuits, and bolts of cloth. But he was more tolerant than he had been with Pele, afraid he might again mix love with pain. He told himself that no one had ever heard of a Samoan going bankrupt. God must take special care of them. He had never quite trusted the Good Book admonition to "take no thought for the morrow." Well, this time he would have faith like a Samoan and stop this constant struggle to make money. Only one thing still bothered him. How would he tell his children about Faafete? He finally decided to say nothing at all.

It was not long before Maggie, who handled household finances, began to encounter difficulties. The rent for their house at Malifa fell into arrears. Sometimes they didn't have enough food. Willie brought less and less home. He coped with the problem temporarily by moving the children back to Lotopa, where they did not have to pay rent and could raise vegetables. But before long he realized he could not support two families at once. He would have to consolidate them.

He decided to present Faafete to his children as a *fait accompli*. He simply brought her and baby Denny home one night after everyone had gone to bed and installed them in his room. He would explain things quietly at breakfast.

Early next morning Maggie heard a baby cry and opened her father's door to investigate. After that there was no opportunity to explain things quietly. Maggie was seventeen. For eight of these years she had been sole mistress of this little household, foregoing her childhood, schooling, and church vocation to be its "little mother." Now without warning she had been displaced by a girl barely older than herself, plus an unrelated baby with whom they would have to share their slender resources. The little world she had organized so patiently exploded and with it her temper. She screamed, tore down the lamps, and smashed Pele's best glasses against the wall as if to make visible the destruction of the family. Aggie and Mary rushed out and watched petrified as their older sister vented her rage. They thought she had gone mad. Willie assured Faafete that Maggie would soon calm down. She always did have a sharp temper.

Maggie reached the end of Pele's glassware but not the rage within her. It grabbed her by the throat whenever she spoke to Faafete after that, leaving nothing but a few curt words. It spilled over at night into a secret diary she called her "Law of Compensation." To its pages she confided her darkest fears and suspicions. She didn't show it to anyone but it helped drain the venom from her blood.

Aggie did not particularly mind the new arrangement. She noted that Willie seemed happier with a woman and that Faafete in her own way was good to him. She would never replace Aggie as Willie's co-conspirator, since she always treated him like a chief with formal deference. In some strange way, Aggie felt even closer to her father now. He seemed more human and she could tease him. Their relationship bewildered Faafete. "Aggie acts more like your chum than your daughter," she told Willie.

"Must be the tomboy in her," he laughed. "She seems to know where it hurts to be a man."

Faafete had her own way of expressing affection. She was fiercely jealous of Willie and absolutely dedicated to elevating his status with the Tuiletufugas. A fine opportunity soon presented itself. The most important Sunday on the LMS church calendar was the *Mē*, when each family presented its annual contribution. The *Mē* in 1910 was especially important to Apia's LMS church members because it was their turn to host the white missionary. The church was overflowing, not so much to watch the missionary as the contribution ceremony.

After the opening prayer, the highest deacon seated himself with great dignity at a table below the pulpit and opened a large notebook. In a stentorian voice he intoned the name of each family. Titleholders rose in turn to call out the couples of which their family was composed, whereupon one of their children would run forward with its contribution. The deacon carefully totalled these and announced a sum for the extended family group. Everyone listened eagerly and compared results. The reputation of the family was in direct proportion to its contribution to the Lord.

For as long as anyone could remember, the Seumanutafas had headed the list. It could hardly be otherwise since they had the highest title, the biggest plantation, and the most couples. In fact, Seumanutafa had invited a whole village from Niue to come live on his land. They presented him with a basket of fish every day and helped with such ceremonies. When the deacon called his name, Seumanutafa rose confidently. It took him some time to enumerate all his couples and the deacon had to check his arithmetic several times before he announced in a monotone, "253 marks!" Seumanutafa was pleased. It was the best they had ever done.

Tuiletufuga's name was called second. He was apprehensive. Judging by the number of children who were running forward with only five marks, this was going to be their bad year with the Lord. He did not call on Faafete. Her elopement with that bounder Lui had disgraced them all and he hoped never to see her again. While everyone was waiting for the family total, Tuiletufuga was surprised to see Faafete herself slip up the aisle unbidden and whisper something in deacon's ear. The deacon straightened up and intoned in the selfsame monotone, "Three hundred marks from Doctor Suani!" His hands shook a little as he added this to the Tuiletufuga total. It was the single largest contribution in his experience, and from a Catholic too!

A wave of surprised murmurs undulated across the congregation. Suani's name was on every lip and Faafete smiled with satisfaction. That would show Tuiletufuga she was not to be written out of the family so lightly. The "distinguished doctor" would again be the talk of the village. Tuiletufuga might even want to adopt him and assign them a house and a plantation on the mountain. Then Willie would not have to work in his dusty little shop any more. Too bad he wasn't here to see all this! His daughters had gone to mass and as usual he had stayed at home.

The news did not reach Willie until next morning. He and Maggie were at the back of the shop scrutinizing three legal notices that had arrived by messenger. They were from Nelson, Moors, and Fabricius, and indicated that these firms had waited as long as they could for repayment. Friendship was one thing but business was another. They had foreclosed on his property, which would shortly be put up for auction.

It was almost a relief to Willie. The endless delaying tactics were over. So were Faafete's contributions, since he could not get credit anywhere. He would lose Lotopa but he still had a green thumb. Maybe he could "go native" back in the bush somewhere, build a hut, shoot pigeons, watch the sunset. That life was not so bad.

To Maggie, on the other hand, bankruptcy was the end of everything: shop, home, friends, balls, parties, and marriage prospects. Swanns would now be numbered among the "fallen" and all because of that little trollop who had bewitched her Dad. In her despair she decided to show Willie what this usurper was really like. She snatched the "Law of Compensation" from her bag and shook it in his face.

"Listen to this!" she cried in a last desperate effort to regain her position in the family. "Then you will see how that girl has been cheating you!" She started to read it.

Willie was livid before she finished the first paragraph. He tore the diary to shreds before her eyes. Wherever he went, he told Maggie, Faafete would go with him.

Maggie had lost. She felt she could live with the family no longer. A few weeks later she left for New Zealand with a friend to study dressmaking. Willie let her go, realizing that otherwise there would never be peace at home. His family seemed to be crumbling around him just like his business. He couldn't bear to watch and started drinking more than ever.

After his creditors had dismantled his assets, he found himself with nothing except one more upcoming mouth to feed. Faafete was pregnant.

At this desperate moment someone unexpectedly took pity on him. Olaf[1] Nelson, born of a Danish father and a Samoan mother, managed an extensive chain of bush stores around the island, which he supplied from a central firm in Apia. When his first Apia store next to the Central Hotel burned down he purchased a large section of Beach Road including Willie's first chemist shop. He built a large warehouse on one side and a copra wharf on the other.

Now he stood with H.J. Moors on the top rung of Apia's ladder.

Calling Willie into his office one day, Nelson said, "I need a manager for a bush store out at Tifitifi. It's a small place but it does have a Samoan house and a well. Business isn't brisk but there's no doctor at that end of the island. Perhaps you could handle calls on the side."

Willie jumped at his offer. As a Nelson storekeeper he had a tentative hold on the bottom rung of Apia's ladder, though it was of little value. Tifitifi was twenty-five dusty miles from the Tivoli Bar, the Turf Club, and the balls at Market Hall. He arranged for Mary and Bill Jr. to stay in town with the Freuans to go to school. Aggie and Faafete accompanied him into limbo.

Aggie found the move exciting. It was like going back to Toamua after hectic years in town. Willie, Faafete, Denny, and her new half-sister Daisy lived on a small thatched platform under the breadfruit trees. The store itself was a two-room shack with a counter and shelves in the front and a storeroom in the back, where Aggie slept to watch over things. Behind the shack was a bin for the coconuts brought in by their customers to exchange for tea, sugar, and kerosene. The only other amenities were an outhouse, a brackish well, and a thatch raised on unsteady poles over an open fire and earth oven. This was their kitchen.

Thirteen is a confusing age, a watershed between child and woman. Aggie alternated. On days when she felt like a child she played *Nonu a togi a togi e*[2] with the village children or marble games using the round seeds of the *pu'a* tree. Glass marbles on the counter in the store were a forbidden luxury. But her favorite playground was the warm, shallow lagoon. At low tide she rose early and waded out to pick up tough black *loli* (sea cucumber), which she hacked into little squares and strung on a coconut leaf midrib. Next day they would be soft and chewy, with the delicious salt tang of the sea still in them.

One night she went torch fishing with a village couple in a small dugout canoe. Their smoky torch of palm fronds was the only speck of light on the whole black sea. Peering into the transparent water, she could see a hole in the coral squirming with lobsters. They were crawling all over each other. In a few minutes they had lifted sixty into their small craft. The hollow log canoe was so full that the man had to swim alongside while Aggie and his wife paddled. They steamed the lobsters that night and drove them to Apia next morning. They opened their baskets on the sidewalk and sold out right away. This was bigger and better shrimping!

Willie took her quail shooting with him at certain times of year. After he sat on the beach and fired into the clouds of birds, Aggie collected the fallen and drowned them in the sea. Baked into little pies they tasted even better than pigeon. What more could a child want?

Grown-up days were different, filled with tantalizing mystery. Something was happening to her, but what? At Tifitifi as at Lotopa she ran around barefooted and barechested, clad only in her little black bloomers. She never thought about clothes until one day a German clerk from the DH&PG plantation nearby galloped up on his horse.

"*Guten Morgen*, Aggie!" he called, hitching his horse to a tree. When he turned she noticed that he was staring not at her but her growing breasts. Strangely embarrassed, she crossed her arms and turned away.

"*Huebsches Maedchen*," (pretty girl) he murmured and ducked hastily into the store.

It was intriguing and confusing. She told Willie about it.

"Is that so!" he responded angrily, uneasy to discover that Aggie was growing up. "Well, I guess that means we must go to town and buy you a dress." He wasn't sure how else to handle this new responsibility.

Aggie was overjoyed. She had always wanted a pretty, grown-up dress. Her body tingled with joy as she put it on. Maybe now Dad would let her go to dances like Maggie! That shimmering thought soon collapsed with a painful realization. Who would send an invitation to her way out here? Who, in fact, would ever see her transformation?

Breasts were not the only portent of maturity. Dad began to give her more responsibilities. Every fortnight after the copra was dried, someone had to take the sacks to town. Aggie was the most reliable person left. Willie taught her to harness and handle two horses. The wagon had benches facing each other in the rear, with enough space between them to carry eight sacks of copra. Her job was to sit on a storage box up front and drive the horses. As soon as she had learned to pound a grommet and mend a brace, Willie sent her off to town with the load.

Galloping down the road at dawn, her black curls flying, Aggie experienced a glow of power as tingling as the thought of romance. She sensed new strength in herself. Maybe she could help Willie climb back up the ladder again. It was a heady thought! By the time she reached town at noon she was hot and tired.

As she drove into Nelson's yard, she noticed the great man himself watching her from an upstairs window. What piercing eyes he had! He came down to check her sacks in person and ordered the clerk to bring her a lemonade and a packet of biscuits. Did he do that for everyone?

After she had made purchases for the shop, she packed everything into the storage box and climbed on top of it for the long trip home. As she left the yard she glanced up. There he was again, watching her from the upstairs window. The power of the man thrilled her. When he ordered, people obeyed!

But Tifitifi had its bad days too, days she hated to recall. Often these began with a visit from Faafete's relatives. Willie's lonely spouse never let her kin go home without a basket with tins of meat, five pounds of sugar, two yards of cloth, and a bag of candies for the children. The frequency of their visits and her unfailing generosity severely tested the bush store's resources. If Willie remonstrated there was always a fight and a retreat to the bottle. Poor Dad never seemed to win!

Faafete no doubt suffered too. All her relatives could see that Willie had plenty on his shelves. When she could stand his parsimony no longer, Faafete would throw a keg of beef and a tin of biscuits into the wagon and go home for a couple of days, leaving Willie in an agony of remorse for fear she would not return.

But she always did; and Willie was always overjoyed to see her. Too bad, Aggie thought — what made life meaningful for one brought ruin to the other. Despite it all the lovemaking went on. The following year Faafete presented Willie with a son they named Fred.

Unfortunately, no amount of forebearance and forgiveness could change the fact that Tifitifi's bush store was in decline. When they got word that Nelson himself was coming out to check the inventory, Aggie panicked. He would soon discover that the income of the little store no longer matched its dwindling supplies. Her father would be fired and that would be the end of their last toe-hold on Upolu. They would forever be doomed to the ranks of the "fallen"!

A few days later, in New Zealand, Maggie opened a disturbing wireless: "DAD ILL STOP COME HOME STOP AGGIE."

Frightened but gratified that the family needed her, Maggie quit her sewing lessons and returned on the next boat. Dashing out to Tifitifi in a hired carriage, she ran breathless into the shop and stopped short in surprise to find her father seated calmly behind the counter.

"Hello, Maggie," he greeted her pleasantly, as if he had seen her yesterday. It was Aggie who had to explain.

As soon as Maggie had a chance to go over the accounts, Willie discovered that Maggie's temper had not improved a bit. She blamed it all on Faafete. But her concern for the family fortunes was as strong as ever. She went back to Apia with the last two bolts of cloth and turned them into dresses on Freuan's sewing machine. During Faafete's absences she brought her dresses to Tifitifi and sold them in the store.

Her best customers were the Solomon Islanders with Samoan wives working at the nearby DH&PG plantation. "Oh, Misi Meki!" cried one small black man running into the shop while she was at the counter. "Me want *lava* for wife-wife."

"Did you bring me one of her dresses?" Maggie asked. "I need to know her size."

"Oh no. Me forget!" he said, crestfallen. "But she big here." With two arms he outlined a wide circle before his chest. "And big, big here! Soon come pikinini." He grinned proudly and described an even larger circle at his waist.

Maggie laughed, tore out a side seam, and sewed two dresses together. He ran out waving it with delight.

Two months later Nelson came for the inspection. His clerk counted and called out all their cash and cans while Nelson himself added and subtracted the figures in his ledger. Aggie and Maggie watched the process, terrified.

Had the dresses made up for Faafete's largesse?

Finally the great man leaned back and looked at them thoughtfully, "I don't understand it," he said. "Tifitifi is the only store I ever had that made eighty-four marks more than it should have. How do you explain that?"

"I changed your yard goods into dresses," Maggie confessed. "I'm a seamstress, you know."

That evening Nelson proffered Willie a drink and asked, "How does an easygoing old codger like you come by such loyal daughters? Good-looking, too! It's more than one man deserves. Here's to your girls!" Willie drank to that.

Nelson lingered on at Tifitifi almost a week. The endless pressure of business had exhausted him. Here he had time to listen to the lapping waves at dawn and watch the twilight creep across the purple mountains. It reminded him of his childhood in Safune years ago. The Samoan half of him felt at peace out here. He could relax.

Willie baked him delicious quail meat pies. Every morning Aggie waded out into the lagoon looking for sea slugs to make him *lolis.* Her natural twinkle revived his tired spirits. How strange, he thought, that he, at the top of Apia's social ladder, should envy Willie, clinging so uncertainly to its bottom rung.

PART III

ADOLESCENT

Aggie — at sixteen.

Chapter 9

Leone

(1912)

ONCE A YEAR the Sisters of Mary had a religious retreat to renew their commitment after a hard year of teaching young girls. The 1912 retreat was held in Apia and Sister Joseph came over from American Samoa on the little coastal steamer with several of her staff.

She visited Tifitifi and took Willie to task about Aggie. Someone ought to prune that rampant young plant before it was too late. It had already proved too tough for Sister Genevieve. "Let me take her back to Leone with me for a semester," Sister Joseph urged Willie. "Aggie's almost grown now and someone should teach her to act like a lady."

"You're quite right," Willie agreed with relief. "I'm certainly not the one for that job. She needs a mother superior!" He was only too happy to turn Aggie's supervision over to his sister. This daughter would never be tempted into the cloister. The only question was whether she would even go to school.

Actually, Aggie leaped at the opportunity. It might give her a chance to get away from poverty and try her wings. This was the first time she had ever been to American Samoa. She wriggled onto the crowded hatch of the small interisland steamer and sang songs and exchanged food with her neighbors as the little vessel lurched eighty miles through the darkness to the neighboring island.

At dawn the bucking deck suddenly steadied and they found themselves in the spectacular harbor of Pago Pago under the square shadow of Rainmaker Mountain. A wagon was waiting for Sister Joseph on the wharf and a priest drove them as far as Nu'uli, a few miles down the coast. Here the road ended at a wide shallow bay. The nuns disembarked and waded in gaily, wimples bobbing and

109

rosaries afloat. Aggie followed and three young men brought up the rear with their boxes.

Laughing and dripping they clambered up the beach on the other side. The nuns squeezed out their billowing black skirts but did not change. Why bother? There were plenty of mud holes and rain showers to come. Sure enough, the day alternated between rainbows and sunshine as they made their way through an endless succession of coconut groves, thatched villages, and dark forests. Finally, in the late afternoon they stopped on top of a hill from which they could look down on the western end of Tutuila. As they ate a piece of taro, Sister Joseph pointed to Leone, with its church steeple and convent school nestled in a valley far below.

The excitement of the trip faded abruptly next morning, when Aggie found herself fastened into exactly the same routine she had managed to escape three years before: starched uniforms, marching lines, hard benches, and chapel. The only difference here was that she had no friends. Before the week was up, she was asking herself how her father ever expected her to learn social graces in a place like this. She was homesick for the freedom of Tifitifi.

One afternoon when she could stand it no longer, she wandered over to Leone's bush store, facing the beach and a small wharf. Its sign read "Pritchard's General Merchandise." A tall slender girl a few years older than herself was stacking cans on a shelf behind the counter. Aggie watched, admiring her tight-waisted dress and carefully set dark curls. The latest fashion! The girl turned with a smile and Aggie knew at once she had found a friend and a real lady.

Lena was from a well-known family in the islands. Her grandfather Pritchard had been the first British consul in Fiji, introducing the long-staple cotton that had lured Aggie's grandfather to the Rewa. Lena's father was a well-to-do shopkeeper in American Samoa. She herself had just returned from school in the States, a gentle, refined, open-hearted girl. Aggie was deeply impressed and soon confided her frustrations to these friendly ears. Lena understood completely and immediately invited Aggie to come and live with her.

"I'll go ask Sister Joseph myself," she said.

Sister Joseph was already in despair. Her niece was not stupid, but she seemed impervious to academic learning. Lena was a well-mannered, deeply religious young woman; if she thought she could teach that little rapscallion something, let her try. The mother superior agreed to let Aggie spend all day with Lena, provided she return to the convent at night.

Lena led Aggie into a new and wonderous world. Aggie followed her new friend everywhere, copying her walk, her talk, her smile. Lena soon sewed up a dainty fashionable frock for her devoted admirer. "Forget that horrid old uniform," she said. "This will make you look more grown up." It certainly did. All of a sudden Aggie looked like a lady, a livelier version of Lena.

"It takes more than a dress to make a lady," Lena warned, and introduced her to activities she had never known existed. Lena was more than a shop girl; she was her father's hostess, and he had many guests. She showed Aggie how to make dainty cakes and sandwiches, pour tea with a raised finger, and maintain a pleasant banter. Lena never used earthy words and Aggie made every effort to swallow hers lest she distress her friend.

Most exciting of all, Aggie discovered that Lena had an admirer. His name was Ben Kneubuhl and he ran a big store in Pago Pago. Every weekend he rode out to Leone to see Lena and often brought a friend.

Lena was by no means a "wild" girl. She planned these occasions very properly and always included Aggie. One Saturday, for example, they hiked down the coast to Atauloma with picnic baskets and ate on the grass by the stream. On another occasion they rode horses to Pu'u Naite and climbed up to the wireless station. In the evenings they turned on the gramophone and taught Aggie the latest dance steps. Never had she had so much fun! She could never seem to get enough. Ben was amazed how quickly she learned. But one thing he could never figure out. Who in the world was teaching Aggie to be such a flirt? Certainly not his polite and modest Lena!

Ben had a young friend named Ewing. Before long Ewing became a weekend regular at Leone. He found Aggie the life of each party but never dared tell her.

111

After all, she was only fourteen. Finally he confided his problem to Lena.

"My parents are sending me to high school in California next week. It may take a couple of years. Do me a big favor, Lena," he pleaded. "Please tell Aggie to wait for me! I'll be back. I really will."

Aggie was delighted to hear of Ewing's problem. Even though she never saw him again, he had told her what she wanted to know—yes, she too was attractive to men!

The rest of the school term sped by unnoticed. Suddenly Sister Joseph announced it was time to return to Dad. Aggie and Lena shed tears, entreating the nun to relent. Having observed Aggie's precocious development, however, the good sister was no longer sure she could handle it all. "No!" she said flatly. "Aggie has already learned enough. Now what she needs is a father!"

Aggie felt her new skills would be wasted in the country and her sister agreed. Maggie was still living with the Freuans. Her sewing enterprise had expanded and Aggie's new flair for fashion might be useful. She let Aggie stay with her in town.

Maggie had a serious suitor now, Peter C. Fabricius II. He was the son of a Danish sailor who had developed a trading station at Poutasi in the days when it was a shipping center. The family later moved with the times to Apia, where they now owned two stores. As far as the social ladder went, Maggie was doing well for herself. Unfortunately, however, Willie would have nothing to do with Peter because of his part in the bankruptcy proceedings. He would not even speak to him. Peter was not discouraged but Maggie was wavering.

About this time an amazing entertainment was introduced at Market Hall. It consisted of a kerosene lamp, a mirror, and a lens. When a roll of film was cranked quickly across the lens in front of the light, shadowy human figures seemed to jerk around on a sheet at the front of the hall. They appeared to be either chasing or kissing each other in utter silence, but a violinist and the audience helped explain it all with appropriate sound effects. The result was so mesmerizing that former jugglers, magicians, impersonators, and poets found themselves out of work, displaced by a strip of celluloid. "Pictures" were the rage of the town.

Peter arranged to take Maggie, John Betham, Mary, and Aggie to the "pictures" a few weeks after her return. Aggie could hardly wait but when the evening finally arrived she had a dizzy headache. That was unusual. Maggie sent her to bed and she went without a word. That was even more unusual.

When Maggie returned from the "pictures" she found her sister tossing, turning, and babbling incoherently.

Maggie had seen fevers like this before on house calls with Willie. Pressing a wet cloth to her sister's brow she told Peter, "Bring your horse and buggy up to the steps. I've got to get Aggie out to Tifitifi right away. If she's got typhoid, Dad's the only one who can help her."

It was midnight before they started the twenty-five-mile journey, holding Aggie upright between them. She was burning with thirst and crying for a drink. At first Maggie refused. Hadn't Dad said typhoid had something to do with water? By the time they reached Puipaa, however, Aggie was shaking all over.

"Peter, please stop!" Maggie cried. "Perhaps she does need a drink." Peter jumped down, woke some boys in a nearby house and came back with a cup; but Aggie was no longer able to swallow.

"We must get her to Tifitifi quickly," Maggie sobbed. "I think she's going to die!" Peter sped through the dark villages like Goethe's "Erlkönig" in the popular German ballad about a father trying to reach home before the angel of death snatches his child from his arms.

One look at Aggie transformed Willie into a doctor again. He lifted her tenderly from the carriage, laid her on a mattress in the store, and worked over her for hours. When Peter left that afternoon, Willie went out and shook his hand. "I never thought I'd say this to you," he told his creditor, "but thanks. You saved her life. Come back and see us anytime." Peter had won himself a wife.

Business, booze, and bickering all ended as Willie fought for Aggie's life. Faafete sat beside her fanning away the flies for hours at a time. Relatives who had formerly dropped in for handouts now brought food instead: a string of tender reef fish, a bowl of chicken broth, or the chunks of black sea slug that Aggie loved so much. For the second time Willie realized that the Samoan custom was not always a burden. In times of need it was a real support. The following months were a time of healing not only for Aggie but her father. As she recovered, so did his confidence in himself. Perhaps he was meant to be a doctor not a storekeeper. Aggie had responded to his touch.

He began setting bones, pulling teeth, and prescribing epsom salts again. Sure enough, his fortunes improved. One night he confided his new resolution to Aggie. "You know what I really want? I want to open a chemist shop in Apia again. Nothing fancy this time, just a few bottles in the cheapest place we can find. At least then we could all be together. I know myself better now and I think I could make it this time."

Count von Luckner and Oesterlich.

114

Chapter 10

Age of Innocence

(1913-1914)

THE ROAD BACK to Apia was not easy. It required more this time than simply finding a shop and supplies; old creditors had to be paid and no one, not even Arthur, was willing to loan Willie money. Aggie took over Nelson's store; Willie went on medical calls; Maggie sent dresses to sell. Even Faafete made a sacrifice; she no longer entertained relatives. But progress was still slow. Few customers were able to pay in cash. It was a chafing time for Aggie. By now she realized that nature had dealt her a great hand for romance: self-confidence, good looks, a sense of humor, and a spark of wickedness. She wanted to play it to the hilt, but here she was, stuck out at Tifitifi where no one would ever notice her!

She had underestimated her visibility. On one of her trips to town with the copra wagon, she spent the night with Maggie. Dora Simpson, an old friend from school, dropped by after tea and suggested they walk over to Bill Tattersall's house at Malifa. Bill's porch had been a magnet for teenagers ever since he had learned to play dance music on his accordian.

Dora and Aggie had just perched themselves on the railing when Dora's friend Werther sauntered up with a German clerk, whom he introduced as Ohle. The four of them discussed the new building DH&PG had just completed out towards Mulinuu. It was a sumptuous affair, a full block long, with a dining room big enough for balls, a palatial lounge, and over a hundred bedrooms! Apia had seen nothing like this before and called it the Casino. DH&PG had built it for overseas employees: managers would stay in the left wing and clerks like Werther and Ohle in the right. After describing its wonders, Ohle invited Aggie to its housewarming ball the following Saturday night.

"I would love that!" she breathed with shining eyes.

"Of course I would need to ask your father for permission," Ohle said properly. "Where can I reach him?"

Aggie's heart skidded. "We live way out at Tifitifi," she admitted miserably. That was the end of Ohle and the ball. Next morning she drove back to that impossible trap in tears. Her life was ruined!

Two days later she was counting coconuts for the drier when she heard a commotion up the road. Looking up, she saw a crowd of village boys whooping along beside a cloud of dust. From inside the cloud came honking and coughing noises like those of an angry stallion. On her last trip to town Aggie had heard of the "horseless carriage" a merchant named Hanson had imported from Hong Kong, but he certainly would not send it way out here!

With a screech of its brakes and a parting shot from its muffler the complaining contraption halted right in front of their store and Johnny Ah Mu jumped out, barely recognizable in a leather jacket and goggles. "Is Doctor Swann at home?" he asked Aggie with a formal bow. "I have an important message for him." His tone implied a death of some sort and Aggie ran to call her father.

"Doctor Swann." Johnny bowed again as Willie appeared, rubbing his eyes. "I have this letter for you." The crowd watched with rapt attention as he withdrew a sealed envelope from his breast pocket. Willie tore it open and read,

Casino Hotel
June 5, 1913

My dear Dr. Swann:

With your kind permission I would consider it an honor to escort your daughter Agnes to the Casino Housewarming Ball on Saturday next.

If you are agreeable I will send this car to pick her up wherever you suggest.

I promise to look after her well and escort her home safely by half after midnight.

Yours respectfully,
Ohle M. Schwartz

"Do you know a man by this name?" Willie asked, sur-

116

prised, as he handed Aggie the letter.

"Yes, Dad," she said, her heart suddenly leaping with excitement. "Dora introduced us at Tattersall's last week!" Willie did not have to ask her how she wanted him to reply. She was already jumping up and down.

"Well," he said, after Johnny's machine had lurched back down the road with his reply, "I guess that means we will have to go to town Friday and buy you some material for a ball gown." Aggie threw her arms around his neck and gave him a big kiss. Dad did understand what things were important!

They reached town earlier than usual that day and visited four or five stores. Finally Aggie spied just what she wanted, a soft beige material with shiny brown satin stripes. It was perfect. Willie spent every penny from their till to buy four yards. She took the package straight to Maggie, who fingered the material critically and pronounced it satisfactory. They smoothed it out on the dining room table and began to snip and baste.

That evening Aggie turned on Freuan's gramophone and taught Dora some steps she had learned at Lena's parties. She was too excited to sleep and rose early Saturday morning to wash and curl her hair as Lena had taught her.

That afternoon Maggie hemmed the last frill around the neck and skirt of Aggie's first ball gown. She tried it on in front of the mirror and could scarcely credit her eyes. A sophisticated woman of the world stared back at her. By the time Ohle knocked at the door and helped her into the horseless carriage that evening, however, the sophisticated lady had vanished. The gown graced a little girl rigid with fright, who couldn't think of a thing to say. Neither could Ohle, immobilized in his first tuxedo. They sat in stiff silence as Johnny drove them down the street. Everyone stared at them, to see what dignitaries might be riding in the "horseless carriage." Aggie squeezed her eyes and her handkerchief tight, afraid to look lest people burst out laughing. Lena had not prepared her for such publicity! What if she did something wrong? Ohle would be sorry he had brought her.

The enormous new Casino was blazing with lights as the car sputtered up its wide drive and stopped with a jerk in the portico. All eyes turned to see who would emerge. Aggie rose with dignity as Johnny opened the door but the frill of her gown caught under her heel as she tried to step down and she plunged headlong into the arms of a portly gentleman who hastily introduced himself as Herr Hanson from Hong Kong. Aggie could not utter a word. What does one say to the owner of a "horseless carriage" one has just fallen out of? She curtsied quickly and ran past him into the lobby.

As soon as she stepped into the ballroom, however, she felt a rush of relief. It was full of girls from Sisters' School. She had known them in middy blouses and they looked so uncomfortable in their new ballgowns that she started to giggle and couldn't stop. Ohle hung a dance program on her wrist and whirled her away.

An endless series of well-scrubbed German faces bowed in front of her every time the music stopped. She had no chance to sit down. When Ohle finally appeared with a "heavy supper"[1] and a glass of wine, she was only too grateful for a rest. Wine was a brand new experience, but she took care to sip it as casually as if she drank it every night. It tasted terrible but she sent Ohle for another glass, hoping to restore the sophisticated lady. He brought it back with word that it was already after midnight. He must take her home right away or her father would not let her come again.

Ohle left her at Freuan's door with a formal bow. She was grateful that he didn't ask to come in. The whole family was waiting up to hear what had happened. She wanted to go right to bed but they pressed her for every detail.

"Did you drink anything you shouldn't while you were dancing?" Maggie asked.

"Only lemonade," Aggie replied, taking full advantage of her sister's wording. The wine had come with supper. She drove back to Tifitifi with Willie next day more determined than ever to get back to town for good.

Willie had underestimated his greatest asset; three lively daughters were not to be discounted in a town over-supplied with men. His creditors, especially Fabricius, softened their demands and finally declared themselves satisfied. Willie was free to try his own business again.

He packed their meager belongings into the wagon, realizing that it would be even harder than before with two more mouths to feed. They moved in with Faafete's relatives while they looked for a place they could afford.

Westbrook's "slate" house[2] next to the British Club had already had its day and was now moldy and cracked with age. No one had lived there for years because it was said to be haunted. Westbrook's son was skeptical about Willie's ability to "make ends meet", but what did he have to lose? He rented it to the Swanns for ten shillings a month.

The whole family moved in: Mary, Aggie, Bill Jr., Faafete, Willie, Daisy, Fred, and a niece named Paese. Maggie did not join them. She and Peter had married[3] and now lived in his fine house up the hill. The slate house had no shop but Willie built some shelves in the front room and set out his bottles hopefully.

There was no rush to his door. It was difficult to compete with Sabiel's freshly painted apothecary from a moldy house at the edge of town. But village mothers still remembered their "distinguished doctor." They brought colicky babies and left gifts of food, so that there was always something to eat.

One late afternoon Willie sat on his crumbling steps with his chin in his hand. One cash customer today and the rent two months overdue! If Westbrook evicted him, where would they go? Suddenly he felt someone sit down next to him in the gathering dusk. It was Maggie. She had strolled over from Fabricius' store near the courthouse, where she had opened a seamstress shop. Willie told her his worries.

"No wonder business is slow," she said brusquely. "Just look at this moldy dump you're in. Who in his right mind would buy medications from a cave?" She waved with distaste at the slimy "slates" behind them. "What you need is a bright, clean shop with no leaks in the roof."

"And where do you think I'd get something like that?" Willie asked hopelessly. "I can't even pay for this 'cave.'"

That was not easy to answer. They sat in silence in the dark. Someone lit a lamp in the British Club and it twinkled at them across a patch of mangroves. The sand strip was so narrow at this point that it could barely hold Beach

119

Road. Waves lapped the shingle beach on one side and crickets sang from the marsh on the other. The British Club was almost like a little island. Willie observed idly that if Heatherington threw in a few loads of fill between them, the club wouldn't be flooded so often.

"But I guess the old man is just too busy making money," he concluded bitterly. "He can't be bothered."

"Why don't you offer to fill the gap for him?" Maggie asked with sudden inspiration, "In return for letting you build a house and shop on it. He'd probably be so grateful he'd let you live there the rest of your life. I could help you gradually with lumber and roofing from what I make at my sewing shop."

The idea seemed improbable but Heatherington felt there was no harm in letting them try. He'd been concerned for years about the Club's foundation on that side.

Filling the gap was by no means as easy as Willie had thought. The rocks he laboriously dumped in from his wagon just disappeared in the next flood. Finally, he discovered that if he dug four-foot-square holes and filled them with rock when the marsh was dry, the bottom stayed firm. But it took several years of backbreaking labor to make the strand wide enough for a house.

Meanwhile, Maggie's sewing shop was prospering. The governor's wife appeared one day with a Parisian fashion book and pointed to her favorite picture. Maggie reproduced it and stylish creations from that book were soon the rage of Apia. What Maggie most enjoyed making was wedding gowns. She even got an order from the queen of Tonga, who wanted her train stitched with thousands of tiny seed pearls. Every penny Maggie earned went to buy lumber, cement, and roofing. Gradually a one-story, wooden house appeared between the old slate house and the British Club. In the process, the Swann girls learned to pour cement and pound on roofing irons.

Willie was proud of every nail. To save space, the two front steps were almost on the road. They led up to a shop about thirty feet square. Behind this were a living room and two bedrooms. A covered walkway connected these to a kitchen shed in the back. Half-way along this passage, steps led down to the back yard. When the marsh was not flooded, the girls could run across the grass to the caretaker's house behind the British Club. He let them use his shower.

At the housewarming, Willie set Pele's jar of swirling water in the window, praying that his fourth shop on Beach Road would finally make the grade. The opening of their own shop signalled full membership in the European community again. The vivacious Swann sisters were always in demand for picnics, masquerades, dinner parties, and tennis matches. "Our prettiest South Sea Island bouquet," prosperous planter Kurt Meyer called them.

Maggie was famous for ingenious costumes. At one masked ball in Market Hall, she turned Peter into Charlie Chaplin, complete with a fly-away wig, baggy pants, and enormous cardboard shoes. He won a prize.

Mary was the most accomplished of the trio. She sang, danced, played tennis, and performed in the repertory theater. Her achievements were described in the social column of the German newspaper almost every week.

Aggie's particular talent, as she said herself, was "playing the fool." She never tried out for leading roles. Why bother? She was not looking for applause but a good time. Even before the final curtain call, she would jump off backstage into the arms of some eager swain who would swing her down, saying, "Let's get out of here, Aggie. Dora and Bill are waiting." While the leading lady was still bowing, Aggie would already be strolling down Beach Road in the moonlight, devising reasons for not getting home on time.

The boys soon agreed that Aggie was the town's worst tease. She had an uncanny knack for devising pranks that would raise excitement to the breaking point and then let her slip out from under without paying off. At the Sei Aute Club carnival, for example, she set up a booth with a sign reading:

(KUESSEN — 50 pfennig)
(KISSES — 50 cents)

It immediately attracted a long line of young men because the face smiling through the hole was Aggie's. But when they slapped down their money in good faith and stepped behind the curtain for their reward, all they got from her was a grin and a tiny German cookie called a *Kusse*. Some found that an unbearable frustration! When one lad tried to insist on his own definition of "kiss," she pointed to the chaperones lined up behind her against the wall. All he could do to get even with her, of course, was to claim to the other boys that he got more than he really did. Such gossip greatly augmented her reputation and might have led to trouble, except that no boy was quite sure whether it was seduction she was after or just a chance to laugh at him. Who wants his manhood mocked at seventeen?

Aggie was presented with endless opportunities to perfect her games. Sociable community life provided the occasions and Mother Nature provided the places: moonlit nights, sheltering palms, and soft sand beaches. But as in any good game there were also hurdles. Victorian parents, watchful priests, jealous spouses, prying eyes, and wagging tongues made the game challenging. Apia's double standard made it especially tricky for women. Aggie became so adept at dodging, however, that she managed to spend two relatively innocent years perfecting her thrusts and parries, still under the impression that romance was nothing but fun.

As her experience with men increased, however, so did her ability to discriminate between them. Unlike checkers, men were not all alike. Most of them were expendable but one or two wore crowns. With them she had to be more cautious, realizing she too was vulnerable.

One face in particular came gradually into focus before Aggie's seventeen-year-old eyes. Strangely enough he was not the gayest of her blades. He was a staid German entomologist in his thirties who had come to Samoa to do research on coconut beetles. His name was Paul Muensch. Aggie liked him because he seemed more mature than the others, always concerned, always polite—someone a girl could trust to keep her out of trouble. The excitement of the whirl began to pall, but Muensch did not.

Willie actually approved of Paul, relieved to find his gadabout daughter showing such good judgment. Muensch was well established and apt to go up in his profession. Sister Genevieve was relieved. Perhaps all those years of painful education were not in vain.

Even Aggie might settle down! The younger set began to refer to Paul as "Aggie's sweetheart." Before long they were calling him "Aggie's fiance." Why not? Aggie thought. Everyone else was getting married. She wasn't one to be left behind.

Chapter 11

Age of Revelation

(1914-1918)

SOLF'S ADMINISTRATIVE talents were appreciated not only at Beach Road but in Germany as well. The Kaiser called him back to serve as secretary general for all his colonies. He was succeeded in Samoa by Governor Schulz, whose first contribution to island progress was a small wireless station.

Without that wireless the small colony might not have known of the storm clouds gathering over Europe in 1914. As it was, few settlers bothered to read the long, dull accounts copied straight from the airwaves into the *Samoanische Zeitung*. Who wanted Europe's troubles? On this island Germans, Americans, and Britishers made money from each other every day and socialized with each other every night. Like his predecessor, Schultz took pains to treat all settlers alike regardless of nationality. Newcomers like old timers took Samoan wives and raised Euronesian children who never set eyes on their respective "fatherlands."

Only one announcement commanded serious local attention. In November, 1913, the price of raw rubber fell from twelve to two shillings a pound as factories in southern Europe were closed by impending war. That spelled the end for Samoa's rubber planters. Everyone else went on as usual.

It was a surprise to most when, on August 14, 1914, the governor's wireless tapped out the message that Britain and Germany had declared war against each other. Neighbors along Beach Road had not thought of the others as enemies for more than a decade. London and Berlin immediately warned their merchant ships to darken their lights and procede at full speed to the nearest neutral port. Pacific waters were free only to warships now. It was rumored that the *Scharnhorst* and *Gneisenau* were already rounding the Horn, hoping to build a base in German Samoa!

In Apia, overseas mail stopped and imported foods disappeared from the shelves. Merchants ceased to buy copra, since there was no way to ship it. The *Samoanische Zeitung* soon dropped to half-size for lack of paper. The colonists finally realized that they were cut off, alone in the middle of the Pacific. With no militia and only twelve unarmed German administrators, they could be snapped up by anyone with a ship larger than a dugout canoe. Residents along Beach Road found themselves with sharp differences as to whose warship should appear next on the horizon.

On the morning of August 29, Apia woke to find eight warships entering the harbor. Racing for binoculars, they soon made out that the names and flags were not German. Two weeks previously, only one day after the declaration of war, two New Zealand troop ships, the *Moreaki* and *Monawai*, with an occupation force of fourteen hundred volunteers had sailed from Wellington, hoping to reach Samoa before the *Scharnhorst* and *Gneisenau*. They were escorted by three smaller ships, *Psyche*, *Pyramus*, and *Philomel*. In New Caledonia they had been reinforced by the *Australia*, the *Melbourne*, and a French warship, the *Montcalm*. The fleet was under an Australian commander, George Patey, but the expeditionary force on board was led by Colonel Logan, a New Zealander.

His volunteers were still edgy as they disembarked on the wharf. For two weeks they had been looking for the *Sharnhorst* and *Gneisenau*. For all they knew, these formidable enemy battleships had already reached Samoa and were waiting to blast them into the sea!

Sitting in their offices in the courthouse, the twelve German administrators were even more uneasy. Since their wireless officer had managed to break the New Zealand code two days before. They already knew the fleet was on its way. But what could they do with only twenty local constables armed with 1872 rifles, and half of them British to boot? Resistance was obviously out of the question. Schultz had paid each of his administrators a year's salary and sent the rest of his treasury to neutral American Samoa for safekeeping. When the fleet was sighted, he told his officers to raise a small white flag and wait for Colonel Logan. He himself went to destroy the wireless.

In the next two hours, without a shot being fired, World War I ended for German Samoa just twenty-five days after it began. By afternoon it was an Allied possession.

The Swann family watched from the chemist shop window as New Zealand troops barricaded the Vaisigano bridge. From her sewing room above Fabricius' store, Maggie saw Colonel Logan land at the Tivoli wharf. Unknown to her, in his pocket was a letter he had just received from a number of prominent British residents requesting that Schultz and his staff be treated with the same consideration they had always accorded British settlers. "Strange place," he thought.

Since no officials appeared to greet the victors, Peter's brother Kurtz went out and shook hands with the Colonel. He showed them around the courthouse and the German officers quietly surrendered at their desks. Schultz was apprehended half an hour later beside his useless wireless. All of them were deported a few days later with the fleet and interned on Motuihi Island in Auckland Harbor for the rest of the war. The occupation force, of course, remained behind. Logan declared Samoa under martial law. His own administrators took over the vacant desks in the courthouse, leaving most German regulations unchanged.

The *Samoanische Zeitung*, however, took on a brand-new face. Its German editor was replaced by one Haylock of the occupying forces and the following week it appeared in English under the name *Samoa Times.* For the rest of the war it conscientiously confined its news to local social events, barely mentioning the war convulsing Europe. As its new editor maintained,[1]

"Samoa's ultimate fate will be decided in Europe and should in no way affect agricultural and social life here. . . . It is our duty as a newspaper to assist in maintaining good feelings between the Germans and British in Samoa [for we] are bound together by ties of blood and the close friendship of long years."

As soon as she heard that German Samoa had become a British possession, Aggie began to worry about her fiance, Paul Muensch. Would he be deported too? A few wary German planters hastily married Samoan wives, hoping to avoid deportation or expropriation, but to Aggie's relief professionals like Muensch were allowed to continue with their work, subject only to an evening curfew.

Monday, September 14, two weeks after the New Zealand occupation, was a misty rainy morning. Residents scurrying to work along Beach Road suddenly saw two huge shapes loom up out of the fog and enter the harbor. The *Scharnhorst* and the *Gneisenau!* In consternation, Willie began boarding his windows and barricading his doors again. Those German warships looked more menacing than Samoan warriors with blackened faces, and his new shop was right under their cannon!

Colonel Logan called a meeting with his provost marshal. With his own fleet gone, it looked as if Samoa would be lost almost as fast as it had been won. His only hope was a bluff. He called up all fourteen hundred volunteers and paraded them back and forth along Beach Road, hoping that the mist would magnify their number.

Apparently it did. After watching for several hours, the German warships turned without a shot and sailed out of the harbor and down the coast. At Mulifanua they anchored briefly, apparently to reach the German DH&PG manager. History does not record what he told them, but a few hours later the warships turned and headed east. Several weeks later, both were sunk by British destroyers as they rounded Cape Horn on their way back to Germany. Allied merchant ships heaved a sigh of relief and began moving again.

The war in the Pacific was over except for the daring exploits of a six-foot German pirate in a little sailing vessel. He continued on single-handed, saving Willie and Apia's other "armchair admirals" at the Tivoli bar from utter boredom during the next four years.

Count von Luckner was an adventurous Prussian who had run away to sea at the age of thirteen. After seven years in Australia as a Salvation Army officer, kangaroo hunter, mercenary, and sleight-of-hand artist, he had returned to Germany as a prizefighter. The Kaiser gave him a naval commission just in time for the Battle of Jutland. When it looked as if the German fleet was beached for good by the British blockade, von Luckner disguised a small captured American clipper ship as a Norwegian lumber vessel called the *Seeadler* and managed to slip by the blockade and out into the North Atlantic. In the next few weeks, ten Allied merchant ships unaccountably vanished in that area, sending Lloyds' insurance rates to impossible heights. No one knew what was happening.

Unable to overtake steamers in his sailing craft, the Count lured them to his side by requesting a chronometer reading. Then he and his men swarmed over the railing with a whoop, evacuated its crewmen to their own hold, and blew up the enemy ship; the Count did not approve of taking lives. This sort of activity, of course, could only last until his hold was full. He finally sailed towards South America and set his captives adrift in lifeboats. Since his identity would be known as soon as they reached shore, he hastened southward.

In no time the race was on. British destroyers chased the *Seeadler* down to Cape Horn, where it vanished in a terrible storm. The destroyers confidently returned home, only to hear a few weeks later that three British merchant ships with forty-five crewmen, one woman, and an opposum had suddenly vanished in the Pacific. The *Seeadler* had escaped around the Horn under cover of the storm and was on the prowl again!

In July, 1916, the *Seeadler* was reduced to matchsticks by a tidal wave while its crew and unwilling passengers were on Mopelia Atoll, replenishing supplies. The dauntless Count laid out a German town for them to build while he and six crewmen went for help in a lifeboat. Their tiny craft reached Wakaya island, but the count and his crew were captured trying to book passage on a larger vessel and interned on Motuihi along with Governor Schultz. The count and governor proceeded to mastermind several spectacular escapes. They might finally have succeeded except that the war ended and New Zealand, relieved, shipped them home.

Meanwhile, the Count's "colonists" back on Mopelia Atoll managed to capture a French square-rigger and continued to scour the Pacific until finally, loaded with silks, perfumes, and parasols, they ran aground. A Chilean vessel rescued them and released them at the end of the war with the loss of only one life — that of the oppossum.

While Willie and the Tivoli "admirals" followed the fortunes of their Count around the Pacific, Aggie was concerned with her own favorite German down the street. Late one afternoon, Lisi Tuataga from Matautu sauntered into the chemist shop to find Aggie. They chatted about their respective sweethearts as Aggie washed the last bottle and closed the cupboards. There was so much to relate that Aggie invited her friend to spend the night. Over tea she confided her greatest trial. Having one's fiance restricted to quarters after six spoiled most of the fun. They sat down on the front stoop to watch the moon rise. Now street lamps could not be lighted, it seemed especially beautiful.

"Let's go for a walk," Aggie suggested. "We could go down and pay a visit to poor old Paul, since he can't go out." Lisi agreed and Aggie told Dad they would be back soon.

Muensch lived with his friend Gefken in a room they rented from the Mann family across from the customs shed. When the girls knocked, it was Gefken who opened the door. He looked somewhat startled to see them and did not invite them in. So they laughingly brushed him aside and stepped into the small sitting room.

It was not an attractive place, lit only by a kerosene lamp on a heavy table. A green curtain was hung across one end to screen off the bed. Muensch was nowhere in sight. "Where's Paul?" Aggie asked, surprised. "I hope he didn't go out."

Gefken mumbled something incoherent and started pacing back and forth in front of the curtain, his hands clasped behind him. His nervousness brought out the tease in Aggie and she started pacing after him, mimicking his gait. Suddenly she reached up and tossed back the curtain intending to make the most of his reaction. But the laugh died on her lips. There on the bed lay Paul, rigid with fright, his arms around a pretty Samoan girl!

With a scream of anguish, Aggie dropped the curtain . and ran out the door. Lisi flew after her. Beach Road was full of goggling eyes. Lisi pulled her distraught friend into a doorway until she could calm down. "How could he?'" Aggie sobbed again and again. "He's engaged to me!"

Lisi couldn't answer that question. She could only lay her cheek against Aggie's and add her own tears at this horrendous betrayal. Finally, as Aggie's grief subsided, Lisi whispered softly, "It's time to go home, Aggie. Your Dad will be worried." She steered her friend out into the street.

Aggie obeyed like a puppet, her mind dull with pain. She paid no attention to where they were going or whom they passed. Suddenly someone called from across the road, "Hey, Lisi! You and Aggie hold up a minute; I have someone I want you to meet." A moment later they were confronted by Lisi's friend Mathison. Behind him stood a man neither of the girls had seen before.

"This is my friend Gordon," Mathison said, "Gordon Hay-MacKenzie. He's just arrived from New Zealand to help set up the new Union Steamship Office here."

Mathison continued to talk but Aggie returned to her pain. All she could think of was the horrified look on Paul's face when he saw her standing there. From now on, she told herself, she would never trust men again.

Finally she heard Mathison say, ". . . then let Gordon and me walk you girls home. You need an escort with all these Kiwis² (New Zealanders) about." He took Lisi's arm and the two of them started up the street. Aggie followed miserably. Gordon looked down curiously at his curly-haired companion.

"I just got in yesterday," he hazarded, since she didn't seem inclined to talk. "Chapper and I were sent up from New Zealand to take over the German shipping routes." When she did not respond, he continued, "New thing for me, being ashore. I've been purser on Union steamships for nine years. It'll be great fun living ashore." As she did not offer to show him around, he continued bravely to fill her silence. "Union Steam has just rented that two-story building on the corner of Saleufi Street. Know where it is?"

"Ought to," she said laconically. "I once lived there." Remembering what she had lost there, she started crying again. Gordon had to put his arm around her to steer her along. Sad girl, he thought, but looked pretty even in tears!

When they got home, Aggie threw herself on the bed, moaning, "It's all over. Lisi! When a man does a thing like that, you know he will never make a good husband!" Suddenly love was no longer synonymous with laughter. The Age of Innocence was over. Lisi spent the wee small hours trying to comfort her friend but it was dawn before they finally fell asleep.

Barely an hour later, Aggie was wakened by the sound of hoofbeats coming up Beach Road. They stopped abruptly in front of the shop. Aggie's heart jumped into her throat and almost strangled her. She heard Willie open the door and an urgent voice began talking.

"It's Paul!" Aggie croaked, sitting bolt upright.

"What are you going to do now?" Lisi whispered anxiously, but Aggie couldn't say.

A few moments later, Willie knocked on the door and called, "It's Mr. Muensch, Aggie. He wants to talk to you."

"Well, I don't want to talk to him!" she called back. "Not now! Not ever! Tell him never to come back!" She sounded as if she meant it. Willie went back and asked Paul for an explanation. The two girls listened breathlessly to catch his answer.

"You know how a man gets when he really loves a girl," Muensch pleaded with Willie. "I had to do something because I didn't want to touch her! I want to marry her like she is."

"I think that's rather nice," Lisi whispered tentatively, but Aggie firmly shook her head.

"If a man really loves a girl, he should be able to hold out forever," she said flatly. Her words hung in the air a moment and Aggie realized they sounded more like Sister Genevieve than Willie. Maybe nuns had a tendency to view men as they "should be" rather than as they really were, because they didn't have to live with them. But fiances should be different, and Aggie was unable to forgive him this disillusionment. When Muensch discovered Aggie's heart had hardened, he went back to Europe to visit his aunt. Aggie and Lisa consoled themselves by walking in the evening with Mathison and MacKenzie.

Samoa's great German corporations were also beginning to fall into British hands. DH&PG became NZRE (New Zealand Reparation Estates) as compensation for its losses in Tripoli. Cut off from the fatherland, many German firms went bankrupt even before they could be liquidated. British and American settlers benefitted from being on the spot. H.J. Moors picked up even more enterprises. O.F. Nelson inherited most of the village copra supply and announced that he was marrying Moors' daughter, Rosie. Sage heads nodded; that man was building an empire.

To Apia's hostelries, however, the occupation was an unmitigated disaster. On December 5, 1914, Captain Tottenham of the occupation forces brought Apia's rollicking social life to a standstill by proclaiming a complete ban on the "production, sale, and purchase of liquor except for medicinal purposes." Samoans were not greatly affected by the announcement; they still preferred kava. But the European community was stunned. How would merchants like Willie recover from a hard day's work? Where would they get the news of the day? The Tivoli became a boardinghouse and the Central Hotel went out of business. Who wants to sit at a bar over a glass of lemonade? Bottles disappeared from store shelves as well. They were not emptied down the drain, of course. Fabricius' £4,000 inventory went straight into Maggie's closet and reappeared regularly at private parties. But everyone chafed at the inconvenience.

One morning Aggie was washing bottles in the chemist shop while her father waited on customers seated at the counter. She looked at him from her new viewpoint on men. He looked older, a bit wasted by his rounds with creditors, spouse, and alcohol. But his gray eyes still held a twinkle. Dear old Dad, he still couldn't be trusted!

Just then a buxom Samoan girl entered from the street. She too had seen her share of hard times. Her dress was faded to a dull gray from frequent laundering on a rock in the river. It was torn under one arm, revealing a firm brown breast as she pointed at the epsom salts.

"How much?" she asked.

"Two shillings," Willie replied, his eyes riveted to the hole in her dress. Noticing the direction of his gaze, the girl burst out laughing. So did Willie. Aggie could see that Muensch was not the only man with temptations. Should she subscribe to the code of Sister Genevieve or come to terms with the masculine condition? Suddenly she saw a glorious opportunity to get a laugh at the whole affair. It was just too tempting! She ran down the passageway calling, "Faafete, you'd better come out here quick or Dad might just misbehave!"

Aggie saw Faafete grab a butcher knife and suddenly realized her humor might have gone too far. All she could do now was turn and run full speed back to the shop calling, "Dad! Faafete's coming with a knife!"

"For whom?" he asked, looking up from the armpit.

"That girl you're looking at!"

The lady in question did not need a second warning. She was out of the door and well on her way towards town before Faafete charged through the doorway with her weapon. They were well beyond Westbrook's store before Faafete gave up. That girl would not come back again!

Back in the store, Willie roared with laughter. "You little devil you!" he said shaking his finger at Aggie. "We'd both better go and feed the chickens before mom gets back with her knife!"

Out in the backyard Aggie asked him curiously, "Are you angry with me, Dad?"

"Of course not," he replied. "You probably saved that young girl's life."

"Are you angry with Faafete?" she persisted, trying to understand his picture of loyalty.

"Why should I be angry?" he laughed. "It's just Faafete's way of showing how much she loves me!"

A few minutes later Aggie found her stepmother back in the kitchen, still panting from the chase. "You should have warned me sooner," that aggrieved lady grumbled.

"I was afraid you might kill her," Aggie replied only half in jest.

"Well, anyone that fools around with my Willie deserves it!" Faafete growled, giving the knife a menacing spin. She was not laughing. Aggie felt a twinge of sorrow for this hard-bitten woman, rejected by her old community and able to maintain her place in this one only by clutching onto Willie. Why couldn't a woman earn a status of her own instead of having to rely on a husband? This faithfulness thing grew more complex every day. To Sister Genevieve it was a moral issue, to Willie a romantic impulse, to Faafete a livelihood. Aggie wondered whether she should react with a belly-laugh or a sob.

Apia's Operatic Society reappeared in 1917 singing Gil-

bert and Sullivan rather than German *lieder*. Aggie joined
the chorus of "Pinafore" not to display her voice so much
as the fetching costume Maggie made for her. It was
a darling little confection with a deep rose bodice and a
fluffy, cream-colored skirt trimmed with red roses.
Maggie even found a wide-brimmed hat and trimmed it
with a band of matching rosebuds. Gordon would love
that. Even before the final curtain call, he would swing
her down from the back of the platform with a kiss and she
would gleefully kick up her shiny patent leather slippers.
Aggie could hardly wait. Dora and Mathison were calling
for her and they would all go for a stroll.

At teatime that evening, Willie and Faafete had a fight.
Aggie could hear loud words in the parlor as she dressed
in her bedroom. She paid no attention until she heard a
crash. Running out, she found Dad on the floor with
Faafete on top of him, lifting his head by the hair and
banging it down on the floor. Poor old Dad! He seemed too
dazed to defend himself. Aggie raced across the floor and
attacked the raging lady from the rear, burying her hands
Samoan-style in the long black hair and twisting it around
her wrists for a good grip. Then she pulled with all her
might.

"Let go of my hair!" Faafete screamed.

"Not until you let go of my Dad!" Aggie grunted, pulling even harder. The older woman twisted around until
she had one hand on Aggie's fluffy skirt and the other on a
puffed sleeve. Soon Aggie's dress was in tatters, pieces of
her costume strewn all over the floor. But she didn't let
go until Faafete released Willie. He jumped up and joined
his little champion. Together they wrestled Faafete to the
floor and sat on her until she finally lay still. Then Willie
got up without a word and went into his room.

"How dare you do that to a man who's been so good
to you?" Aggie blustered. Faafete burst into tears. She
felt so torn she needed to lash out at someone, but Aggie
was quite right—why Willie?

There was a knock at the door and Dora called that it
was getting late. All Aggie could do was snatch an old
dress from the trunk to cover her scratches. It was lucky;
that she would scarcely be visible in the back row. Faafete
got up slowly with new respect for her stepdaughter. That

133

kid was one hell of a scrapper!

The war in Europe was not the only agent of destruction in 1917. Nature gave a few heaves of her own. One evening in June, Aggie was dressing up for a party. Gordon would stop by soon to pick her up and she wanted to look her best. She wrapped herself in a *lavalava*, tying its ends around her neck, and ran across to the caretaker's house for a shower. His ingenious little facility consisted of a water tank on a wobbly wooden platform with a tap which opened into a cubicle below.

Aggie had closed the flimsy door and was just soaping herself under the drizzle when the earth gave a strange shudder. This was followed by a terrible jolt that knocked her to the ground. Dazed, she looked up and saw the water tank dancing wildly over her head. She heard Dad shout, "Aggie! Aggie! Earthquake! Get out of there quick!"

The shower door was swinging open and shut by itself as soon as she dashed through. Her flapping wet *lavalava* caught on a nail and she spun into the backyard wearing exactly what she was born in.

Willie immediately dashed out with a towel and wrapped her up, but the detail in which the waiters of the British Club could describe that fleeting moment was indeed impressive. Every one of them claimed to have been an eyewitness to the event and recounted what he saw at least a hundred times. It certainly reenforced her growing reputation.

It was amazing what a two-minute shock could do to other things as well. The chemist shop was a shambles of broken bottles, strewn powders, and spilled liquids. The place reeked with iodine and the jar of swirling waters was reduced to a brown puddle on the floor. Only Nelson's crockery department rivaled their debris. Professor Augenheister of the German-built observatory at Mulinuu registered the quake at 8.3 on the Richter scale, with an epicenter about seventy miles southeast.[3] British Club waiters insisted the center had been right in their backyard!

Even the sea was affected. Next morning it looked as if a giant mouth had sucked the harbor dry. The rusty ribs of the *Adler* stood high and dry in the sunshine, and children ran out on the exposed reef to pick up stranded fish.

Frantic elders called them back and sure enough, the giant mouth suddenly disgorged the water again, sending wave after wave crashing across the beach and up the Vaisigano. As the swollen swamp waters lapped around stone platforms that night, old ladies in the village told their huddled grandchildren about Mafuie, the volcano god, who shakes the pillars of the earth when he gets angry.

Not a few young men offered to mend the heart that Muensch had broken. But the winner was Gordon Hay MacKenzie, perhaps because he had taken Aggie home the very night of her disillusionment. In some ways he resembled his predecessor, a tall, blond, good-looking man in his thirties, already well established in his profession. But he was gayer than the stolid German. He joined the clubs, played tennis, and was in great demand for parties. Life at sea had not dulled his wits and he was a charming dinner partner. Aggie was flattered to discover she had the attention of one of the most popular bachelors in town, and her grief over Muensch was soon forgotten.

At first they went out with Dora and Mathison, but one evening Gordon dropped by alone and they sat together on the front steps talking. He told Aggie that Robert Tattersall had recently hired an old woman to play his accordian and was teaching the porch crowd a new strut.

"They say it's terrific," Gordon urged. "We really ought to try it. Shall I ask your Dad to let us stroll up there tonight?"

"Wonderful!" Aggie cried, jumping up ready to go.

Willie agreed. "All right, you two, but be sure to be back here by twelve-thirty. That's my rule, you know!" Gordon assured Willie he would cooperate.

The new strut more than lived up to its reputation and they had to review their old steps as well. "I say, Aggie," Gordon cried suddenly. "It's after midnight! We'll have to start home right away." Aggie wanted one more dance but he pulled her down the steps and out into the moonlight.

"Let's walk home by way of the hospital," Aggie suggested, heading up the hill instead of down. He guided her over the detour by putting his arm around her waist.

Circling back across the Malifa playground, she stopped in the middle to look at the moon. She looked so lovely he had to put both arms around her to steady himself. That led to a long kiss that seemed to bewitch them both. In fact, it was so sensational that they retested it under every shady tree after that. When they finally reached the LMS church corner, they dallied even longer to watch the moonlight on the water. Time stood still.

But not Willie's gold watch! Gordon had just given Aggie's patent leather slippers a final spin on the doorstep when Willie's fist sent him sprawling. "That will teach you that when I say twelve-thirty I mean twelve-thirty, not two!" he yelled at the dazed young man.

"But, Dad—!" Aggie cried desperately, trying to think up a good excuse.

"You shut up and go inside!" Willie shouted. "This is between Mr. MacKenzie and myself."

Gordon motioned her to obey and she did, blinded with rage. Hadn't she always championed her father in his affairs? How could such a kind and gentle man suddenly fly off the handle like that? Why hadn't he punched Muensch, who deserved it? She flung herself into her room and cried herself to sleep on the bed. Now she had lost an even more important person—and on the very night that she had discovered how much she loved him!

Next morning she refused to speak to Willie. She sat on the front steps brooding, with her chin in her hands, bitterly resenting Willie's interference. Her tear-blurred eyes followed the bend of the bay back to the corner by the LMS church where she and Gordon had so recently watched the moon across the water. Suddenly her wandering mind snapped back into focus. There was Gordon himself, a smile on his lips and sunlight in his hair, peddling his bike up Beach Road in her direction!

She jumped up hastily and ran inside to splash water on her face. He musn't see her in this condition. "Did your Dad beat you up?" he asked as she opened the door. The question took her by surprise. Dad had never whipped her in his life; but she loved Gordon's concern.

"Of course not," she smiled. "But I'm sorry he hit you. Sometimes he loses his temper over nothing at all."

"What we did wasn't nothing!" Gordon replied in stout defense of her father. "A man is supposed to be boss in his own house and he was quite right. I got you back later than

I promised and it was all your fault for leading me on!" He gave her a wink and they both started laughing.

"Can I see you again tonight?" he asked.

"Do you want to get punched again?"

"Of course not," he said, rubbing his jaw. "That's why I came to apologize to your father. He should have cooled off by now." Gordon was right. Willie not only forgave them but gave permission for another twelve-thirty walk.

That evening they didn't go anywhere. They just sat on the low sea wall across from the shop and watched the moon. It was even more bewitching than before, a path of light beckoning them across the dancing water. Forgetting Dad completely, they slipped down to the soft sand and lay among the creepers.

Once reassured that his parental word was respected, Willie realized that Aggie was again doing very well for herself. What more could a man want of a son-in-law? Gordon treated him with dignity. He held a steady job with a sound firm, and was certainly in love with Aggie.

Aggie herself looked more radiant than ever. In fact, she and Gordon were the talk of the town as they dashed around to tennis matches, cakewalks, and tea parties in Gordon's new trap with its swishing golden fringe. Sometimes Willie did miss his black-bloomered, hooky-prone little companion. In this new incarnation, Aggie was a great responsibility. She was not at all like her shy and delicate mother. Unlike her father, she had drive and confidence. In a way she reminded Willie of that perky go-between, Eliza. Maybe it was the *afakasi* (mixed blood) in her.

Before long, Aggie confided to Dora that she had "known" Gordon and that sex was the ultimate thrill. Dora was a bit shaken, not because she was surprised (rumor had claimed her friend an expert years ago) but because Aggie was so forthright about it. Sisters' School had apparently failed to impart any sense of guilt. Sex was something natural.

On the first Saturday of February, 1918, Tattersall's porch and parlor rollicked to an engagement party for Gordon and Aggie. Apia's "younger set" all turned out for the occasion. The *Samoa Times* reported that the Misses Boyd and Johnson sang. Captain Booth gave a rendition, and the happy couple was presented with a bank draft to help furnish their new home.

The wedding followed on Friday and was heralded as the "principal social event of the week."[4] It was held at the Apia Protestant Church in deference to the groom's persuasion. The bride's dark curls were covered in a cloche-like veil caught up in orange blossoms and she wore a white silk gown edged in lace. Her bridesmaids, Dora Simpson and Gladys Syddal, wore blue and white. Willie's relief at passing on responsibility for Aggie to some other man endangered his slender pocketbook. He threw a wedding feast for everyone at the Papaseea Cafe at Lotopa.

Old Huche owned a two-story building on Vaea Road across from the now defunct Central Hotel. It had a store downstairs with an apartment above and was reached by a flight of wooden stairs. Up these Gordon happily carried his pretty new burden, kicking her patent-leather shoes with delight.

Encampment of the New Zealand expeditionary force, 1914. The German hotel and the Nelson store are in the rear.

PART IV

MOTHER

Aggie and Charlie Grey in front of their house on the hill. Circa 1929.

Chapter 12

The Grim Reaper

(1918)

AGGIE SOON became pregnant. Huche's apartment did not face seaward and its airless rooms sweltered in the March heat. It was unbearable except in the evenings, when Gordon returned and the hot, dusty town cooled off. By six o'clock Aggie usually felt ready for a party.

The biggest event of the 1918 social season was Olaf Nelson's jubilee and housewarming, held on March 9 at his new manson at Tuaefu.[1] That was exactly fifty years since his father, August Nelson, a Swedish prospector fresh from the Australian gold rush, had stopped off in Samoa on his way to California. Island life enchanted August, and he opened a small bush store at Salailua in Savaii. Before long he married Chief Tugaga's daughter Sina from Safune on the north coast, and built an even larger store in her village.

It was there that Olaf was born. He grew up with the village boys until he was eight. Then his father sent him to the Marist Brothers' school in Apia for five years. He was big for his age. The Brothers found him an exceptionally bright lad and felt he should go on. But since secondary education was not available in the islands, his father apprenticed him to DH&PG for training as a clerk. He already spoke Samoan, German, and English. Olaf was a natural leader. At sixteen he founded Apia's first brass band and persuaded H.J. Moors to supply it with uniforms. At seventeen he took over management of his father's store at Safune with an inventory worth £365. Three years later he had done so well they were able to open Nelson & Son in Apia, next to the Central Hotel, retailing to townsfolk and wholesaling to village stores.

When the New Zealand military government liquidated DH&PG, Olaf was right on hand to take over its

141

German bush stores, including Tifitifi, and was soon handling most of Samoa's village copra. The price sky-rocketed in Europe and he soon became the wealthiest man in Samoa. When he also married H.J. Moors' daughter, Rosie, he was able to incorporate many of her father's holdings as well. By 1918 he was a well-known business-man in the entire South Pacific. Not bad for a part-Samoan! All he needed now was an heir for his empire and a castle to display his wealth. So far Rosie had provided him with three daughters; he still prayed for a son.

The castle did not require divine assistance. On the hill at Tuaefu he erected a magnificent mansion, larger than Robert Louis Stevenson's former home at Vailima. It was approached up a long drive winding past a private chapel, tennis courts, and terraced gardens up to a stately portico. Gazing at its three stories and many windows, awed villagers whispered that his mother's chiefly blood had given him royal inclinations but his father's blood was responsible for the wherewithal. Everything he touched turned to gold!

By sunset on March 7, 1918, everyone who "counted" on Apia's ladder was turning up the drive to Tuaefu. Gordon and Aggie reached the scene in their shiny trap and felt they were entering fairyland. The terraced gardens on the hillside were ablaze with Japanese lanterns. The great mansion looked like a castle. On the widest terrace a tent had been erected for a sumptuous feast. Rosie and Olaf were standing in front of it, welcoming their guests.

When Nelson heard Aggie's name announced, his mind flashed back to the curly-haired child in black bloomers driving a loaded copra wagon into his courtyard. Now here she was appearing in his life again, a glowing bride in a soft-flowing gown. She was indeed good-looking, but it was her brash sparkle that still tingled his imagination. She offered him her gloved hand but he drew her to him instead and gave her a kiss island style.

The band struck a dramatic chord and fifty couples, the elite of Apia, began a grand march under the stars. This was followed by five hours of toasting and dancing, interspersed with frequent trips to the bar and food tables in the pavilion. It was after midnight when Judge Roberts finally thanked the host and hostess on behalf of the guests and the Hay-MacKenzies drove home through the cool dark streets of Apia. Aggie made every effort to prolong the wee small hours. Daylight was her favorite time for sleeping.

In June they attended another gala. Everyone on the island was invited to this one. The King's Birthday had replaced the Kaiser's as a day for national celebration. Beach Road and the Courthouse were garlanded with flowers.

"Well, what do you think of Samoa's newest king?" Moors asked Willie as they watched three boys construct a triumphal arch. "When I first came, it was Malietoa. When you arrived, we had Mataafa Iosefo. In 1900 it was Solf and his Kaiser. Now look whose royal birthday we're celebrating — the king of England! All I can say is that it's lucky Samoans like lots of kings!"

Four thousand people gathered on Tiafau, the *malae* (meeting ground) of "All-Samoa" at Mulinuu. To honor their most recent royalty, High Chief Fiame of Lotofaga presented an impressive *taalolo* (gift giving ceremony) to the British monarch, represented by Colonel Logan. The grass was covered with roast pigs, rolls of fine mats, tapas, shell necklaces, kava bowls, and bottles of scented oil. Faga and Saluafata bands played martial music. This was followed by sports contests and *fautasi* (longboat) races from five miles out at sea. Samoans knew just how to elevate a royal ego. That evening the Laumosooi Club, led by Rosie Nelson and her sister Priscilla, presented a concert at Market Hall for the benefit of Samoan-born soldiers wounded in the European war.

H.J. Moors refused to be outdone by either Nelson or the English king. His gift to Apia's 1918 season was a party to dedicate his new Alcazar Hotel.[2] Weakened by prohibition, the old Tivoli had finally succumbed to one of its own acetylene lamps and burned to the ground. Hoping to avoid the same fate for its successor, Moors climaxed the evening by throwing a switch which set three hundred dimly flickering bulbs aglow, the first electric lights in Apia! Unable to toast this amazing phenomenon in their customary manner, his guests settled for "ices" and rides on his new carousel.

"Electric lights are just a start, my dear," Moors told Aggie. "Remember that motor car you rode in to the Casino ball? Apia now has fifty-six of them! Colonel Logan has set a speed limit of twelve miles an hour, but they still bump into each other now and then. My next venture is a motor repair shop. I am encouraging the governor to build a motor road all the way to Falefa. Think of what will happen to your father's business if that many more village mothers could ride into town! It pays to keep an eye on newfangled contraptions, my dear!" Aggie never forgot his advice.

The war in Europe was finally dragging to a close. By now the victor was clear and in Apia German stores were following the German plantations into oblivion. Grevsmuhl sold his to a rising British firm known as Burns Philp for only £1975. The charming little teahouse at Lake Lanutoo was rotting away, and Malololelei Resort, where Germans had spent their weekends in the cool mountain air, was up for sale.

With Maggie and Aggie married and his business reviving, Willie needed another hand at the chemist shop. Four years before he had sent Mary to school in Sydney. The convent sisters in Apia had felt that she was the one girl in his family who could benefit from further education. Now she was eighteen, holder of a school-leaving certificate and the best educated of Willie's daughters. He wrote and asked her to come home.

Mary was delighted. She had missed Apia's congenial social life. As soon as she disembarked, she dived into the swirl of tennis matches, teas, and dances. Scarcely a month after her return she landed the part of the major general's daughter in "The Pirates of Penzance." Aggie, thanks to her pregnant condition, was relegated to "goddess of poetry—a living statue."[3] Maggie had no time for such frivolities at all. She had just given birth to a daughter.

The *palolo* (October) rains never arrived that year. Rivers and roof tanks ran dry and dust covered everything. Only Tufuiopa, the cold blue spring near the cemetery, continued to provide Apia with fresh water. Aggie sent her house girl over early every day, but the waiting line was so long it took her all morning to fill her pail.

On October 9, word flashed around the world that

Germany had finally surrendered. Samoa's former governor, Dr. Solf, who had risen to the post of German chancellor, was now involved in establishing a new republican government in Berlin. In Apia, news of the armistice outshadowed another brief announcement in the same paper —a few cases of influenza had been reported in Auckland.

Aggie and Gordon were too involved to read the paper at all. Aggie was in labor and Gordon had rushed out to call Dr. Atkinson. It was not an easy birth. The doctor had to use forceps but finally delivered a fair-skinned, blue-eyed baby girl. Aggie called her Peggy, short for Margaret of course. Gordon kissed his exhausted wife and promised her a good vacation as soon she could get around.

"I've booked us on next month's *Talune*, darling," he said. "A week of sea air and rest on shipboard will do you no end of good. We'll go down to Wellington to stay with my parents for three months. That should be lots of fun."

"You need a rest too, Gordon," Aggie murmured and fell asleep. It was almost three weeks before she got up.

Apia selected Tuesday, November 12, for its Peace Celebration. By the eleventh, Beach Road was again decorated with garlands and triumphal arches but Aggie was too busy packing for her trip to help out.

At dawn the *Talune* entered the harbor on her monthly round. As usual, Dr. Atkinson went out in the pilot boat to check her for quarantine. "Anything serious?" he asked the *Talune's* captain.

"Not that I know of," he replied. "One old reverend told me he had been sick back in Auckland but he seems fine now. Two Samoan kids, Tau and Faleolo, had headaches yesterday but are up and around again today. I'll run up the yellow flag, however, in case you want to take a look."

"Just run the passengers by my table as they disembark," the doctor said. "I'm sure they want to get off in time for the Peace Celebration. It starts at noon."

He questioned the pastor and two boys as they went by, but no one complained of being ill. Two hours later the yellow flag was lowered. The *Talune* had a clean bill of health.

Schools closed before noon and a great crowd gathered along Beach Road to watch the peace parade. The Vaimoso band marched out to Pilot Point, turned, and marched back down the full length of town, followed by carts, honking motor cars covered with bunting, marching school children, and dancing girls in gay costumes. Church bells rang as they passed and thousands of spectators cheered them on through the clouds of dust. In a drought like this it was impossible to water the road but who cared about such a minor inconvenience? The war was over! The world was at peace again! The procession stopped at the customs house to burn an effigy of the Kaiser and went on to Mulinuu. That evening there was a great ball at Market Hall to welcome young Private Meredith home from the front.

Next day many of the celebrants stayed home with headaches. Only a "touch of sun," they said. By afternoon, however, the hospital at Motootua was filling with cases of "pneumonia" so virulent that some were dying.

The following day was Thursday and Gordon returned to the apartment at noon. Aggie was full of excitement about her first trip to New Zealand. She had their bags all packed. They were to board the *Talune* that evening, since it was sailing at dawn. The apartment was so hot, however, she was hoping to board early. "Hurry and eat, Gordon," she called. "Don't go back to the office. Let's go now."

Instead of sitting down, he put his arms around his wife gently and said, "Aggie, I'm afraid you will have to sail without me. Now don't start fretting. Something is happening to this town. Everyone at the office is sick except me, so I have to stay. I've wired my parents to have my sister pick you up in Auckland. Don't worry, I'll join you next month when whatever this is blows over."

"If you don't go, I won't either," Aggie pouted, kicking over their suitcase.

"Oh, yes, you will!" he said firmly. "I wouldn't let you and Peggy stay here now for a million pounds. You're damned lucky to have tickets!" He looked so worried that Aggie stopped fussing. He picked up her bags, saying, "I'll drive you over to your Dad's place right now. Stay there until it's time to go. He'll send someone out to see you aboard."

Scarcely able to believe her bad luck, Aggie picked up

146

the baby and Gordon drove them to the chemist shop. To her astonishment, it was full of people. "What's going on, Dad?" she asked, pushing her way behind the counter.

"Looks like some kind of lung fever," Willie replied. "I never saw anything like it. People just start coughing and a couple of hours later they suffocate with their lungs full of fluid. Gordon is right to get you and the baby out. Mary will see you aboard. I'm stuck here at the shop."

By evening it was clear that the ailment was Spanish influenza, the same grim reaper which had claimed fifty thousand lives in the United States and was now stalking the world. Samoa had assumed that two thousand miles of ocean was sufficient protection, and had opened its door at the worst possible moment, as thousands of its people stood cheering in a cloud of dust. Gay celebrants were even now carrying the fatal germs back to every village on the island. American Samoa, by simply refusing to let the *Talune* dock, had been spared. With no known cure, Western Samoans could only pray and count their dead. At sunset Mary escorted Aggie and the baby out to the *Talune* and returned home with a splitting headache. Willie gave her a dose of quinine and sent her to bed.

By sunrise Friday morning, Beach Road was in panic. All its stores and offices had closed, their keepers either dead or fighting for the lives of those they loved. Hearing that seven soldiers at the garrison had expired, Colonel Logan wired Australia for a medical team, but for some reason he did not respond to an offer of help from American Samoa, a few sea miles away.

"That man has mistrusted Yanks ever since his son was killed at the front," Peter fumed to Maggie. "He could never forgive them for joining the war so late." He was helping his wife lift a feverish houseboy into the back of their open Ford. She had dosed the lad with everything she had on hand and wrapped him in a blanket, but he still seemed to be choking. He had pleaded to be taken home to die.

On the return trip, the car suddenly swerved as Peter put both hands to his eyes. "Maggie!" he cried suddenly, "I can't see!" She grabbed the wheel as he fell back helpless on the seat. All she could think of was to get him to Dad as soon as possible. She turned the car west towards

147

the Vaisigano. Rounding the bend towards the bridge, she caught sight of a huge crowd of Samoans filling the street in front of Dad's shop. Instead of cheering as they had on Tuesday, they were wailing. "Suani, *fa amolemole, ua vaivai lo'u tama*" (Dr. Swann, please help! My father is dying!). Some lay on the ground, unable to reach the door. For the first time, Maggie realized that what was serious for Europeans in their large houses was desperate indeed for Samoans huddled on little platforms with the blinds down. She wondered what it was like in Toamua right now, with no doctor and no one to explain what was happening. No wonder they believed in evil spirits!

She parked the car at the far end of the bridge and pushed her way through the crowd to the back door. Faafete was rolling in agony on the floor of the passageway. Mary tossed on a bed, delirious. Maggie ran forward into the shop. Willie was standing alone behind the counter, facing the clamoring crowd. A bottle of quinine was in his hand and he was dispensing it drop by drop on little pieces of waxed paper. His eyes were dull with exhaustion and he was not asking for money.

"Dad! Dad!" Maggie cried. "Peter is terribly sick! What shall I do?" Willie shook his head like a zombie and poured half an ounce from his bottle into a tiny cup.

"Give him just enough of this at a time to cover a sixpence," he said. "This is the last bottle I've got."

"What will you use when it's gone?" Maggie asked.

"Whiskey," he mumbled. "What do you think is keeping me alive?"

Back at the car, Maggie dosed Peter from a teaspoon. Then she rubbed his arms and wrapped him in the blanket. His fever had soared and he was already coughing. As she drove home through the deserted streets, she could hear the same sound from behind the lowered blinds of every Samoan house. The scythe of the grim reaper was snipping off lives like blades of grass.

Despite the heat, Maggie lit a fire in her wood stove. All night long she forced scalding Bovril down Peter's throat to "keep up his strength." In the next room, her two-month-old daughter fretted and Maggie listened anxiously, dreading the first sound of a tiny cough.

Next morning all three of them were still alive, though

Peter was too weak to move. Maggie changed his damp sheets and the baby's diaper, and took them down to the Vaisigano to wash. Horrified, she found that even the river was dead! No bird sang. No rustling leaf or gurgle of water broke the blistering stillness. The stream that had blessed Aggie's perfect day had vanished. Dead shrimp lay everywhere, rotting on the sunburned rocks. Without thinking, Maggie set down her bundle and began to sweep the decaying little carcasses into a pile with a coconut frond. It consoled her to be able to do something, anything, in this hopeless situation. She set the noisome remains ablaze with a brand from the stove and watched them burn, realizing she had no more control of this situation than a shrimp. Why didn't she too lie down and die? Instead, she stiffened. Until the reaper claimed her, she vowed, she would doctor the sick, clean up the mess, and spit in death's eye!

For the next three weeks she kept a soup pot boiling on her stove, ladling out portions not only to Peter and his three sisters but to Aggie's old admirer Muensch, who lived alone in the house next door. Soup was no cure for the flu, but it did prevent death by starvation. She also visited the thatched platforms across the street. Samoans did not have supplies of tinned food in their cupboards the way she did. Stores were closed and most villagers were now too weak to get back to their plantations. All they could do was lie on their platforms and await the "will of the Lord." When Maggie lifted the blinds of one *fale*, six corpses stared back at her! Kind neighbors had taken away the orphaned children, but no one had strength to bury the dead.

At Papauta School for girls, Hilda Small, the missionary headmistress, was frantic. Only one of her 104 pupils had escaped the 'flu, which had invaded their compound about a week after the celebration. In every one of her sleeping *fale*, girls and their teachers tossed on mats. All Hilda and her helper could do was wrap the dead and whisper a prayer before the New Zealand soldiers arrived with the burial wagon each day. What concerned Hilda even more was the girls who did *not* die. They needed nourishing food and good care for several weeks before they could struggle to their feet again. Usually the girls supplied their own food from tidy school gardens and weekly fishing expeditions. Now there was no one to handle these essentials. Hilda entreated the soldiers for soup from their messhall and they brought her their own rations. A few days later she asked them to take a note to their commander requesting twenty-five pounds of meat. Her reply was a sharp note from Colonel Logan, asking her to appear before him in person.

As soon as she entered his office, she realized that something even worse than the 'flu was wrong with this man. He was no longer the cheerful, vigorous commander who had marched his troops up and down the waterfront under the guns of the *Gneisenau*. He looked as if he had not slept for weeks and his personality had changed.

"Why do you ask me for meat for your lazy schoolgirls," he shouted, "when everyone is starving? You could have eaten one of your horses, you know!"[4] She gazed at the broken man for a moment, then turned without a word and left the room. The reaper claimed minds as well as bodies. Shortly thereafter, Logan was recalled and replaced by Colonel Tate.

The bottles of whiskey Peter had concealed in his closet were now considered a national treasure. "Best doctor in town," he winked after he had recovered. He handed out doses without charge to anyone who asked. Even the teetotaling Methodist missionary, the Reverend Mr. Mueller, begged a bottle for his children. New Zealand soldiers on the burial wagon stopped in for a daily ration. Maggie could see their grisly load when they parked in her driveway, bloated bodies rolled in sheets or mats and stacked like cordwood. After being thus fortified, the soldiers proceeded to Vaimea Church, where they dug a mass grave. Peter's whiskey was their only protection.

Aggie kissed Mary goodby on the deck of the *Talune*, trying to hold back tears of despair. This was hardly the send-off she had anticipated. No garland-throwing, kiss-blowing, hand-waving friends. Not even Gordon! What was happening to her fun-loving world? As Mary's head disappeared over the side, Aggie suddenly felt terrified. She would be met by complete strangers in New Zealand, if she made it that far. Gordon, Willie, Mary, and Maggie might all be dead when she returned! Now she could well understand why her mother had sobbed beside the smoke-stack of the *Taveuni* on their flight to Fiji.

Peggy began to fret and Aggie stopped a steward who was rushing by. "Could you show me to my cabin? I want to lie down." The distraught man stopped and looked at her flushed face. Another sick passenger and this one so recently a mother! He realized that neither she nor the baby would survive the voyage if left in that fetid hold.

"I'll tell you what, miss," he said, relaxing into a kindly voice. "It's cooler up in the dining room. I'll just settle you up there where there's a breeze. You look as if you could stand some sleep."

Aggie stumbled after him blindly. Her head was beginning to throb and all she wanted to do was lie down. The dining room was already crowded with passengers. The steward led her up some narrow stairs to the balcony above and found a dim space behind a piano. At least it would shelter them from the sights and sounds below. He dragged in a mattress, and Aggie sank onto it to nurse Peggy as he piled the bags around them.

That night Aggie could not sleep because of the groaning and coughing below. She was burning with fever but whenever she felt it would be better to die, she looked at the tiny mite sleeping beside her and realized that death was a luxury she could not afford. Without her breast, Peggy would not have a chance. The world slipped into confusion, but Peggy's bleat managed to penetrate the haze. Aggie tossed over on her side and let the baby nurse.

Next morning she did not even hear the *Talune's* parting whistle. She recalled only that the steward appeared with a mug of bitter stout. Later he returned to pick up Peggy and bathe her in his own cabin. "You know what?" he joked on his return. "I think this baby's drunk!" Aggie didn't laugh.

The following day Aggie woke long enough to hear a hundred voices in the dining room below, intoning the Samoan funeral hymn.

Talofa uso e, tofaina oe.
Ua sau le itula e malolo.

(Brothers, we have gathered to say farewell.
The hour has come for eternal rest.)

151

For an instant she was back in an upstairs living room, a child of five, kissing the cheek of a beautiful mother lying at rest among the candles. Now again that hymn made her realize that she was not alone in this terrifying world. Others were there to hold her in her hour of need. She was part of a great family that even included the steward.

As the hymn died away, she realized that the *Talune* had stopped in mid-ocean. In the stillness she could hear the call of the frigate birds and short commands in English on deck. There was a splash, then another and another.

"Where are we? What's happening?" She cried to the steward, who was staring out the porthole.

"Near the Tongan islands, miss," he said. "Don't worry about nothin' else. Just take care of baby; that's your job."

By the time the *Talune* docked in Auckland four days later, Aggie's fever had broken but she still felt terribly weak. The steward helped her pack her bags and kissed the baby goodby. "Would you look at this wee thing!" he marveled. "Still fit as a fiddle!"

Aggie tottered down the gangplank with Peggy in her arms. Waiting at the bottom was Gordon's sister, a motherly woman who had come up from Wellington to meet them. She took the baby and after one look at Aggie decided to change their train seat for a sleeping compartment. It was clear Gordon's wife could not sit up all night.

Next day Aggie found herself in bed in a strange house on Tinacorrie Road. Gordon's mother was very kind to her pretty daughter-in-law from Samoa, but for several weeks Aggie was too weak to get up. She lay exhausted between the white sheets, wondering if her mother had felt this lonely too. No, she would never be a keen traveler like Mary.

A month later the world brightened; Gordon arrived. "I'm thankful you came on first," he told her. "People are still dying in Apia, but the worst is over. Your Dad and Dr. Atkinson have been working like heroes." Gordon took her to Paraparamo to visit his older brother, and the rest of their leave passed like a honeymoon. Before they started the trip home, Aggie realized she was pregnant again.

During the first month of the holocaust, even the voice of the *Samoa Times* was silent. Its editor had died. When the little paper struggled into print again, it tried to assess the damage. One Samoan in five had died in the past four weeks! Casualties were particularly heavy among the elders. The grim reaper had done more than cut down lives. He had stabbed deep into the heart of a culture. A generation of chiefs, orators, and grandmothers rich in oral lore had been wiped out before they could transmit their treasures. Twenty-four of the thirty-one members of the Samoan legislature were gone, leaving it unable to function. Hundreds of leaderless families and orphaned children were left drifting on a turbulent sea of change without their traditional rudders.

The local European community also mourned its dead. For weeks obituaries replaced advertisements in the newspaper. In one of these black-edged boxes the Meredith family announced that it had lost its grandmother, her daughter Jane, her son Thomas with his wife and child, another daughter Eleanor, and James Jr., son of Joseph. The enterprises of S.H. Meredith, deceased, would henceforth be handled by Freuan. Five of its bush-store managers had also succumbed.[5]

Despite Willie's medical skills and Peter's whiskey, the Swann family had also suffered losses. Faafete was dead. Mary was recovering slowly and had offered to take over responsibility for Faafete's children, Daisy and Fred.

O.F. Nelson had lost his mother, a brother, and a sister. He himself was sick for a year. But he had one consolation. Rosie finally bore him a son. His empire could go on! As soon as he recovered he took his family to Europe to buy "the best of the West" to refurnish Tuaefu. It was worthwhile now he had an heir.

Food was short until March, but the merchant families shared what was left on their store shelves as generously as they had once shared parties. Samoans consolidated their kin and reseeded their plantations. Blame had to focus somewhere, and poor Colonel Logan got the brunt of it for his refusal to accept medical help from American Samoa. One hundred and twenty-six irate chiefs signed a petition asking the New Zealand government to help with Samoa's orphans. They further suggested that the islands be turned over to the United States or Britain.[6]

When a New Zealand Royal Commission arrived in

June, 1919, to investigate, the official death count was set at 7,542 out of a population of 30,636.[7] Colonel Logan claimed he had received no offer of help from American Samoa and that the whole story was a political move by H.J. Moors. Dr. Atkinson claimed that the captain of the *Talune* had never warned him of the quarantine at Suva. But everyone agreed on one thing: the New Zealand garrison had performed above and beyond the call of duty during the crisis. Since the dead could not be restored, the island community finally accepted its fate and life began again. The chiefs withdrew their petition, empty titles were gradually filled, merchants restocked their shelves, and the birth rate climbed. Samoa's ship of state sailed on, even though its course would never be quite the same.

Huch's house.

Chapter 13

Bereaved

(1919-1925)

GORDON AND AGGIE jumped back into Apia's social circuit as if to make up for lost time. The first wedding they attended on their return was Mary's. She had settled on a young accountant named Robert D. Croudace, who, like Gordon, was a New Zealander rising in the commercial community. The Swann sisters did not intend to risk banishment to Tifitifi again.

This newest son-in-law had the right religious credentials for a wedding in the cathedral. Gordon stood up for the groom, but Aggie was too far along in her second pregnancy to be maid of honor. Dora Simpson and Clara Passi caught the bridal bouquet. Within the next few months, Dora wedded Frank Meredith and Clara became Mrs. Ralph Tattersall. Almost everyone in the old crowd was now married.

One afternoon Gordon raced up the apartment stairs with exciting news. Union Steamship had just bought a manager's residence in Vaiala and they could move out of Huche's airless rooms. The new house was right on the ocean, a one-story wooden cottage with a wide porch, set in a garden shaded by palms. Aggie felt she could breathe again. She could even wade out on the reef to gather sea slugs. Two months later Ian was born, blond and blue-eyed like his sister.

Gordon was made honorary French consul the following year, even though he had never seen Paris. Now that the days of international intrigue were over, consular responsibilities were not demanding. Few Samoans asked for French visas and there was little trade. Gordon's primary function was to entertain officers from visiting French warships and represent France at Government House balls.

For this he and Aggie were eminently qualified. Within a month they mounted a garden party for the officers of the warship *Aldebaran.* Aggie supervised every step of the preparations, showing her girls how to shine silver, make dainties, and serve tea just like Lena. Her teaching was spurred by the fact that she had no intention of remaining in the kitchen herself. She preferred to be the life of the party.

Apia even aspired to connections with Europe's social circuit. In 1920 the Prince of Wales himself stopped by on the H.M.S. *Renown.* When local matrons heard he was still a bachelor, they organized a gala reception at the British Club to introduce him to their eligible daughters. If European royalty were so keen on this island, why not catch a prince? As it turned out, the royal lad was a very shy young fellow. The only person he warmed up to was Willie, who introduced himself as "your father's interpreter in Fiji thirty years ago." The prince remembered hearing his name. That was about as close as anyone in Apia came to the British throne!

Gordon's sister Lyla came from New Zealand to visit them. She was a confirmed "old maid" and fell in love with Peggy. She begged to take the little girl back with her.

Just as Aggie began to feel secure on the ladder, the ground again dropped out from under her gay little world. At thirteen months, Ian was a lusty toddler digging in the sand with a spoon by the back steps. At sixteen months he lay helpless in his crib, too weak to even raise his head. Aggie was frantic.

"It's earthworms!" Maggie declared in her forthright manner. "Every baby gets them when they begin to crawl. I give mine a good dose of crushed garlic. Then I turn them bottom-up on my knee and go after the little buggers with a hairpin." Aggie winced.

"No, it's intestinal roundworms," Willie told her; "an everyday problem in the tropics. I'll send over some Cospos pills. Ian will love them because they taste like lollies."

When Ian responded with convulsions Aggie sought the opinion of her controversial neighbor, Dr. Virginia. Apia's most eligible bachelor, the American consul, had met and unaccountably married an unusual, middle-aged woman doctor on a recent trip to the Russian border. Instead of trying to placate Apia's disappointed matrons, she spurned their invitations and spent her time touring the villages, doctoring Samoan mothers and babies without fee. She handled difficult deliveries and handed out extra bandages to make tiny singlets. Such a woman was a target for gossip. Who ever heard of a Russian lady doctor? But Aggie was desperate.

Dr. Virginia led Aggie into a spotless "examining room" full of strange instruments and smells. Willie's shop was nothing like this and it made Aggie uneasy, but she was willing to try anything. The doctor seemed remarkably self-assured. She prodded the baby's stomach, examined a sample from his diaper under a magnifying glass, and finally gave Aggie her version of Ian's problem.

"Parasites are found everywhere in the tropics. Most children learn to live with them, and both worm and baby go on using the same intestinal tract in mutual tolerance. But some children don't seem able to control their worms. The parasites multiply wildly, even entering the brain and causing convulsions. I'm afraid that is what's happening to Ian."

It was too late for medication. The following evening Ian had another attack. Aggie rushed him to the chemist shop, where he stiffened and died in her arms. As she and Maggie laid out the little body, they saw six horrible white worms wriggle out of his tiny nose! Maggie went after them with her hairpin, but Aggie threw herself screaming on the floor. Her gay world was completely shattered, leaving only Job's eternal question. Why, God? Why my lovely innocent child? She couldn't bear the thought of parties after that. Even Gordon and Peggy seemed unimportant. She stayed on with her father at the chemist shop for weeks.

Willie knew something about grief. "You know, Aggie," he said one evening as they sat together on the stoop. "After Pele died I spent two years asking God that same question. How could He take a beautiful young mother like Pele when we all needed her so much. Finally I realized that question is only a trap, something one uses to avoid accepting death. Sooner or later you have to look it in the eye, pull in your gut, spit on your hands, and get on with life again."

157

"Oh, Dad!" Aggie laughed for the first time in months. "The way you do put things!" When she tried spitting on her hands, she caught sight of her belly, pregnant for the third time. Maybe I *do* have to go on living, she realized, and trudged back to Vaiala. Two months later she gave birth to Gordon Jr.

The "golden couple" at Tuaefu had its own encounter with death but did not fare as well. Olaf returned from his year abroad laden with lavish furnishings for his mansion. Nothing but the best would do for his son and heir. One afternoon the toddler disappeared. After a frantic search they found his little body floating face-down in a stream at the bottom of the hill. Nelson was inconsolable. He built a rose garden and buried his son under the statue of an angel. Rosabel was equally distraught. She never had another baby.

Nelson handled grief as he handled everything else, by drowning it in hard work. When his father-in-law, H.J. Moors, died, he amalgamated their interests and founded O.F. Nelson Ltd., Samoa's first indigenous corporation. This was so unusual that a local corporations code had to be written for that purpose. Other merchants followed, but Nelson's was always known as the "senior firm."

Having witnessed the rise and fall of his German counterparts, Nelson was aware that favorable political soil is essential for economic blooms. Would Samoa's new rulers from "down under" fertilize the garden as assiduously as Solf and Schultz had done? It didn't take him long to detect a disturbingly different motivation in Tate and Richardson, New Zealand's civilian administrators following Logan.

In 1922 the League of Nations had declared Samoa a Class C mandate, a role reserved for societies "too primitive to handle their own affairs in the foreseeable future." The education of this "splendid but backward race," as Tate described Samoans,[1] was entrusted to New Zealand, an island still young enough and white enough to thrill at the prospect of parenthood. The "backward race" lived in grass huts and subsistence villages, so that was where Samoa's new parents focused their humanitarian concern. The commercial settlers in the former protected area suddenly felt abandoned by their own kind. Not only did Tate and Richardson continue prohibition of liquor for the sake of the "backward race,"[1] they brought in seventy-one Kiwi constables to enforce it! Even worse, they refused to import the Chinese labor essential to run European plantations, lest these "coolies" take root and crowd out indigenous enterprise. Apia's roads, bridges, water supplies, and wharves fell into lamentable disrepair. The merchants still paid taxes, but these now went to pay teachers and agriculture inspectors "to bring backward peoples into the twentieth century." Far from fertilizing the soil for Beach Road's new corporations, the regime even proposed to establish a government agency to purchase village copra!

Nothing could have been a greater threat to the merchant community on Beach Road. Copra was the life blood of their bush stores. When incensed local businessmen tried to protest, the new administrators pointed to clause 102 of New Zealand's Constitutional Order of May, 1920, forbidding criticism of the government.

That was too much! Politics would have to take precedence over economics until the garden could be made fertile for productive enterprise again. When the New Zealand parliament sent a mission to inspect the progress of its mandate, Nelson organized a local citizen's committee to present the merchants' grievances. Gordon Hay-MacKenzie headed its sub-committee on censorship, and Mary's husband Robert Croudace chaired the sub-committee to protest the government copra store.

Apia now boasted several thousand permanent European and part-European residents. Most joined Nelson's citizens committee. Just what is an *afakasi*? It is risky to make assumptions about either his social class or his cultural behavior. Nelson, for example, had grown up in a traditional Samoan village and experienced the comforts of a Samoan extended family. He held the title of *taisi* in the traditional hierarchy and participated actively in Samoan ceremonies. He conducted his business affairs like a shrewd European merchant, but at times of crisis or exhaustion he found solace with his mother's people. After the death of his son, he spent more and more time in the villages, and not just to check on his bush stores. As at Tifitifi, he lingered long after the accounts were done.

159

Close contact with the forest and the sea relaxed him and put the pressure of business and death in more perspective.

He spent long evenings listening to village elders. Their legends, proverbs, and genealogies gained in meaning. He marveled at the delicate nuances of the chiefly language, which allowed an orator to elevate a human ego—or rip it to shreds with the turn of a phrase. But what fascinated him most was the social game his mother's people had invented. The more he got into it, the more intriguing the *faa Samoa* became. Its hierarchy and rules were far more intricate than the *faa palagi* ladder he had been climbing in Apia. Only someone who had never played the Samoan game could call it "backward." As far as Nelson could see, neither game was more natural, more moral, or more advanced than the other. Both were human artifices, like chess, which defined how players should interact and what their objectives should be. By following the rules, participants could constantly gauge where they stood *vis a vis* each other and make rational decisions about improving their positions. Without some such game to play, no one would know whether he was "getting ahead."

The only astonishing thing was that these two games were so different. Europeans in Apia ranked individuals on their ladder by the wealth they could accumulate and display. Nelson's mansion and parties at Tuaefu had proclaimed him at the top. Hard work and skill at turning a profit had put him there. The *faa Samoa* on the other hand, ranked people by the dignities others were willing to accord these at ceremonies: titles, fine mats, serving order, seating, prerequisites, legends. Samoans were as deft at inventing dignities to pamper the psyche as Europeans were at producing goods to pamper the body. The only catch with dignities was that they had to be offered by others. They couldn't be stored. Therefore, chiefs had to constantly work on each other, repairing their human relationships.

The games were alike in only two ways. They were addictive and required everything a player could muster: wit, time, and substance. Such resources being limited, it was almost impossible to play both games at once. Nelson smiled at New Zealand administrators who assumed

Samoans were just "backward *palagi*" yearning for the "light." Actually, most chiefs were not yet convinced that the *palagi* game was more rewarding than their own. The two games were now going on within a stone's throw of each other under cover of mutual "darkness." With a little more "light" they might easily collide.

Unlike Nelson and her husband, Aggie had given up gaming for the moment. She was pregnant for the fourth time herself, but even more concerned about Gordon's health. He was affable as ever but he tired easily and kept losing weight. Perhaps he was working too hard on all those committees. When he developed a persistent cough, a terrible fear swept back from her childhood and grabbed Aggie by the heart. She insisted that he see a doctor.

Gordon returned from the visit with a prescription and assured her that his cough would soon be better. "Don't worry your pretty head about me, honey," he laughed. "Just get down to women's business. I want a girl this time."

With the manager at Union Steamship he was more candid. The doctor had diagnosed his cough as a virulent form of TB known as "galloping consumption" and advised immediate treatment in New Zealand. Without telling his wife, Gordon wired his brother in Hauroa and arranged to sail on December 18, 1924. On the evening of his departure, friends gave him two stag parties, one at Loible's office and the other at the British Club.[2] Covering their concern with gay admonitions about "behaving himself in New Zealand," each group presented him with a purse of bank notes to take along.

Aggie was not aware of either function. She was in labor at the chemist shop. She woke next day, exhausted but happy. Beside her lay another baby girl. Gordon would be pleased.

He came in to see her with a cup of tea and sat on the edge of the bed. He admired his new daughter and returned her gently to Aggie's arms, explaining that he was leaving on the *Tofua* in an hour. He hadn't told her before for fear of complicating the delivery.

"Don't fret, sweetheart," he said in his usual cheerful manner. "As soon as you can travel, I'll send for you and we can have another great vacation. It's just my turn to go

161

first this time." He kissed her and was gone.

Aggie lay back unable to come to grips with what was happening. Her mother's death, Willie's bankruptcy, the 'flu ship, Ian's passing, and now Gordon! All she had asked of life was some fun and it was turning out to be a series of calamities. At mid-morning Willie came in and found her standing at the window in tears. He put his arm around her and together they watched the *Tofua* give a parting blast, turn seaward, and disappear around the point. Their throats were too tight for words. "I'm going to call this baby Pele Jr." Aggie murmured. Willie nodded that he understood.

The house at Vaiala was needed for Gordon's replacement. Aggie stayed on at the chemist shop with her three children. Prosperity was still around the corner for Willie. It was not easy for him to support them all, as well as Daisy and Fred. For Aggie, parties were a thing of the past. It felt more like Tifitifi. Gordon waited six months to fulfill his promise but time was getting short. "TICKET ARRANGED TOFUA NEXT," he finally wired. "BRING PEGGY."

The *Tofua* was heaven compared to her trip on the *Talune*. Peggy was seven now, a beautiful child with blonde ringlets and blue eyes. She romped around the deck, her white frock snapping in the breeze, while Aggie watched from a sunny deck chair. They both loved New Zealand milk and butter and were first in line at the dinner gong. It was such a release from washing bottles and diapers that Aggie felt young and gay again. After all, she was still in her twenties. Perhaps Gordon was already cured. They would have another honeymoon and put this ghastly interlude behind them just as they had the 'flu.

Her heart sang with relief when she saw him gaily waving his hat on the dock at Auckland. He had caught the train from Hauroa despite dark warnings from his brother, and was determined to have a good time. "You two are just what the doctor ordered." He laughed as he kissed his wife and eldest daughter. "Just look! I am a new man again."

He certainly acted like one. Their two-week spree in Auckland made up for the last six months. They dined out, danced until midnight, made love, and slept until noon. "All the things the doctor told me not to do," he quipped, "are just what's making me feel better."

He was enchanted with Peggy. He told her funny stories to make her giggle and couldn't keep his fingers out of her ringlets. But the idyll couldn't last forever. One morning he started coughing blood. "Too bad," he sighed with a weak smile. "It's back to Hauroa for me."

"I'll go with you," Aggie proposed. "I'm a good nurse, you know. We can come home together when you're well."

Gordon refused. "Pele and little Gordon need you more than I do," he told Aggie. "There is nothing you could do in Hauroa, anyway. Auntie Lyla has me cooped upstairs in a little house in the garden. She wouldn't even let you up the stairs, and that would be hard on both of us. But I could take Peggy back with me. Lyla wants her and it's time she went to school."

Aggie remembered Gordon's kindly "old maid" sister and her attachment to Peggy. Schools *were* better here and leaving her eldest would mean one less mouth for Willie to feed at the chemist shop. She reluctantly agreed and walked up the gangplank of the *Tofua* alone.

Peggy and Gordon stood on the wharf and waved good-by. As they turned to leave, Peggy was surprised at the sudden change in her father. He seemed to have spent his last ounce of energy on that farewell. On the train to Hauroa he looked like an empty shell. Her uncle whisked him off to an upstairs room the moment they arrived and sent her to live in the back with Auntie Lyla.

She did not see her father again for weeks. Auntie said he was up there getting treated. When Peggy finally mustered enough courage to creep up the stairs to peek at him, all she could see was a motionless figure in a great white bed, staring vacantly at the ceiling. Her gay young father had vanished.

Receiving no word from Gordon for several months, Aggie knew that something was amiss. It haunted her to think that Gordon might die alone in his upstairs room, unable to reach her. How would she ever know? Watching her distress, Willie wondered what he would have done if denied his last hour with Pele. "Aggie," he finally said, "you will have to go back to Hauroa. Otherwise you will always feel guilty."

"But, Dad," she cried, bursting into tears, "how can we

afford the ticket? I should never have listened to Gordon and come back here!"

She never knew how Dad had arranged it, but a few months later she found herself on the *Tofua* again. This time no one met her at Auckland. She took a coastal steamer to New Plymouth and the train to Hauroa.

It did not take her long to realize she should have made inquiries first. She found herself in a strange household completely dominated by Gordon's elder brother, a retired banker with gimlet eyes who lived alone in the front room. He managed the lives of Gordon and his two maiden sisters with about as much compassion as he had run his bank. He had built a small two-story cottage in the garden to isolate his dying brother, and Gordon lay upstairs too weak to move. Lyla went up to tend his needs, but otherwise he had no company and had ceased to care. For him the outside world had already fallen to ashes, consumed by the fire in his lungs.

Aggie tried to win him back with gaiety, funny stories, and flowers on his tray. He did not even see them. Unfortunately, the elder brother did. The banker's beady eyes followed Aggie everywhere, down to the kitchen, out to the garden, upstairs to Gordon's room. They made her very uneasy, but she said nothing until his corpulent body began to follow his gaze. She would turn from the stove to find him close behind her, or open a door to find him staring at her from the other side. She tried fending him off with sarcastic wit but that only seemed to lead him on. What was it about her, she wondered, that seemed to twist this man's mind in her direction? Didn't he realize that she was a young wife with three small children and a dying husband?

All the banker could see was that a playful butterfly with a soft irresistable body was fluttering around his garden. He couldn't help trying to catch the bright and tempting creature. He swiped with his net again and again but Aggie always managed to dodge. After a week of sleepless nights, he decided to set a trap. Instead of following her to the kitchen as she made Gordon's tea, he hid in his office next door. As she passed he suddenly pounced. The tea cup shattered as he dragged her inside.

Aggie was terrified. She suddenly realized how vulner-

164

able she was in this secluded house with two helpless old ladies in the back and her husband confined to an upstairs room in the garden, unable to lift his head. She reacted instinctively, sinking her teeth deep into the banker's arm. With a howl of pain he jerked it back and hit her full across the mouth. The blow gave wings to her feet. She was out of the house, down the street, and into the train station before her heart stopped pounding.

On the returning *Tofua*, Aggie cowered miserably on a deck chair in her steamer blanket. She tried conjuring up memories of that happy trip with Peggy six months before, but it wouldn't come. All she could recall was the porcine eyes of that hateful banker. She knew she would never see Gordon again, nor her gay old life as wife of the French consul. She would spend the rest of her days as a widow, raising her children, fretting over bills, and washing bottles for Dad.

The prospect was unbearable. What was it Dad had recommended when Ian died? "Look death in the eye, pull in the gut, spit on each hand, and get on with life again." Maybe he could manage that with a few drinks in him, but she couldn't afford even that recourse. She was penniless.

"Aggie! Fancy finding you here!" a voice suddenly boomed above her head. "Why are you burying your curls in that old blanket? Hop up, pretty lady, and let me buy you a drink! It's a much better way to keep warm!"

Aggie peeked out with one eye. There stood Charlie Grey, a gay young gentleman who in happier days had rivaled Gordon as Apia's most avid party-goer. A sharp-witted accountant, he had managed to inherit Meredith's store when it went bankrupt and was now doing very well for himself. Charlie tossed back the steamer rug and gallantly helped Aggie to her feet. A few moments later, over a gin and tonic, she was confiding her dark experiences to his friendly ear. It began to seem more like an exciting adventure now that she could joke about it with a member of the old crowd.

Charlie listened, feeling warmly masculine towards this damsel in distress. Aggie could soon feel the warm glow rising in him. "How's Daisy?" she asked teasingly, to remind him of his pert little wife back home.

"We'll know soon enough," he laughed; "but let's spend

these four days getting *you* back on your feet again."

The rest of the voyage was a delightful dream suspended between two unbearable realities. Charlie saw to it that she thought only of the present. He was generous, humorous, attentive, and ever the cavalier. She responded as if she had just got out of jail. She felt wild, giddy, free, greedily cramming into four days enough laughter to last the rest of her life. She drank, she danced, she flirted outrageously with everyone, including a shipboard count. She made full use of the very talent she had bemoaned in herself the week before—her ability to capture men's attention. Gentlemen swirled around her with their nets, pouncing this way and that while she dodged and twinkled with laughter. For some reason the chase was no longer horrifying—it was lots of fun!

The excitement of the trip did not make it any easier to go back to the dull routine of the chemist shop. Uncertain whether Aggie was a wife or a widow, Apia's hostesses solved the dilemma by not inviting her at all. But their eyes and tongues were more alert than ever to note how she conducted herself. Willie sensed how difficult this must be for his liveliest daughter. He regaled her with stories about that other *afakasi* girl, whose husband went off to sea and never returned. Aggie appreciated Emma's position and pondered her solution.

Only Charlie Grey and his sociable wife Daisy saw that she got out now and then. Unfortunately, Daisy soon succumbed to the bane of heavy drinkers and was rushed to New Zealand with a liver ailment. Like Gordon she never returned.

When Aggie's formal release finally arrived, it was delivered with a sting she would never forget. The following Christmas time she received an envelope postmarked Hauroa. Inside was no letter, no sender's name, no word of condolence, only a clipping carelessly torn from a local paper. Gordon Hay-MacKenzie was dead.

Chapter 14

The House on the Hill

(1926-1931)

ONE LATE afternoon, Aggie was standing at the tub in the chemist shop scrubbing bottles. Doors had already closed for the day but this obnoxious job seemed to go on forever. When she was through, there would be tea to prepare, children to bathe, and prescriptions to make up for the morning. For a few months this mindless routine had been a help, but now it was a grave she was digging for herself. Maggie and Mary were up there in the world of sunshine and laughter but she was down here buried alive, slowly suffocating.

Suddenly she could take it no longer. She straightened up, looked at herself in the mirror, and then slowly and deliberately spit on her palms. It was like a shot of adrenalin. She grabbed a soapy bottle and flung it across the room, feeling like the rebellious child who walked out on Sister Aloysia. The glass crashed in the corner; she flung back her curls and marched to the sitting room door. She threw that back with a bang—and found herself staring straight into the astonished eyes of Charlie Grey on the other side.

"I thought I heard an eruption in here," he said, as startled as she was.

"You did!" she replied flatly. "Why do you always seem to appear at moments like this?"

"Psychic," he laughed, recalling the defiant eye that had peered up at him from the steamer rug. "I say, you do look as if you needed another stiff one!" She nodded and they walked out the front door arm in arm and headed towards the British Club.

It wasn't unusual to find Charlie in the Swann's sitting room. He had dropped by often since his wife left, to sit and chat with Willie. But this time both he and Aggie knew it was different. Over their drinks he admitted that she was the one he really came to see. He couldn't seem to forget her. Aggie was convinced she had conjured him up when she spit on her hands. Actually, the moment had been lurking about, waiting to happen ever since their trip on the *Tofua*.

To Aggie it was like being sixteen again, slipping out past Dad's door to keep tryst with her lover. This time Willie did not even bother to watch the time. He just went to bed.

Charlie was different from Paul or Gordon, Aggie thought, trying to pinpoint her attraction. Paul was like a rock, something firm one could hang onto. Gordon had been a seabird, sweeping her into sunlit skies. This Charlie was a gambling man, rolling for high stakes, and he made her feel that *she* was his greatest prize. Maybe it was the way he bought her silk dresses and showed her off to his friends. He called her his "crown jewel" and polished her to a warm glow with unfailing gallantry. His generosity provided a fourteen-carat setting for her good looks and flashing wit. Both of them shone with greater brilliance in combination.

Charlie seemed as lucky in business as he was in love. Arriving in Apia with an empty pocket, he had managed to parlay himself from a lowly accountant to liquidator and finally manager of the Meredith firm. Now he was also a partner with Nelson and Riley in a lightering venture known as Apia Stevedoring. He had managed this rapid ascent without making enemies because of his deft social touch. After worsting a business rival he was able to invite him out to lunch and leave him feeling that the whole thing was a lark.

Before long Aggie discovered she was pregnant again. At first she was afraid to tell Charlie for fear he might vanish. Men often did such things. Her bright new world, like Cinderella's, would soon be transformed back into rags, pumpkins, and ashes. She couldn't risk that again!

But she had underestimated his attraction. When she could keep her secret no longer, he was upset only that she had not let him know before. "Why didn't you tell me right away?" he cried, pained at her lack of trust.

"I didn't dare," she admitted. "I was afraid of losing you."

168

"Lose me!" he laughed, sweeping her up in his arms. "What would a gold ring be without a crown jewel? I've just been waiting to buy that big new house below Vailima so that I could ask your father for your hand in proper style! I didn't intend a public announcement quite like this," he chortled, pointing at her swelling figure. "But you women always manage to do things your own way!"

They giggled themselves silly with relief and planned the wedding. Under the circumstances it would have to be a small one, just family and close friends. The old problem of churches arose again. Charlie was Anglican, but when Aggie explained she needed better luck this time he agreed to let the children become Catholic. They were married in the cathedral.

Aggie felt like a queen, moving into Charlie's new mansion on the hill. Never had she dreamed of being mistress of a house like this! It was every bit as elegant as the one on the marble steps in Levuka. Willie had struggled for a lifetime, unable to acquire what had befallen her in a few short months. Charlie wasn't the only successful gambler in the family!

Wide steps flanked with sentinel flowerpots led up to a double door shaded by canopied windows on the second story. From the upstairs balconies she could look out over five acres of garden to the sweep of the harbor and Mulinuu peninsula far below. It wasn't Vailima or Tuaefu of course, but it was the next rung down and had something neither of those great estates could yet boast of—a swimming pool, the first in Apia! This symbol of success with its thick cement walls stood proudly on the front lawn where everyone could see it. Charlie never discussed business with Aggie or his guests. He did not need to. The pool said it for him; he was one of Apia's up-and-coming gentlemen.

Aggie sent Gordon Jr. to join Peggy in New Zealand. It was time for him also to begin his education. But Pele Jr., who was only three, moved into the house on the hill with her mother, to be joined shortly by a half-sister named Maureen.

Aggie could hardly wait to get onto her feet again, so that she could organize her new household for entertaining. There were girls to train, tables to polish, and brand-new crystal glasses to arrange on the shelves. She intended to make her new home a center of Apia's social life.

For the next five years the Grey's house and pool were to Apia's young married set what Tattersall's porch had been to its adolescents. A party started at Grey's could have finished up next morning at an F. Scott Fitzgerald estate on the Hudson without the slightest change of mood. With her bobbed hair, cloche hats, and low-waisted dresses, Aggie was Apia's most authentic "flapper." She danced, she flirted, she laughed, she drank 'til the small hours. Tate and Richardson could have their prohibition. It was irrelevant at her private parties.

Charlie couldn't get over his good fortune. This new jewel of his flashed with ceaseless energy and brought his house to life. When he woke with a dull hangover, she was already up, directing her girls to polish the brass and shine the silver for the next party. She was an excellent house-keeper and able to inspire the girls she brought from Toamua to help her.

Even the birth of her sixth child failed to slow her down. His name was Edward but she called him Sonny. She hired old hunchbacked Auntie Tauili to look after him and his sisters so that she and Charlie could keep stepping out.

Aggie could not get over her good fortune either. Charlie was just what she wanted: gay, rich, generous, and ever the cavalier. He gave her everything she needed to display her talents, and she rewarded him in turn with the tenderest word a flapper could bestow—she called him "Daddy."

If there were any counterbalance to this heady world, anything that even vaguely resembled either of her roots, it was her garden. An afternoon spent training bougain-villea over a trellis or planting cucumbers brought her back into focus before she started the evening's party. Pigs and chickens reminded her of Lotopa, a calm glimpse of reality. As a result the Grey's five acres began to flourish with bananas, avocados, pineapples, tomatoes, lettuce, and cab-bages, far more than they could possibly eat.

"You know, if I could get these things to town," she told Charlie, "I could make good money from our garden."

He smiled. It always amused him when an attractive

woman like Aggie talked about money. Why should she worry her pretty little head about things he, a man, was ready, willing and able to provide? But if a truck would please her, so be it. Next day he appeared with a pick-up purchased from a friend and she gave him his reward, a squeal of delight and a kiss. "If you ever manage to earn anything, my dear," he laughed, patting her curls, "buy yourself a ball gown."

The truck inspired a flood of energy in Aggie. First she had to find some place to keep it out of the rain. There was a small wooden shed in the back, but its door was too low for a truck. Next day while Charlie was at work she asked a boy who was repairing the laundry to cut a large triangle above the shed door.

"Don't waste the lumber," she told him out of habit. "Store it out behind the shed with the old laundry windows."

As soon as the truck was housed, she started her vegetable business. She had her girls weave several dozen coconut-frond baskets. A pineapple, a hand of bananas, and some bright vegetables in each made them very attractive to homesick New Zealand administrator's wives. Several times a week she sent the boy to town with a load. The money he brought back she just stuffed into a jar.

When she finally counted it at Christmas, she could hardly believe her eyes. It came to £684! She had been making about £57 a month. A full-time foreman on the Reparations Estates was lucky to make £18! With money so easy to come by, she wondered why her father had ever chosen to be a chemist. Having no immediate need for it, she just let the money accumulate to prove what she could do.

Chapter 15

The Mau Rebellion

(1926-1931)

ON SEPTEMBER 24, 1926, the Apia business community held a reception at Market Hall to welcome Olaf Nelson back from a vacation in Australia. On his way home he had stopped in Wellington to present the grievances of the citizens' committee to Nosworthy, New Zealand's current minister of external affairs. It was Beach Road's latest effort to protest Richardson's copra scheme and the traders were anxious to hear if it had succeeded. Judge Gurr gave a welcoming speech and Nelson reported with some bitterness that his mission had fallen on deaf ears.

"Charlie," Aggie asked on the way home, "did Olaf seem different to you tonight? He sounded personally affronted by whatever happened down there. I wonder if Nosworthy insulted him or something. He's a very proud man, you know."

Next day Nelson attended a second reception. His fellow chiefs had gathered to give him a traditional welcome feast at Vaimoso. At this affair he sat crosslegged in a thatched meeting house on the *malae*, his back against the post of honor. The chiefs addressed him by his Samoan title, *Taisi*, son of the great *tafaifa* Galumalemana. They gave him the first cup of kava and a feast followed.

Lealofi, the current Tamasese, spoke bitterly of his recent humiliation. Richardson had banished him to Savaii for refusing to cut the hedge around his house in compliance with the government's beautification plan. The chief had immediately returned home, of course, but felt he had been treated with great indignity. Whose village was it? Another chief complained that his village council could no longer make important decisions about the life of its own people. Its meetings were now concerned only with carrying out directives from above: tax collectors,

172

court clerks, and agriculture inspectors. A third was distressed by Richardson's new postal-savings plan. The administrator was urging young men to save their money to buy land and businesses of their own so that they could "free themselves from their feudal chiefs." What would that do to Samoa's great extended family groups? Adolescents were the arms and legs that fed and protected them! A fourth chief objected to having to build schools. What would be taught there? Was it possible that these foreigners were trying to capture not only the village council but the hearts and minds of their children?

Finally the chief orator arose and delicately came to the point. "We rejoice that you have returned, Taisi, and can resume your rightful place beside Tamasese, protecting our way of life. The Germans wanted only land for their coconuts; these New Zealanders want to run our families and villages. You learned the white-man's game from your father, but we know that your heart is with your mother's people."

Nelson listened, deeply moved. How beautifully these orators soothed a wounded spirit! Nosworthy had scolded him as if he were a backward child. These chiefs were treating him as their champion! Until this moment he had felt torn between his two worlds. Now for once they were speaking with a single tongue. His colleagues on Beach Road and the chiefs in this Samoan council house were both asking him to lead them against the same enemy. How could he refuse?

The following evening he was guest of honor at yet a third welcoming function, a banquet at Vailima hosted by Richardson himself. Nelson and the governor had been "official" friends ever since the latter had added "locals" to his advisory Legislative Council (LEGCO). Five of its members were New Zealanders, heads of administrative departments. The other three—Williams, Westbrook, and Nelson—had been elected by local property owners to represent the business community. These eight composed the guest list tonight at Richardson's party.

The long polished table in Robert Louis Stevenson's banquet hall flashed with candlelight on crystal as smartly uniformed houseboys with VR (Victoria Regina) buckles slipped silver trays of food between the guests. Nelson eyed the service critically and adopted a slightly condescending air to indicate that Vailima did not quite match up with the latest at Tuaefu. Richardson sensed it immediately. This haughty merchant had always made him uneasy.

Nelson noticed his host's malaise and hoped it was the result of his mission to Nosworthy. At their recent meeting in New Zealand, the external affairs minister had stoutly defended the governor's programs in Samoa, but the merchant hoped that at least he had sowed some seeds of doubt. Perhaps one of these had sprouted into a confidential cable ordering Richardson to restrain his ardor for advancing "primitive people."

Since the three "local" guests were strangely silent, the five New Zealand officers loyally shouldered the buren burden of dinner conversation. The director of agriculture reported that, thanks to his inspectors, the villagers were finally destroying more pestiferous beetles and copra production was improving. Now the government had forbidden village chiefs to go on fine-mat visitations, they also had more time to plant coconuts, and Samoa's economic future looked brighter than it had since German times.

The director of communications reported rising deposits in Richardson's postal-savings plan. Soon ambitious young Samoans could buy land of their own and free themselves from "unpaid bondage to their feudal chiefs," and Samoa would finally "emerge from its Dark Ages."

The director of education pointed out that he would soon have an elementary school in every district. Teachers were already being trained in Apia to follow a "good solid New Zealand curriculum" that would bring Samoa's children "into the twentieth century." One officer proudly passed a clipping from the *London Times* reporting that New Zealand was running the most enlightened mandate in the League, thanks to Richardson's "grasp of the native mind." A knighthood was in the offing because of his "outstanding contributions to backward races." All the officers clapped.

Nelson listened in stony silence, trying to picture what would happen if the chiefs at Vaimoso yesterday could understand English and listen to the conversation at this

174

table. Even more unlikely, what if these eager white men could speak Samoan and understand what had been said on the *malae* yesterday? It seemed incredible that intelligent people could view the same events through such different lenses that they reached opposite conclusions. No wonder Samoans and Europeans passed each other like ships in the night! He shook his head helplessly at the thought of trying to explain something like this to the man at the end of the table, who regarded himself as an "authority on the native mind!"

Richardson, for his part, eyed his quiet guest apprehensively, wondering how to handle this pretentious and ruthless merchant whose bush stores robbed his own people. This imposter had actually built a mansion to rival Vailima, hoping to become governor, himself, no doubt! According to a recent confidential cable from Nosworthy, Nelson even had the nerve to complain about village development projects! Obviously he wanted to keep his people backward so that he could continue to enrich himself. How ironic to find this unscrupulous local tycoon elected to his legislative council the very first time he opened it to the business community! Fortunately he had appointed a Samoan Council of Chiefs *(Fonoa a Faipule)* to advise him on how the "natives" felt. He had hand-picked the "best and brightest" young Samoans he could find for that post, and was diligently preparing them to replace Samoa's "hidebound" traditional hierarchy. Their touching words of appreciation always warmed his heart and made him more determined than ever to "free this noble race."

Nelson said nothing until dessert was being served. Then he reiterated his long-standing proposal for bridging the communication gap. Perhaps if an English-speaking chief of high traditional status were included on the European Legislative Council, the governor would finally get to hear a real authority on the Samoan mind.

"May I repeat my suggestion, sir, that you appoint High Chief Malietoa to our august body here. He might be able to keep us in touch with another important segment of island opinion."

Richardson could see through that ploy fast enough! This demagogue wanted to gain popularity in the villages for seeming to promote their feudal hierarchy. "May I remind you, sir," the governor retorted coldly, "that you were naturalized a British subject in 1924 and elected by local Europeans to represent *their* interests, not Samoans. The welfare of the 'natives' is my responsibility, not yours, thank God! I have Samoans of my own to advise me. I would thank you to stay out of 'native' affairs after this!"

Nelson's face stiffened and he stood up. That was the end of even "official" friendship. The administrator had thrown down the gauntlet and Nelson was only too happy to pick it up. The eyes of the two antagonists met for a moment. Which one of them would emerge as Samoa's true champion? Then Nelson gave a curt bow and strode out of the room, followed by Williams and Westbrook. Everyone realized that something had just happened but no one was sure quite what.

That night both champions lay awake selecting their weapons. Guns and warships were out of the question in these days of enlightened mandates, but each had political, economic and legal resources and knew how to use them.

Next morning Richardson called a meeting of his hand-picked Samoan council *(Fona a Faipule)*. As usual, its members expressed gratitude to God for sending him to enlighten their minds and promised their support. Thus reassured as to the "native mind," he went back to his office and studied the Native Affairs Ordinance recently passed by the New Zealand parliament to help him through difficult times like this. It defined as seditious "any organization which spreads dissatisfaction and disobedience among the natives."[1] He wired Nosworthy for legal advice on his power to banish, deport, and imprison such offenders. Upon reading the reply, he sat back with a smile. He should have no difficulty taking care of one pretentious *afakasi.*

Nelson also rose early that morning. He sent a messenger to Vaimoso, inviting the traditional chiefs who had spoken so eloquently about their grievances to a secret meeting at Tuaefu next day. They were overjoyed that Taisi was taking such prompt action as their leader. Three *tamaaiga* attended the meeting: Tamasese, Tuimaleaiifano, and a prospective Mataafa (Faumuina). The current Malie-

176

toa was absent, indicating that, as always, Samoans would be able to hedge their bets.

The upshot of the Tuaefu meeting was the creation of an organization known as the Welfare League of Samoa. Its objectives were to bring an end to administrative banishments, title deprivations, fine-mat restrictions, and meddlesome inspectors. Control of village life would be restored to local chiefs and the dignity of the traditional hierarchy restored.

On October 16, 1926, Nelson convened a meeting of the citizens' committee at Market Hall. Williams, Westbrook, Cobcroft, Meyers, Smythe, and Stowers assured the unhappy business community that vigorous action on their grievances would soon be under way. The most unusual thing about this meeting was that it was translated into Samoan for the benefit of some brown faces in the back row. The traditional chiefs of the Welfare League had joined Apia's businessmen! For the first time in Samoa's history, the two communities were taking joint action.

The meeting elected an executive committee composed of six local Europeans and six chiefs. Its next decision was to invite Nosworthy to visit Samoa in person, to hear the grievances of both communities. After he had mailed the invitation, Nelson sat back with a smile. Those signatures might make Richardson think again about the Samoan mind.

As soon as the governor learned of the joint meeting, he sent a strong letter warning the local European members of the citizen's committee that "mixing in native affairs" could be seditious. He sent an equally strong letter to the chiefs of the Welfare League, directing them to channel any grievances they might have through his handpicked Samoan Council.

The affair was reaching proportions that made old-timer settlers like Willie nervous. They had lived through the hurricane, the one-day war, and Solf's meeting with Lauati and felt it was risky to incite traditional chiefs. "I don't like that man at Vailima any more than Olaf does," he told Aggie uneasily, "but I don't think Olaf should heat up those high Samoan titleholders. They're not as easy to control as he thinks. If H.J. Moors hadn't died last year, he could have told Olaf what happened when he armed Mataafa Iosefo back in the eighties. Those warriors could have killed us all in an hour. There's something about *tamaaiga* that stirs Samoan blood. If Olaf were wise he'd let them be. Samoans don't need a champion!"

Peter told Maggie he also had trepidations. "I deliberately stayed away from the citizens' committee meeting last night. When Olaf stopped by this morning to ask me where I stood, I told him, 'right on the fence looking down at both sides.' And that's where you'd better stay too, Maggie, if you want to continue making dresses for both Mrs. Richardson and Rosabel Nelson!"

Some prominent businessmen and planters like Cobcroft and Kurt Meyer prudently withdrew from the combined executive committee. But others like Westbrook, Williams, Gurr, and Smythe openly flouted Richardson's warning. In the secrecy of the ballot box, the business community overwhelmingly returned Nelson, Williams, and Westbrook to Richardson's Legislative Council.

Out in the villages, Samoan families also hedged their bets in time-honored fashion. The chiefs of Falealili continued to support the government, not because of Richardson's welfare projects, but because of their historic loyalty to Malietoa, who had decided not to take part in this affair. At the same time, however, many of them regularly attended Mau meetings as members of the Safenunuivao political family, which historically supported Tamasese. Neither Richardson nor Nelson could be blamed for claiming to represent a majority of Falealili as judged by turnouts at their respective meetings!

A second meeting of the combined committee was held on November 12. Like other members of the cautious business faction, Aggie and Charlie did not attend but drove back and forth in front of Market Hall to see who did. On the stage they could spot the three members they had elected to LEGCO and the three Samoan *tamaaiga*. That was expected. What really surprised them was the audience. At this second meeting, brown faces outnumbered white faces three to one! No wonder Willie was uneasy about stirring up the Samoan heart. Richardson explained the Samoan turnout to Nosworthy as due to Nelson's demagoguery.

Whatever it was, Samoan morale was rising. Out in the villages, chiefs began visiting each other again with fine mats and kava sticks. Polite oratory reverberated again on the *malae*.

Meanwhile, in town their two would-be champions addressed each other less politely through the local press. The *Samoa Times*, like its German predecessor, addressed itself almost exclusively to the local European community. Pat Brown, its current editor and fifty-five per cent owner, vehemently supported Richardson. But the other forty-five was owned by Nelson himself. He had no intention of losing this potent weapon to his enemy. In May, 1927, he sold his share of the *Samoa Times* and founded a rival weekly, the *Samoan Guardian*, with his friend Gurr as editor. Not only its politics but its intended audience was a new departure. Half of every issue was written in Samoan!

After several delays, Nosworthy agreed to come for the king's birthday celebration in 1927. Richardson organized for his superior the grandest parade, regatta, and Vailima ball the island had yet seen. A good turnout would attest to his popularity in both communities and a poor turnout was inconceivable. What Samoan could resist a celebration?

To the governor's intense chagrin, the streets were virtually deserted that year. He couldn't understand it until he discovered that Nelson had scheduled an even bigger celebration and feast at Tuaefu.

Nosworthy was in no hurry to listen to the grievances of the combined committees. He waited until the last day of his visit for the hearing. Their complaints were nothing new. Tofaeono was upset because the administrator had seized some of his land for a road. Alipia accused him of hand-picking his *Fono Faipule*. What was unusual, however, was the size of the crowd outside his window. Two thousand Samoans sat sullenly in the street! Richardson had already explained to Nosworthy that "simple-minded natives can be readily influenced if certain methods are used to appeal to their lower instincts."[2] He could easily guess who had organized this demonstration, but the faces did not look friendly. Nosworthy hastily closed the hearing with a warning, "There is room in Samoa for only one administrator, not two. . . . There will be no toleration of any further aping of the governor."[3]

Nosworthy left for Wellington next day, saying he would report his findings later; but it was already clear that he had concluded that Nelson was inciting the "lower instincts of these simple-minded natives" and that something would have to be done about it. Ideally he should be deported along with other disruptive Samoan chiefs; but unfortunately, he was a British subject and member of Apia's Legislative Council. Deporting him might not look like the spirit of democracy to a New Zealand electorate bred on the Magna Charta. Nosworthy and Richardson prudently decided to confine their punishments on dissident Samoans. Lagolago, Faumuina, and fifty other Samoan leaders were deported to the small island of Apolima near Manono, and thirteen had their titles removed. That should take care of the Mau!

Actually, nothing could have aroused traditional Samoa more effectively. By the time the chiefs got back to Vaimoso two days later, their titles had gained historic dignity. They were greeted with kava and feasted like heroes. Samoans did not gain or lose their titles in accordance with British law; they had rules of their own.

Shortly thereafter, Richardson's department heads began to report disturbing incidents with the welfare programs. In a number of villages, Samoans were removing their children from the new public schools, failing to show up for court dates, seeking local healers instead of clinics, and selling their copra to Nelson's stores. Worst of all, they were refusing to pay their taxes. The treasury was able to collect only £2,000 of £19,000 due that year![4]

Non-cooperation was indeed distressing in a model mandate. Village welfare projects were at a standstill. Obviously Nelson would have to go if Samoa was to continue into the twentieth century. But that was easier said than done. Legally it was not too hard to banish a Samoan from one island to another. Their rights had never been clearly defined anyway. But it was something else again to deport a *bona fide* British subject from the land of his birth, especially one fully cognizant of his rights and able to pay the best English lawyers. Richardson and Nosworthy proceeded with due caution, requesting that the New Zealand parliament send a royal commission to investigate the situation. Then they carefully set the stage.

All went well. In September and October, 1927, the commission held its hearings in carefully selected "loyal" villages. The citizen's committee and the Samoan Welfare league were not able to make disruptive speeches or clutter the streets, because they were notified at the last moment. In December the commission returned its findings: the governor had every right to deport disruptive agitators regardless of nationality.

Richardson lost no time in taking Nelson, Gurr, and Smythe to court. They were found guilty of sedition forthwith. The first two were deported to New Zealand for five years and the latter for two. Richardson sighed with relief and waved goodby to the problem as their ship disappeared around Pilot Point. Now at last he could get back to his welfare programs.

To his astonishment the village boycott continued to spread! In January, 1928, five hundred chiefs gathered at Vaimoso and changed the name of their organization from Samoan Welfare League to Mau (our belief). It was now completely different from Apia's citizens' committee. Tamasese Lealofi III, the *tama aiga*, emerged as its leader. Deporting Nelson had apparently not excised the movement's "brain" at all. It had just made the Medusa more Samoan! A Mau executive committee began meeting every Wednesday in a round house about the size of a grandstand on Vaimoso's *malae*, a few minutes from downtown Apia. The Mau had a headquarters!

The Mau proceeded to organize mass meetings of villagers from all over Samoa. Everyone came dressed in blue *lavalava* with white stripes. The Mau had a uniform! Some guards identified by purple *lavalava* kept the crowd in order. This movement now even had a police force of its own! When these participants returned to the villages, they began organizing their own courts, raising their own money, and banishing government inspectors and teachers. Good heavens! This was no longer a protest; it was beginning to look like an independent government! The Mau confirmed this by producing its own flag, inscribed *Samoa mo Samoa* (Samoa for Samoans).

Now on his own, Tamasese Lealofi felt no particular obligation to Apia's business community. Mau police appeared on the steps of some Beach Road stores, turning back Samoan purchasers. "If we stop spending money on imported goods," Tamasese had told his people, "these foreigners will run out of money and their government will run out of taxes."

In a panic, the administrator wired New Zealand for military assistance. In February, the *Dunedin* and *Diomede* sailed into Apia harbor with two hundred and fifty marines aboard. "Didn't I tell you?" Willie said to Aggie as he prepared to board up his shop windows again. "That's what comes for fooling with the *faa Samoa!* Chiefs are not children. They've got their own thing going on this island and the numbers are still on their side."

The following day the marines arrested four hundred Mau at Vaimoso, only to find one hundred and more on the *malae* within hours. Since Apia's jail could only hold a dozen, all but the leaders were loaded on trucks and dropped seven miles outside of town.

Richardson finally realized he would have to make some concessions on Samoa in the twentieth century, and tried to negotiate with the *tamaaiga*. He offered to suspend their sentences, hold an open election for his *Fono a Faipule*, and allow districts to go on fine-mat excursions if they wished. He even invited Tamasese to sit on the Legislative Council. Lagolago and Faumina felt that this concession was sufficient, but Tamasese and eighty-year-old Tuimalealiifano refused to settle for anything less than complete self-government. The latter was soon released from jail anyway. It was just too risky to hold the frail old man behind bars. The following month Tamasese ended his own incarceration by simply walking out the door, assuming, quite correctly, that the marine on duty would hesitate to shoot a *tamaaiga* in cold blood. The Mau uprising continued. In 1928, two-thirds of the villages paid their taxes to the Mau and the administration was able to collect less than £1,000.[5]

At this point, New Zealand decided to try another administrator. Nelson had submitted a formal complaint to the Mandates Commission of the League of Nations and Richardson was sent to Geneva to defend his policies. Colonel Allen, a man of more military and less humanitarian inclinations, was sent to Samoa as New Zealand's administrator. He arrived with an escort of seventy-four armed New Zealand police. They were billeted in the former British Club, next to Willie's chemist shop. With their assistance, Allen soon rearrested Tamasese and sent him to jail in New Zealand for six months, hoping that action would finally quiet things down.

Actually it only compounded his problem. The administrator had underestimated the political sympathy an imprisoned *tamaaiga* might engender "down under." A Samoan Defense League was formed in New Zealand, claiming to represent twenty-two thousand voters, including the leader of the opposition party and Sir Maui Pomare, a prominent Maori. This Mau was like a hydra; whenever one head was chopped off, more appeared! By now Samoa was being referred to as "New Zealand's" India."

Samoa's two original champions went to Geneva to battle it out. The Mandates Commission took testimony from Richardson but refused to hear Nelson, claiming he "did not represent a legally constituted government." Its final report faulted the New Zealand administrator in only one regard, "lack of firmness in dealing with dissenters."[6] Nelson hired the celebrated Sir Stafford Cripps to take his appeal to the British Privy Council, but the case was dismissed. The British Empire was not yet in a mood to give in.

With its leaders defected or in exile and the rise of a pro-government faction in Samoa known as the *Malo*, the Mau might have faded from view except for the events of "Black Saturday," December 28, 1929. Tamasese Lealofi had been allowed to return home. He requested that he and his followers be permitted to march down Beach Road that day to welcome Smythe, who was returning from his two years in exile. Since the Mau seemed quiescent, Police Chief Braisby granted permission, provided no Mau police or tax evaders appeared among the marchers to force him to make arrests. Smythe's ship arrived at dawn. By six a.m., seven hundred Mau members in blue uniforms had materialized and were marching from Vaimoso towards Apia. A short time later, an equally large Mau contingent set out from Matautu and crossed the Vaisigano bridge. They planned to converge at the Tivoli wharf to greet their hero. Tamasese and Tuimalealiifano led the procession and Mau police and tax evaders were quite visible among the marchers.

That was too much. When the parade reached the courthouse, Braisby sent out policemen from his station across the street to make arrests. Angry marchers defended the wanted men with sticks and stones. Braisby tried to rescue his beleaguered police by sending in two sergeants and twenty-five more armed men. Pandemonium ensued, and the outnumbered police were forced back to the station without their quarry.

Nervously, they positioned a Lewis machine gun in the yard and sent warning shots over the heads of the crowd. The two *tamaaiga* shouted to their followers to "keep the peace," but it was too late. The angry mob pressed towards the station, throwing stones. The police panicked, lowered their sights, and fired directly at the leaders. Tamasese fell with a wound in the groin; old Tuimalealiifano was shot in the arm. Followers who tried to cover them were riddled by a second round. Faumui and Tapei died outright. Leota, Migao, Vele, and Tamasese died within a few hours. The final Mau toll was thirty injured and eleven dead. Six policemen were injured and one killed.

The marchers withdrew towards Matafele, bearing their casualties. The bush wireless crackled like lightning across the island—an unarmed *tamaaiga* had been mowed down by New Zealand police in the streets of Apia! Immediately every Mau heart in Samoa beat strong again.

No one knew what might happen next, but Colonel Allen took no chances. He wired New Zealand immediately for a cruiser, one thousand pistol rounds, and a box of Mills bombs. He also toughened sedition regulations to prohibit Mau uniforms and meetings. He expanded the jail and reinforced the police. The *Dunedin* arrived shortly with not only marines but New Zealand's minister of defense in person to direct the operation.

These new administrators were in no mood for welfare projects; they just wanted to end the Mau forever. Unfortunately, they could find no Mau to arrest! Vaimoso and Lepea were empty except for women and children. In the next four days the marines scoured the north coast as far as Mulifanua and were able to make only one capture. Old Tuimalealiifano was found sitting in his *fale* (Samoan house), his arm in a sling, proudly wearing his Mau uniform. The others had taken to the forests like their fathers in the days of Mataafa Iosefo!

The defense minister sent to New Zealand for an airplane, the first in the islands, to locate Mau hideouts in the hills and to scatter leaflets on the villages. With this eye in the sky, the marines were able to locate thirty bush shelters in late January (1930) and took twelve prisoners. The rest of the Mau had scattered in small parties which were difficult to find under the trees. The Tamasese title and leadership of the movement fell to Lealofi's younger brother, Meaole, reportedly somewhere in the mountains above Safata. Bishop Darnand of the Catholic mission gained contact with him and transmitted a government offer of safe conduct, but he refused to come down.

Strangely enough Mau uniforms still paraded down Beach Road on steamer day. The police were completely at a loss with this newest phenomenon. Rosabel Nelson and her sister Priscilla had organized the wives and sweethearts of the men of the hills and formed a Woman's Mau! Unable to fight them with guns or planes, Colonel Allen resorted to the only anti-female tactic he could think of. He described them to external affairs as "a band of known prostitutes."[7]

Finally, in March, 1930, the Catholic bishop was able to arrange a face-to-face meeting between the defense minister and the new leader of the Mau. Life in the dripping rain forest, with its myriad mosquitoes and meagre diet, was taking its toll. Like Pepe, Mau warriors were beset by fevers. Tamasese Meaole drafted their grievances in the form of seventeen queries, including:[8] Does the mandate allow you to declare war on Samoans like this? What have you done to prepare us for self-government? Why are we being treated like a former colony when the Treaty of 1889 made us a protectorate? How can the Savaii chiefs return home when you have taken their boats?

Fifty Mau chiefs met with the minister of defense and three government representatives in Tamasese's *fale* in Vaimoso to get New Zealand's answer to their queries. The defense minister, who was leaving next day, praised Samoa's climate and beauty and assured the chiefs of his undying friendship. Old Tuimalealiifano replied that this was not what was in dispute.[9] He said: "The Mau is like a ship with the cargo still in it. When the ship reaches land, the cargo will be discharged. You have said to end the Mau. But what about the objects of the Mau? . . . Let us wear our uniform until we get what we are fighting for. The Mau will not say 'yes' until you have given it a crown."

Colonel Allen responded by having both Tuimalealiifano and Tamasese re-arrested for seditious language. He dismissed the four hundred Mau representatives and explained the failure of the negotiations to External Affairs by cable as follows:[10] "It should be understood that we are not dealing with a civilized or intelligent people and negotiations which would (normally) be conducted in such a case are not possible here. Samoans are devoid of reasoning faculty and success or failure must therefore depend on a few simple issues."

Neither side changed its perception of the other, but both were now tired of fighting, and a period of quiscence ensued.

Rosabel Nelson gave up on her marriage. Olaf had been gone for several years now and the girls were with him in New Zealand. His firm was getting deeper into debt every year. Even the Mau seemed to be dying. The golden couple separated and she retired to a house in Papauta.

Colonel Allen assumed he was victorious. "The Mau has ended as swiftly and imperceptibly as it began," he reported confidently to External Affairs.[11]

But Baxter, the Mau's solicitor, did not agree. At a farewell breakfast Aggie mounted for him at her house on the hill, he explained to guests that he was going to Wellington to urge the prime minister to negotiate with Nelson before his five-year exile was up in December, 1931. "Otherwise trouble is apt to break out again," he told them. "The Mau isn't dead. It's resting. Samoans are enormously persistent people."[12]

Aggie politely steered the conversation to less controversial grounds by proclaiming herself a hostess, not a politician. "Otherwise how would I be able to invite all of you to breakfast together?" she laughed. "Now, who wants to see my swimming pool?" It was the response of a light-headed flapper, but the guests were relieved. The issue had factionalized the town and its families for too many years.

186

Aggie was by nature non-political. Where others saw causes, she saw only people. Take Olaf, for example. Everyone else looked at him as the embodiment of the Mau. Aggie looked at him and saw a breathtaking person. Never had an *afakasi* aspired to the top of both hierarchies at once! Olaf had parlayed his father's £365 into a fortune and then tossed it all on advancing his mother's family title towards the "crown." It was not the cause that intrigued her; it was the sheer nerve of the man!

Mau parade gathering on Nelson waterfront. Circa 1929. Customs house and public wharf can be seen in the rear.

Mau leaders at their Vaimoso headquarters, Tamasese Center. Circa 1930.

Chapter 16

The Great Depression

(1931-1933)

THE TIFAGA Playhouse, Apia's new movie theater, replaced Market Hall as the center of Beach Road entertainment. Apia's first electric sign above its door usually blazed with this week's film, but on the last day of December, 1930, it read: NEW YEAR'S COSTUME BALL. Aggie and the other ladies of the Sei Aute Club spent the day pushing back the chairs and transforming it into a night club.

The ball was a great success. Everyone who counted was there in disguise. Sam Meredith won first prize as a seven-foot whiskey bottle. Aggie's sister Mary, bless her heart, came in second, as a rainbow complete with tissue paper raindrops.[1] Everyone laughed and chattered as if this fantasy world would last forever. Only one person failed to catch the mood. Charlie Grey stood with his back to the crowd, staring vacantly into a corner. That certainly wasn't like him. "Sweetheart!" Aggie cried, running over to him between dances. "Are you sick or something?"

He shook his head as she whirled away with another partner. Then he slipped out for a "nip" of comfort. When Aggie and the house boy finally located him at dawn, they took him home and rolled him into bed. He had always liked to drink, but she had never seen him like this before. Something must be on his mind. Oh, well, nothing a little pampering would not cure. Hassling men about alcohol was a waste of time as she had learned long ago.

A week later he was still on the bottle. He had not been to work at all. "Poor old Daddy!" she worried. "Perhaps it's really something serious!" If so, he never mentioned it. Why worry a pretty little head? A woman wouldn't understand. Finally he came home sober one morning and asked in a tight voice, "Aggie, could I borrow a few pounds from your vegetable jar? I'll pay you back as soon as I get to town."

"Of course, Daddy!" she replied, surprised. He had never asked *her* for money before. It just wasn't like him. She dug £120 from her cache and laid it in his hand. He gave her a wan kiss and disappeared for three days. Then he returned only long enough to ask her for some more.

"Important debt. Can't wait," he mumbled. "But don't worry. My money's coming tomorrow." He went off with another £100. When he returned a few days later, he was incoherent and she put him to bed. He acted so much like Willie at Tifitifi that she ran and checked her jar. Only £64 remained. When she went back to ask him about it, he was already gone.

On Thursday she and the girls were cleaning the parlor when two men she did not recognize drove up and knocked at the door. She invited them in and offered them tea, but they declined. Instead of sitting down, they began to wander around the house, opening cupboards, lifting brass, and pinging her crystals as if they owned them. Finally one of them got out a pencil and began to attach stickers to her things.

"Just what do you think you're doing, sir?" she cried angrily. He looked up in surprise.

"If you don't know, lady, I suggest you ask your husband."

"Do you know where he is?" she quavered.

"Klinkmiller's office, last I seen him," he said, winking at his partner. This pretty little lady was in for a big surprise. Didn't look like she had a brain in her head!

Klinkmiller was a lawyer on Beach Road. When Aggie reached his office, she found Daddy slumped over in a chair with his head in his hands. "Charlie!" she demanded angrily. "Sit up and tell me what's going on!"

She shook him by the shoulder until he looked up. "Bankrupt!" he mumbled and twisted himself away.

The dread word went through her like a dagger. She felt as if it had suddenly slit her new silk dress from neck to toe, leaving her in black bloomers again. The drudgery and hopelessness of Tifitifi flooded over her, even harder to bear this time. She sat down heavily on a stool, only half listening to the lawyer's explanation.

"Stevedoring contract . . . lost to another firm. Farm mortgage New Zealand . . . never paid. Old ladies foreclosed . . . Worldwide depression."

She really didn't care to know any more. What difference would it make? All that mattered now was what to do next.

"Your house on the hill," the lawyer explained, "has already been sold to young Jackson for £1,000. You're lucky to get that much these days, my dear. And your furnishings?" He handed her a clipping from the paper.[2]

NOTICE
Public auction March 23. 9:30 a.m. Drapery, soft goods, hardware, plantation requisites. Inspection Friday 20th and Saturday 21st.

"You must vacate the place by next Thursday," Klinkmiller warned her. "You can take only the things you brought with you into the marriage or purchased with your own money. Everything your husband bought or gave you is entailed."

"But where will I go?" she asked. "I have three small children!"

"That is not a lawyer's concern," he replied. "Ask your husband." Aggie turned and stared at Charlie. His head was in his hands again, lost in alcoholic oblivion.

"Charlie! Charlie! Why didn't you tell me?" she cried, trying to rouse him. "Why didn't you leave the vegetable money? That was mine. Then at least we'd have had something to start on!" He didn't answer.

Appalled at his weakness, she suddenly realized that any future he and the children might have now rested entirely on her. She got up and stumbled out onto Beach Road. The flapper had suddenly vanished. In its place stood a penniless woman responsible for three children and a broken man.

The shops and crowds that had excited her so much yesterday looked shabby and dusty now. What use were they? She had no money to buy things, no house to put them in, no friends to admire them. She felt as shopworn as last season's merchandise. Her hands felt sore, as if they had been washing bottles again.

190

Her old friend Bill Links did not notice the change. He was just stepping out of Burns Philps with Mabel Yandall, his current girlfriend, on his arm. They waved and beckoned Aggie to come over.

"Good news!" Bill grinned. "We've just hired a launch to take us to Fagaloa Bay for the weekend. Why don't you and Charlie come along?"

Aggie could not face her future yet, even less explain it to good-time Bill. For one last weekend, why not keep the idyll going?

"Sounds lovely, Bill," she smiled. "Charlie's busy, but I'm not. When will we be back?"

"Good show,' he said. "We'll return by Sunday evening. It'll do you good."

He was so right! The timeless peace of Fagaloa Bay, with its towering, brooding cliffs, made her troubles seem less significant. Ribbons of water tossed over its precipices, flashed for a moment like jewels in the sunshine, and plunged towards the abyss, only to find themselves at rest in the quiet bay. Maybe things would end like that for her.

The awesome world of nature kept her sane for forty-eight hours while the gay world of Apia slipped from her grasp. The first night she tossed sleepless on her mat in a small thatched house at the end of the bay. If she closed her eyes for a moment, she felt that her lovely clothes, shining crystals, and precious swimming pool would be snatched from her grasp. She struggled to stay awake, resentful at the world, and especially Charlie, for leaving her in this position for a second time.

Just before dawn she got up and waded into the bay. The brilliant orb of Venus *(Tapuitea)* hung in a shimmering sky. It had not looked that bright since Tifitifi! The majestic bay with its tall black cliffs was silent, shrouded in darkness. Suddenly a finger of sunlight slipped down one sheer face and touched the water at her feet, illuminating a black sea cucumber sitting right there next to her big toe! She swept it up with a cry of delight. It had been so long!

Running to the oven house, she grabbed a rusty knife to scrape and cut up her treasure. She pushed the rubbery chunks onto a coconut midrib except for two, which she popped straight into her mouth. The salty tang filled her with comfort. Wait a moment! Tifitifi hadn't been that bad after all!

A young boy came in swinging heavy baskets of taro and green bananas at each end of his shoulder pole. He had just scrambled down a narrow trail from the family planting on top of the cliff. Lowering his burden to the dirt floor, he smiled shyly at the stranger. A moment later his brother appeared with a brace of pigeons shot in the forest. Laughing and joking, they showed her how fast they could split kindling, rub up sparks with a little stick, and start a fire. When it was blazing, they laid rocks on top to heat, using a bent coconut stalk for tongs.

Aggie lay on her elbows and watched them work, still chewing her rubbery *loli*. She felt more at home than she had in years. How secure she felt here with the fruits of the sea and forest all around her and strong young shoulders to bring them in. This family had lived for generations without a penny. Their world had never cast them out or let them down. Her fears relaxed. She yawned, closed her eyes, and fell asleep. The boys covered their oven with leaves and tiptoed out.

Aggie's sleep was suddenly rent by a vivid dream. A terrified two-year-old was toddling around the stone platform of a Samoan house, desperately seeking its mother. Suddenly, there she was beside a post, not the wan Pele of the chemist shop but a radiant, laughing Pele. She was stuffing kapok into a burlap sack, but she stopped and held out her arms to the frightened child. "Did you think you were lost, little one?" she cried, sweeping the baby into her arms and snuggling with her nose. "Stop crying! I am making you a nice soft bed." The little girl plunged her chubby arms into the soft warm tufts. They tickled! She looked up at her mother and giggled with the tears still wet on her cheeks. She wasn't lost after all!

Aggie woke up refreshed. She was the first to board the home-bound launch that afternoon, laughing and joking like herself again. Life with a swimming pool was no more. Well, let it go. She still had the river and the sea!

During their last four days in the house on the hill, Charlie stumbled off towards town each morning. Aggie knew where he was going but made no effort to stop him. Poor Daddy! When a white man's world is gone, where else can he turn? Thanks to her Samoan mother, she had another option.

She set an old sunbonnet on her curls and ran down the hill to visit Trood, the retired British consul who had once signed her parents' wedding certificate. He owned ten overgrown acres just down the road. Too old to farm, he now made ends meet on a small pension. Before long she was pouring her tale into Trood's fatherly ear. Bankruptcies were an old story to him. The residents of Beach Road were always a prey to them. When Aggie asked if she could use the crumbling cement platform in his upper field where the horse shed had stood, he was not dismayed.

"Of course, my dear. Of course. Just the thing! Fix yourself something cozy and stay as long as you like. There are some old fruit trees around, and shrimps in the river. Help yourself."

At the word "shrimp," Aggie smiled. She had not been shrimping since that day she had played hooky from school so long ago. The memory was still redolent with the delicious smell of curry. She gave old Trood a grateful hug and ran back up the hill. She had so much to do before the men came to take her truck.

The first thing she needed was material for a house. Among the weeds in back of the shed, she found the triangular piece of wood the boy had cut out for her garage. Beside it were the old laundry windows, several old four-by-fours, and a few shingles. She hadn't realized how important such things could be. Her eye also fell on the old iron stove with a broken leg, on which she had boiled her clothes. And there were her bush knife, shovel, and hammer. Up in the attic she dusted off the old sewing machine and the black iron pots she had brought with her from Dad's. Years ago she had hidden them up there in embarrassment. Now she treated them like treasures.

Her former house boy from Vailima dropped by with two of his friends and they helped her load the truck. When everything was on, he slid behind the wheel and Aggie jumped in beside him, wishing she had learned to drive. Well, too late now! His two friends threw a piece of pig fence over the load and clambered up with a couple of piglets in their arms. They whooped at passers-by as the truck backed out the driveway and turned down the hill. When the triangular piece began to list, they stopped the truck to rescue it. Then they had to chase a scampering piglet. By the time they reached Trood's pasture, the boys were calling Aggie "auntie" instead of "ma'am" and acting like part of her family. She invited them to visit any time. She needed more strong arms.

They returned next day. At one end of the platform they helped her dig holes for two four-by-fours. While they held the triangular piece aloft, she braced and nailed it. They set in the laundry windows below and filled the spaces with shingle. "Auntie" seemed to know exactly what she wanted and gave orders like a chief. A front door was unnecessary, since the other three sides were open, but at least from the road it began to look like a house.

The third day they all went to the forest to look for *poumuli*. Aggie remembered from Toamua that this tree made the best posts. They set these in holes around the other three sides and nailed a runner across the top. By evening they were pounding on a ridgepole. All it needed now was a roof.

Johnny Hellesoe, from across the road, stopped by next day to see what was going on and he contributed some rusty sheets of corrugated iron from a long-gone chicken coop. That was enough to cover the front half. They finished the rear with thatches from a toppled oven-house in the village. Aggie's house was now a community effort.

At the end of the week, nine eager "carpenters and architects" stood back to assess their new creation. "It looks like a *fale vaa* (boat house)," said one of them, looking at it from the side.

"No, it's a Samoan cookhouse," insisted another, standing in the rear, "with one modern touch — that black iron stove with its foot on a box!"

"Look at that sweet little English cottage with four casement windows!" cried a homesick New Zealand housewife to her husband as they motored up the main road. "All it needs is a bit of ivy."

After walking slowly around the low edifice, Aggie summarized the achievement quite aptly, "*palagi* in front, Samoan behind, an *afakasi* house just like me." She celebrated its housewarming with shrimp curry for everyone and planted bougainvillea instead of ivy under the windows.

When Charlie finally located his family a week later,

the garden was planted, the piglets had a fence, and his two daughters were playing hopscotch barefooted on the platform with some village children. He took one look at the scene and burst into tears.

"Aggie, how could I have brought you and the children to this?" She put an arm around him and gave him a kiss. Poor Daddy! How could she tell him she had had more fun in the last week than she had for years. She felt even prouder of it than her swimming pool.

Far below them, down in Apia, a depression as vicious as the influenza stalked Beach Road. This time it was Samoans who brought food to the settlers. By Christmas, 1933, many well-known faces along Beach Road were missing. The survivors decided to jeer at this new reaper by mounting a "Hard Times New Year's Ball."[3] They transformed the Tivoli Playhouse into a Parisian Boulevard this time, with outdoor cafes along its walls. While Bertie Mann's band wailed the blues, guests arrived dressed as hobos, swagmen, and other assorted down-and-outers. They sustained themselves on fish and chips, and prizes were awarded to those who looked ugliest, neediest, and most miserable of all.

For the first time in years, the Greys were not on hand. They had no need to pretend. Few of the gay crowd had noticed their absence during the past year. Most of them had been too busy holding on to their illusions. Actually, only two good friends had even tried to locate them. One was Bill Links, still the perennial bachelor. Almost every Sunday he drove up to the pasture with a chicken, a string of fish from the "fish tree,"[4] or a suckling pig. He asked Aggie to cook his Sunday dinner and left enough in the pot to last for several days. As he watched her cook, Bill marveled at the change in Aggie. The giggle and flash had vanished. Instead, she seemed to shed a subdued, and competent glow. The high shrieks of laughter were gone, replaced by a deeper voice of almost masculine timber. She was more like a mother than a sweetheart now—someone a man could tell his troubles to, feeling she would understand.

Johnny Hellesoe from across the road was another frequent visitor. On his way home from work at Nelson's he often dropped in with a bag of flour or a remnant of

195

calico. "Leftovers," he insisted. "I wouldn't know what to do with them." Johnny found the change in Aggie more disconcerting. The body of a flapper had emerged with the mind of a man! Here was the hostess of Apia suddenly building houses and foraging for food in the river. It disturbed his image of the stronger sex. What if women learned to do without them?

"Well, there's one thing to be said for bankruptcy," Aggie told Charlie. "When the bottom falls out, you discover who your real friends are."

The depression continued to deepen. On New Year's Day, 1932, Beach Road did not even mount a Hard Times Ball. With copra at an incredible low of £2/10 a ton, planters could not afford to pick up nuts at all, and let the weeds take over. Merchants priced what was left on their shelves lower and lower to catch the last few pennies in circulation: a tin of salmon for ninepence, meat fourpence a pound, rice one pence ha'penny, and still no takers! Money had vanished. Even bush stores were closing down. Samoans looked on in wonder from their subsistence plantings. The once proud game of the merchants seemed to be collapsing! Was their golden magic gone?

Brigadier General Hart replaced Allen as New Zealand administrator and Mau villages, intent on subsistence, now gave him little trouble. Nevertheless, he orchestrated Nelson's return with care. He did not want another Black Saturday. Just before the merchant's release, Hart invited Lord and Lady Blenisloe to tour Samoa. It was the first time a New Zealand governor general had visited the islands, and everyone turned out to welcome the next best thing to British royalty. The crowds waved at them gaily. Not a single Mau uniform was in evidence.

In May, 1933, Hart was informed that Nelson was on his way. Overnight the blue *lavalava* with white stripes reappeared. By the time Nelson disembarked on May 16, a parade a mile long marched to the wharf to greet him. Fifteen hundred Mau women sang a hymn and whisked their hero off to a church service in Vaimoso. Next day a crowd of seven thousand gathered for a *taalolo* (gift-giving ceremony) and welcome feast for their beloved Taisi. Where in the world had they suddenly come from?

Nelson made no secret of renewing his meetings with

the Mau, but the chiefs soon realized that his resources were hardly what they used to be. They offered him a retainer of £1,500 to act as their adviser. Hart refused to let Nelson attend any negotiating meetings with the Mau, but despite repeated warnings Olaf continued to advise them.

The upshot was a proposed constitution for an independent Samoa, with Vaimoso as its capital.[5] That was the last straw! This stubborn man would never learn. Chief of Police Braisby began collecting evidence to re-deport him.

By September the Mau was in full swing again, and Braisby had plenty of grounds for convicting Nelson: meetings of seven hundred in Lufilufi, four hundred in Palauli, and two thousand in Vaimoso. Hart was even afraid that Samoans in their enthusiasm might declare Nelson their king!

In October, Nelson's eldest daughter, Irene, married Tamasese Meaole, Samoan leader of the Mau. A month later the police raided Tuaefu and seized Nelson's correspondence. There was little doubt of his Mau activity. On November 21 he was re-arrested and three weeks later brought to a second trial. Unable to afford legal assistance this time, Olaf handled his own defense.

Aggie slipped into the back row of the courtroom on the last day of the trial. It was clear that Olaf would be convicted, but that was not her concern. Her eyes were on the figure in the dock. She had not seen him for five years and was profoundly shocked. The regal bearing was gone. The tall, strong body had thickened. The once sharp eyes were dull. His words were no longer arrogant, incisive, commanding. Instead they sounded almost petulant. Had he too been drinking? The once proud *afakasi* who had tried to play both games at once had gambled and lost. It broke her heart. She could see that neither his business nor his sanity would survive another deportation.

Chief Justice Luxford pounded his gavel for silence. The prisoner rose and the sentence fell: guilty on all three counts. Nelson was sentenced to eight months in jail and ten more years in exile. He was deported on the *Maui Pomare* and Governor Hart penned an epitaph as follows:[6]

"It is a curious fact that in the last hundred years of

Samoan life there has been no outstanding personality among the Samoan race — the islands do not breed such . . . . If you class Nelson as a Samoan (and at heart he is), then he is the one outstanding personality that has appeared. . . . He is outstanding in personality, in ability, in business, in brains, and in money. He could have been a great influence for good. But unfortunately he is a very vain man, leading him to suppose that he could take the reins of government into his own hands, that it was possible to oust New Zealand from control of Samoa so that the Samoans would have a form of self-government. If such had been brought about, Mr. Nelson would have sought to make himself 'dictator', and I think he had a good chance of success."

That did not say much for full-blooded Samoan heroes Mataafa Iosefo, Lauati, and Tamasese Lealofi. Some white men could ascribe greatness only to those who shared their blood. She sighed. As long as that attitude prevailed, the Mau could not afford to die.

Nelson left Samoa in despair. When, on final appeal, Prime Minister Forbes refused clemency, the fallen champion wrote his daughters, "My sap has run out."[7]

Not even Nelson foresaw what would happen in the next few months!

Col. Richardson.

PART V

ENTREPRENEUR

Chapter 17

The Happy Hour

(1933)

THREE YEARS passed quietly on the platform in Trod's pasture. The bougainvillea grew lush around the laundry windows and covered the rusty roof in purple glory. The Grey family lived without money except when Aggie could sell a basket of vegetables or Charlie could find an odd job for a few days. But somehow food always appeared from the garden, the river, or the neighbors. Portly ladies from the village dropped by with a basket of baked taro or a fish hot from their earth ovens. After a friendly exchange of gossip, they left for home with a pineapple from Aggie's garden or a packet of shrimp from the river. Pele, Marina, and Edward ran around the pasture barefooted. Cousins and would-be cousins joined them in the little hut for a day or a month. An extra mouth to feed was no problem as long as it came equipped with two hands for catching shrimp, scraping coconuts, or planting taro. These time-honored relationships with Samoan relatives and neighbors happened without effort or design. Aggie did not have to send engraved invitations, serve staggering buffets, or push people into swimming pools to feel "in." The Samoan community accepted her simply because she was Pele's daughter. Personal success or failure was not a factor. Poor Charlie had no second option like that and withdrew from everyone.

For a year the challenges of subsistence and extended family living kept Aggie busy. But as she managed to resolve them into a routine she noted a growing restlessness in herself. This kind of life was depression-proof and pleasant enough, but it didn't seem to lead anywhere. The years would go on and on and nothing would change. She was born in a thatched house and would die in a thatched house, just like the others. So would her children and children's children. That was no challenge. She longed for a sense of progress, some ladder to climb that would mobilize her energies and give her a goal. Both her cultures provided ladders, but she faced formidable handicaps in mounting either one. If she followed her grandfather Pepe and tried to elevate her family title connections, she was limited by having only half a Samoan genealogy. Her father had brought no titles into her bloodlines. Her husband was no help. His kin would not gather fine mats, food, or money for her ceremonies. They would think she was crazy.

She could follow her grandfather Swann in building and expanding a profitable business, but who had ever heard of a woman entrepreneur? Even Emma had inherited hers from her father and husbands. Charlie could not help that way either. He had just lost everything he had. For her, neither route would be easy. Which route would she choose? Such matters are usually answered not by reason but by opportunity.

Her future soon became apparent in the weaving of a basket. One day as she was sitting with the village women, weaving floor mats, boredoom overtook her and she tried for a laugh by squaring her corner to form a lopsided basket. That was hardly a new idea, and the others promptly showed her how to do it properly.

"Why do you always weave floor mats," Aggie asked, "when you could making shopping baskets and purses to sell them for money on boat day?" The problem, they told her, was the handle. Their baskets looked nice but when they were filled the handles pulled out. Who would buy a thing like that?

Aggie relieved monotonous moments after that by experimenting with handles. She tried weaving them on around the rim and further down the side. If she could make money on vegetables, why not baskets that could be taken to town even without a truck? She stopped and laughed at herself. "I must be like my grandfather Swann," she thought, "always thinking up a new business. Why can't I just relax? I'm not hungry."

But the old business itch just wouldn't go away. What kept triggering it was watching her children run around happily in bare feet and *lavalava* (sarongs). Was this the end of the line for them too? Didn't six-year-old Pele deserve an education just as much as Peggy and Gordon in New Zealand with the Hay-MacKenzies?

She finally wrote to Sister Joseph, who was still mother superior of the convent school in Leone. The good nun felt she had failed with Aggie but that her six-year-old daughter might be more tractable. She sent Pele a ticket. Three months later Aggie heartily regretted letting her daughter go. A telegram from Sister Joseph brought word that Pele had come down with typhoid fever and had been admitted to the hospital in Pago Pago. Next to TB and worms, no disease could have frightened Aggie more. She remembered her own mad ride with Maggie to Tifitifi and her father's patient nursing. Now it was her turn to rescue Pele. Mary bought the tickets and the two of them set off for American Samoa, leaving Auntie Tauli in charge of the platform in the pasture.

Pele was a delicate child and recovery took months. Mary had to return, but Aggie stayed on to nurse her daughter. That would not have been possible except for her old friend Lena, who had married Ben Kneubuhl and was now living in town above his prosperous store. Kindhearted as ever, Lena invited Aggie to live with them.

That still left the other half of the problem, however. Who would support Auntie Tauli and the children back home? Charlie hated that platform in the pasture. Gardening and fishing depressed him and there were no jobs in Apia. How would the family get along?

Ben gave Aggie an idea. Prohibition had just been lifted in America and Shimasaki, the Japanese storekeeper with the large Samoan family, was going to open a public bar in Pago. He had already leased a wooden shack next to Kneubuhl's store and was looking for a manager. Aggie promptly went to see him. She had never run a bar, but she had been in plenty of them looking for Willie and Charlie. Shimasaki had already heard of her pre-depression skills as a hostess in Apia. Hiring a woman had never occurred to him. But didn't western movies feature frontier bars kept in line by strong-minded ladies? Yes, Aggie looked as if she might be that type: capable, cool-headed, tough, but kindhearted. In fact, she might be even better than a male. She knew how to set men singing, a trait that might be good for business. He decided to give her a try.

Shimasaki's entertainment facilities were a far cry from Aggie's former mansion, consisting of a decrepit wooden shack with two small rooms. The room in front was equipped with a splintery counter and a few shelves on the wall. It was too small to hold tables and chairs. Customers would have to sit on the windowsills or the curb outside to enjoy their beers. A door in the back wall led to an even smaller room, which contained only a few torn mats and a window covered with rat-wire high in the wall. This was to double as manager's dwelling and store-room for beer cases. Beer was the only beverage the Navy allowed.

That was not much to start with, but Aggie approached her new job as energetically as she had her house on the hill. She hired two village girls to help her and had them bring the floor and counter to a clean shine. Crystals, even glasses, were out of the question. Her customers would have to drink straight from the bottle. She was, however, an old hand at bottles. She set three basins under the counter, one for washing, one for rinsing, and one for dregs. To top it all off, she put a broken mirror on the shelf behind the counter. For some reason, Hollywood westerns always showed mirrors behind bars. She named her establishment the Happy Hour. As soon as its sign was dry, she nailed it above the front door and opened for business.

The Happy Hour was a success from the moment of its birth. Whether due to a pent-up yen for beer or a wise-cracking hostess, from four in the afternoon until eleven at night it was the busiest place in town. Sailors, dock-workers, store clerks, and roustabouts leaned shoulder to shoulder at its counter and crowded the window sills and the curb outside. By 8:30 they were usually in full song and it took a couple of six-foot Navy guardsmen to remove the holdouts and close the door at eleven.

Each evening, Shimasaki's wife sent a plate of food to Aggie and her girls. They took turns eating in the back room so that there would be no interruption in business. At the end of the first week, Shimasaki put $10 in Aggie's hand, more than she had seen since the days of her vegetable jar. She ran over to Kneubuhl's store to buy a box of groceries for the family in the pasture, and stuffed the remaining $2 in an envelope. Her friend Bill Steffany, captain of the small interisland steamer, offered to place both of these personally in the hands of Auntie Tauli, and he was as good as his word.

For the next four months, she sent her earnings home. After one trip Steffany returned with a note from Charlie saying that, with the money she sent, he had moved the children from the pasture to a couple of rooms at Hiedland's place. "At least it has four solid walls," he wrote; "that makes me feel more respectable."

Aggie regretted her garden, the shrimps, and the bougainvillea, but if living in a real house would bring Charlie to himself again, it was worth it.

The Happy Hour continued to flourish. Aggie directed its nightly activities with a laugh, a lusty tongue, and a strong hand. Men did not frighten her. In fact, if truth must be told, they were more apt to be frightened by her. She knew how to rub up a spark of manhood in a jaded spirit, fan it to glorious flame, and then blow it out like a candle in a burst of laughter. She left many a poor braggart feeling like a fool.

Only the stouthearted dared take another step but there were always some willing to try. They soon discovered that as far as Aggie was concerned, sex was a matter of inclination rather than economics or morality. She pragmatically decided each opportunity as it arose. Neither money nor political ambition could persuade her. She went ahead only when she felt that the experience would be more fun than laughing at it. That wasn't as often as it looked but it kept everyone gossiping.

Those who cared to look found something else in this forthright hedonist — a surprisingly soft heart. Aggie was vulnerable to people who were down on their luck. She was not afraid of men who were sick, lonely, or depressed. Plenty of troubled men haunted the Happy Hour, trying to quench their sorrows in alcohol. Instead of avoiding them, her impulse was to sit down and listen. At such times she neither joked nor scolded. She simply proffered a pat on the shoulder, an encouraging word, or a dollar from her purse. She did not regard trouble as a punishment for bad luck. Like sex, misfortune just swept over one from time to time. All one could do was look it in the eye, spit on each palm, and march on. Now where had a silly flapper ever come by wisdom like that?

While Aggie could cope with men, women took her by surprise. Not all of them used gender the way she did. Her two helper girls, for example, seemed inclined to settle for material rewards. If she had realized this earlier, she would have made better use of the broken mirror, positioning it on the front wall to reflect the storeroom door. Her problem with the girls was compounded by another group of women who never came near her establishment, but described in vivid detail what went on behind her door. Aggie's storeroom seemed to fascinate everyone in town.

Early one afternoon, as Aggie was wiping the counter in preparation for a busy evening, two policemen sidled up to the counter. She knew them both well. They often dropped in after work for a beer and a laugh, but today they were much too early and fidgeted around with crooked smiles until she took pity and offered them "a free sample." They declined.

"So sorry, Aggie," the elder blurted, "but we are on duty. Our orders are to lock both your doors and put you on the boat back to Apia tonight."

Aggie froze. "What's the charge?" she asked.

Neither of them was willing to put it in words, but their eyes wandered towards the storeroom door. It was closed.

"Oh, I see!" she cried, flying across the room and flinging it open. "Well, why don't you come and look for yourselves, if you have such filthy minds!"

Neither of them moved. They just stared at their feet.

"It's not us, Aggie. You know how much we like this place. We didn't make any charges."

"Who did?" she snapped.

"How should I know?" one of them answered weakly. "Our department gets its orders from the attorney general."

"Then take me to see him right now!" she demanded, picking up her purse.

There were eyes behind every store window as she strode down the street with the two men in uniform behind her.

The attorney general was a white-haired Navy officer with a worn but fatherly smile. It was not the first time he had encountered a problem of this type. It happened on every base. It was just the first time he had encountered Aggie.

Actually he had agreed with Shimasaki's proposal to open a bar. Sailors had to do something on small islands and it was easier to let them drink beer together near the police station than to chase them all over the island. All he envisioned behind the bar, however, was a mousy little man with sad eyes that emanated insufferable boredom. What did he get? An Aggie who set Navy boys to buzzing like bees and Pago matrons to stinging like hornets. Personally, he didn't give a damn what went on in Aggie's storeroom, but he did care about his commission. What if one of those female hornets called for a congressional investigation?

Under the circumstances, he took the precaution of calling Bill Steffany to sit in on his meeting with Aggie. Bill was a friend of hers and could calm her down. The last thing he wanted was legal action. If only she would quietly go home!

When the three of them were seated at his desk, the attorney general explained to Aggie that his real concern was not her back room but peace in the community. Wives and church members were upset at having a Happy Hour practically under the eaves of the cathedral. A prominent businessman had complained that he couldn't sleep at night because of all the noise down there. Whatever might or might not be going on, a strategic base on a small island could not afford community unrest. The Happy Hour would have to close down.

Aggie was livid. She immediately identified the businessman by name and the real cause of his insomnia. She had turned down his advances.

The attorney sighed wearily, "You may be right, my dear, but it only corroborates my opinion that unless you go home there will continue to be trouble around this town. It's just too small a place for a woman of your capacities."

Steffany laid a kindly hand on her arm. "I believe you, Aggie," he said. "But with women in bars, you know, it is 'damned if you do and damned if you don't.' Rumors like this are as bad for your children as they are for a military community. Just go buy your family another box of goodies and be at the wharf by six. The trip's on me."

Since the attorney general had authority to deport non-residents anyway, Aggie submitted to the inevitable. But she felt this time Fate had been particularly unkind. Her business had not failed. It had just been too successful!

Packing was no problem; everything she owned could be put in one basket. After buying groceries, there was only one other thing to do before she left — say goodby to Lena, who had been so kind to her. Lena was in the last months of pregnancy and Aggie could see her rocking in a chair on the porch above the store. Her head was in her hands and Aggie could hear her sobbing! She must have heard the news.

Lena's trust meant a lot to Aggie. More than ever she needed it now. She called to ask if she could come up and explain her side of the story, but it was Ben who leaned over the railing.

"Forget it, Aggie," he said icily. "I don't want my wife associating with a woman of ill repute."

Visit by German Ambassador in 1938. Herr Matthes' Samoan Nazi Party in rear.

Chapter 18

The Brown-Paper Bar

(1934-1940)

AGGIE FOUND Charlie and the children still being mothered by Auntie Tauli. But unlike the pasture, Heidland's place required rent. Aggie had to go to work, but no one in Apia was hiring at times like these. She went to consult her father.

The depression had pushed him also to the brink of subsistence. He could not possibly feed more mouths and she did not ask him to. They just sat on the front stoop together, looking at the empty street and wondering what to do next. Aggie's eyes wandered towards the deserted British Club across the grass. The New Zealand police had gone home the previous year and the grand old structure was listing towards the Vaisigano, its paint peeling and its windows broken. No one could afford to support it anymore.

"Who owns the old place now?" Aggie asked idly. "Whoever it is should provide a decent burial."

"When old Heatherington left for New Zealand, he asked Carruthers to rent it for him," Willie replied; "but as far as I know, no one ever even inquired. Too bad to let her go like that. There's good kauri timbers in those walls, you know, saved from the old International Hotel."

They fell to reminiscing about the Club in its prime. What a splendid place it had been! Remember that reception for Prince Edward? The grand old institution had never recovered from prohibition except for one exciting three-month revival just before the New Zealand police moved in. They chuckled at that brief reincarnation. Willie had talked his Turf Club into renting the house as a "watering place" for horse lovers. A couple of months later, the police had pulled a raid. It wasn't water they

209

found in Willie's homemade contraption in the attic. They closed the Turf Club down.

"Too bad!" Willie sighed. "We need it more than ever this year, with everyone's spirits down." Suddenly his eyebrows lifted with a thought. He turned and stared at his daughter. "I say, girl! You were doing well in Pago Pago! Couldn't you run a club here? Carruthers would rent the place to you for a song."

"Haven't you forgotten something, Dad?" Aggie laughed. "Prohibition's never been repealed on this side of Samoa, and don't think you're going to get away with your contraption again. If anyone even got a smile on his face, the police would be into your attic!"

Willie leaned over conspiratorially and whispered his newest solution in her ear. "You know that Gentlemen's Club of Annie McFagan's down behind Tauese store? I hear those gentlemen give her their medical permits!"

Aggie looked at him and burst out laughing. Of course! Last year the biggest men in town had all come down with identical symptoms, for which kindly old Dr. Monahan had issued the same prescriptions: 1 whiskey, 1 gin, and 30 bottles of beer a month, refillable at the "bond" warehouse. Who could object if they wanted to take their medicine together at Annie McFagan's place? There was no reason why Aggie couldn't provide a similar service for a less exclusive crowd. Still laughing, she ran back into the shop for an old exercise book. Together she and Willie listed the names of everyone they could think of who might feel in need of medication. Charlie Grey was first on their list.

The required symptoms soon appeared around Apia in epidemic proportions. It was almost as contagious as the influenza. Within a month, Dr. Monahan had issued one hundred and fourteen new prescriptions requiring alcohol. Patients forwarded these to the "bond" with identical letters:

Dear Sir,
    Kindly allow Aggie Grey to withdraw my medical permit allocation from bond for the month of_____.
                                        Yours sincerely,

She agreed to have their doses waiting for them every afternoon and evening between four and ten.

Given his experience with Willie's Turf Club, Carruthers was somewhat hesitant to rent the place again. Emilio Fabricius' cafe had recently been raided and fined for having one bottle of whiskey, two bottles of port, and sixty-two beers behind the scenes for his Hawaiian Night party. But when Aggie explained that hers was merely a medical service, Carruthers promptly produced the required symptoms himself. When she also reminded him that the town's new beautification plan made it mandatory for each resident along Beach Road to repair his dwelling and plant flame trees along his waterfront, Carruthers even agreed to reduce the rent to twenty shillings a month if she would keep him in compliance.

Propping up a sagging two-story house was not as easy as thatching Trood's platform, Aggie soon discovered. For safety's sake, she moved her family into the steadiest first-floor room, just left of the front door. The room to its right was reserved for her new club, since it was closest to the building's only water tap, located in the back yard. Unlike her rule at the Happy Hour, there were no girls to help her, no capital, no evening meals, and no paycheck. Under these circumstances, restoration required more energy and imagination. She managed to construct a counter of sorts out of two loose boards and a bit of facing she pulled off the back steps. She borrowed three basins from the chemist shop and set them underneath the counter—one for washing, one for rinsing, one for dregs.

Other furnishings proved more difficult. Her guests might be able to do without tables for a while but she could hardly expect them to sit on the floor. For chairs, she begged some benzene crates from Burns Philps. These were solid enough but when she finally stood on one to survey the total scene, she could only admit it was depressing. Everything looked as if it needed paint. Unfortunately no one was giving away paint.

On the morning of opening night Carruthers, bless him, stopped by with a roll of brown wrapping paper. She hastily pasted that on the walls and counter front and it did manage to freshen things up for the occasion.

Almost every one of her one hundred and fourteen patients turned up for their doses during the first evening —fortunately, not all at once. They raised their bottles "to the health of members sitting on benzene crates" and hooked arms when Aggie tuned up a song. The only casualty of the evening was Abner Duffy, whose foot went through the floor while making a triumphal march. Aggie patched the hole in person with a piece of tin. "Here's to our Aggie! Beauty, brains and a way with men!" someone called in appreciation. Willie started suddenly. The words reminded him of another toast made long ago. But this was not Emma they were honoring. It was his daughter Aggie!

Unfortunately, more fundamental repairs, like propping up the second story, were quite beyond Aggie's repertoire. As happened so often when she was up against it, help materialized from an unexpected source. This time it was a knock on the door a few days later. A stocky little New Zealander was standing there.

"Name's Fred Fairbairn," he said laconically. "Heard you might have rooms to let."

It had never occurred to Aggie that anyone would want to live in this place. But with a little probing she discovered that Fred was new in town. Burns Philps had brought him to Samoa recently to help build its splendid new store on the corner of Vaea Street. A real carpenter!

"Do come in, sir!" she cried, immediately. "I'll show you my upstairs rooms and you can have your pick!"

Fred eyed the sagging floors with a professional eye. They seemed to strike him as a challenge rather than a menace and he and Aggie soon concluded a deal involving repairs rather than cash.

Within a few months he had managed to jack up the whole east side of the house in his spare time, working only by himself. Aggie couldn't believe it. How could one little man no bigger than herself lift a house? He never told her, but it seemed to require only a little hand jack that he set on concrete blocks where the posts had rotted away. He had some sort of magic with things like that. Her part was to talk people into donating supplies, a task at which Fred had no aptitude at all. It was the makings of a good team. Together they managed to accomplish what neither could have done alone.

Evenings in the brown-paper barroom continued festive but not rowdy. Just how far could a man get on a medical permit? And with copra at sixpence a hundredweight, many couldn't even afford that.

"What's the name of this place, Aggie?" someone asked one evening. "Still the British Club?" Aggie could not afford to limit her clientele to one nationality in such a mixed community and proposed "Cosmopolitan Club." But that didn't seem to fit her wrapping-paper decor. Everyone just continued to call it "Aggie's," a name that indeed summed up the spirit of the place.

Once a month, Aggie went over to the "bond" to draw out their prescriptions. Her friend Tom Leban usually threw in a few extra bottles for his best customer, and even helped her drive the load home. But with supplies so limited and profits running at threepence a bottle, Aggie discovered she could barely feed her family, much less pay rent. Carruthers feared the worst. Fred finally managed to prop up two more rooms upstairs and Aggie took on two more boarders, Amby Gilboy and Jack Gatby. That helped.

Fred never ceased to amaze her. She had known all sorts of men in her life but never one like this. He was eager to do anything she wanted around the house and asked nothing in return. But he absolutely refused to join her parties. He wouldn't even pass the time of day with her customers. After the evening meal, he climbed the stairs and sat in the dark in his own room, listening to the laughter below. To Aggie such behavior was incredible. She invited him down again and again without success and finally tried a different tactic.

"Fred," she asked one evening, "could you help me wash glasses tonight? I'm dead beat." He didn't answer but later she found him hidden behind the counter, working over her three basins. He appeared almost every night after that, but she could see it was not from social inclination. He was grouchy as a bear if anyone spoke to him. Only personal loyalty to her could bring him there.

Though he did not talk to guests, he apparently observed them closely. After a few weeks he gave Aggie a suggestion. "Why don't you set up a billiard table on the back porch? Then they wouldn't have to talk so much."

"Great idea, Fred. But where in God's name would I

get a billiard table? They don't grow on palm trees, you know."

He did not reply, but the next afternoon Aggie saw him crawl under the back porch with his tool box. A few moments later, she heard him wrenching off its twelve-by-two reinforcing beams. "Gotta get rid of that rotten porch floor anyway," he explained at supper. "Might as well use those good kauri pieces for a billiard table."

Unfortunately he paid a price for his efforts by straining a muscle in his shoulder. He couldn't sleep that night and was in such agony next day that she had to take him to the hospital. Four days later he was still there and feeling worse. He could not sleep and lay propped up rigidly on pillows, unable either to sit up or lie down. Nothing the doctor gave him could relax that muscle.

Poor Fred! Aggie could not bear to watch him suffer. She went home and came back with the children's jar of Mentholatum. Hour after hour she kneaded his shoulder the way Kala had done when she was a child. Gradually the tension faded and Fred finally fell asleep. He did not wake up even when she and the nurse pulled him flat.

Next morning he sat up refreshed and ate a good breakfast. Dr. Hudson asked Aggie to give him another massage and take him home. She nursed Fred as carefully as if he had been one of her children. As soon as he was able to get up, he expressed his gratitude by completing the billiard table and even the porch to go with it.

His idea was right. Her clientele expanded now that she could offer billiards as well as booze. She added her own favorite sport—dancing—as well. Fred repaired an old gramophone, and her upstairs verandah outdid Tattersall's as a spot where boys could meet girls.

For some reason, her boarders never referred to her as their "landlady." Dancers and drinkers never asked for the "manager"; everyone just called her "Aggie." Perhaps it was because she was never a single functionary—she was an institution, something like a mother. She sensed what a fellow needed before he knew it himself, and took practical steps to supply whatever it was. She would make a sandwich for a tired plantation foreman arriving at midnight, introduce a shy clerk in the corner to a "friend of hers," or scold a sailor for "getting involved with the wrong kind of girl." She gave endless attention to affairs of the heart without telling wives or girlfriends. She laughed at dirty jokes, but only if she really found them funny. The fevered one she sent home to bed; the financially strained she trusted with "chitties"; the pretentious she deflated with gusto. Many men were grateful to her for the candid manner with which she "set them straight." They needed a woman honest enough to do that. Hers wasn't any conscious therapy, just a natural by-product of understanding and enjoying men.

A woman with these gifts was as disturbing to Apia's community as it had been to Pago Pago's. Unsure matrons and disappointed Casanovas had to do something to defend themselves and began a menacing buzz. When she took in Fred, of course, they found an irresistible target for their stingers. By now Aggie looked at town gossip as an occupational hazard rather than a personal disaster. If she closed her bar everytime someone gave a sly wink, she would be back in Trood's pasture for good. Now she just went on without a word. This kept everyone guessing. Actually, a little speculation turned out to be good for business providing nothing could be proved.

When dancing began upstairs, however, community curiosity demanded satisfaction. A few months after Aggie's youngest child, Allan, was born, Braisby's uniformed police swept into the house one evening. They were not looking for "medicine"; her permits were in order. They were looking for "closed doors." They found one immediately—Aggie's, right beside the entrance. It was not only closed but locked from the inside!

Spurred by duty, curiosity and righteous indignation, the officers forced it open with a few good shoves, and peered eagerly into the dim-lit room. The bed was neatly made, its ruffles discreetly lifted to show its innocence. The only adult inside the room was Aggie, sitting in a rocking chair calmly nursing her child. The domesticity of the scene caught the officers off-guard. Faces reddened and feet shuffled as they tried to think of something appropriate to say. "Sorry, Aggie," one of them blurted. "We didn't mean to interfere."

"Is that right?" she said unkindly. "Then why don't you get out and close the door behind you!"

They backed out apologetically, repaired the door and guarded it punctiliously for the rest of the evening. A nursing mother mustn't be disturbed! Inside Aggie winked at the baby!

When Annie McFagan married Captain Jones and closed her Gentlemen's Club behind Tauese Store, her elite clientele transferred as a body to Aggie's. By 1935 the great depression was lifting and "the gentlemen" were beginning to prosper again. Men of means like Eugene Paul, Kurt Meyer, Cobcroft, and Carruthers certainly did not need Aggie's "chitties," but they had heavy burdens of their own. They were only too happy to lay these down on Aggie's stoop and walk through to the back porch for a few relaxing drinks with her. In June, 1936, the Gentlemen's Club was astounded by the reappearance of one of its most famous members—Olaf Nelson! Aggie rubbed her eyes. Hadn't he been sent away for ten more years in exile? This was only eighteen months!

Just after Nelson's second deportation, New Zealand's Labor Party had suddenly come to power. The new prime minister promptly reversed New Zealand's policy on the Mau and paved the way for Nelson's return by sending a Goodwill Mission to the islands. It promised the obstreperous island rapid progress towards self-government and backed its word with some immediate changes. Mau chiefs formerly booked as "seditious" now found themselves on the *Fono a Faipule*. Tamasese and Malietoa were both appointed members of the governor's Legislative Council and more public-service posts were opened to local recruits. When the victorious champion himself sailed into the harbor, the New Zealand administrator greeted him at the dock with a garland of flowers; the chief of police let off a gun salute instead of a hail of bullets, and the Sei Aute Club mounted a community reception. Faumuina put on a welcome feast and the Mau arranged a gift-giving ceremony at Vaimoso.

Nelson was restored to his position on the Legislative Council but, as he explained to Aggie, his concern from now on was business, not politics. Both his firm and Tuaefu were a shambles, but he hoped he could still save them. Copra had risen to £13/10 a ton and coconuts were worth picking up again.

216

Olaf spent long hours at his desk and in his warehouse, but after work he hated to go back to Tuaefu. With no wife and so many memories it seemed like a haunted shell. Instead he regularly attended Aggie's Gentlemen's Club. Her warmth and friendly ear were just what he needed. She was no longer the tomboy of Tifitifi, the tender bride at his Jubilee, or the flapper on the hill. He could scarcely credit what he saw now, a thirty-eight-year-old woman of the world with a family to support and an enterprise of her own! She worked hard, negotiated deals, laughed from the belly, and drank beer like a man. Fortunately, no one could possibly mistake her for a man! She dressed well, loved to flirt, and had a gay twinkle about her. But it was her personal concern that drew him in. She was the only one who seemed to realize that he did not feel like a champion at all. He was really a depressed and lonely man, unsure of himself and his future. When she put her hand on his arm and looked into his eyes, he realized that with her he did not have to pretend. She loved him anyway. He had known many women in his time, but never one as honest as this. They became great pals and, before long, lovers.

What more could a gossip ask? A prince and a barmaid! Apia buzzed with speculation on every possible nuance of their relationship. But speculation was as far as it could get. The principals weren't talking. They weren't even listening! Perhaps they had lived so long in this hive they had become immune to stings.

Actually, Aggie had more pressing matters to worry about. She and Willie had just received a letter from old Heatherington in New Zealand. He still owned the property under the chemist shop and the British Club but was going blind and needed money for his treatments. Would they be interested in buying him out? £500 for the Club, £300 for the shop. For years Willie had wanted to own his shop. But where would he ever get that kind of money? Aggie would have given anything she had to own her Club, but everything she owned amounted to less than £100. She wrote to ask Heatherington if he would consider installments, but he was desperate too. He needed at least £35 on the first of every month. She would have to get it to Carruthers before noon that day. If she defaulted, he would repossess the land together with all her payments.

217

To Aggie, £35 was an astronomical sum. She was having difficulty coming up with a monthly rent of twenty shillings. But if she didn't buy it now, someone else certainly would, and what would her enterprise do then? More than one member of the Gentlemen's Club offered to purchase it and keep her on as manager. She flatly refused. This business was her own!

She signed Heatherington's agreement and redoubled her efforts, taking on more boarders and "patients" as fast as she could find them. It was soon obvious that she couldn't handle them all alone. Fred helped out in the evening, but she needed help all day as well. She finally wrote Sister Joseph asking her to send Pele home. Her daughter was thirteen now. She could attend school in the morning, help cook in the afternoon, and serve drinks in the evening. The little girl pitched in like an adult. She seemed as concerned with the business as her mother. They dropped every penny they could muster into the mortgage jar.

Olaf acted as their "ace in the hole." Before noon on the first day of each month, he called Aggie on the phone. "Counted your pennies yet? Enough? Need a loan? Just be sure to get it down to Carruthers on time." With help like that she managed to stay afloat.

Two years later she invited boarders, customers, and gentlemen to a victory celebration and burned the mortgage. The old British Club and the land under it belonged to her. She was now what Willie had always dreamed of becoming, a proprietor on Beach Road!

At midnight after the party, she and Olaf sat alone on the upstairs porch. She had looked so radiant all evening, he felt he had to ask her the prime question. "Life hasn't been easy for either of us these last two years, Aggie. It's just lucky we had each other. Your plucky laugh has kept me going, but I can support both of us now. Divorce Charlie—he's beyond any help you can give—and marry me. You need someone who can love you as you deserve."

Proposals were not new to Aggie. She had become an expert at saying no. But this was Olaf, the man whom she had admired since she was a child. She had known gamblers, but never one who had tried to play two games at once with such audacity, risen so high, fallen so low, and staggered to his feet again. Her own expulsion from Apia, the house on the hill, and the Happy Hour were nothing compared with his two banishments. During the last two years, while she had struggled to buy one house, he had rebuilt an empire.

Marry Olaf Nelson? How she would have leaped at such a proposal twenty years ago! Hostess of Tuaefu and Jubilees; nothing could have suited her better. But now she realized that she had changed. Adversity had somehow shaped a different Aggie. Her little enterprises, shabby and gossip-ridden as they might be, had proved she could be more than a crown jewel for a man. She too could raise roofs, drive bargains, buy houses; and she liked herself this way. Fathers and husbands kept fading away, but her own skills had only grown stronger. She had no desire to be a butterfly again, even to someone who could put her on the top. Marriage to Olaf would pose a problem he would never comprehend. A man like Fred would be perfectly happy as her assistant. But Olaf, dear Olaf, would always be the boss!

She had another reason he was more apt to understand. Marrying her could risk what he had just won back so unexpectedly. But how could she tell him?

"Olaf," she said tenderly, reaching for his hand, "you know how much I love you. Maybe that's what gives me the courage to say no. The real trouble is not with Charlie but with me. An attorney general in Pago once told me my presence disturbed the town so much it would jeopardize his career if I stayed. That made me angry but maybe he was right. You've shaken up this island a bit yourself, Olaf. It's just now returned you to its pedestal. Would you risk all that again to marry a barmaid?"

"To hell with Apia!" he cried petulantly. "We can go to Australia and forget this place."

"Not me," she smiled. "I wouldn't be happy anywhere else. Neither would you, Olaf. Why don't we just go on being friends and lovers and give this bunch of hornets a rest?"

She cried herself to sleep that night. Where had she ever found the guts to turn him down? But she knew she had made the right decision.

Now it was more important than ever for her enterprise to expand. She ordered a brick-making machine from New Zealand. When the bright red contraption arrived, she thought she had found the key to success. She could just see it spewing forth bricks to build houses, shops, sheds, and swimming pools all over her new property! She bought a bag of cement, mixed it with sand and water, and pressed herself a nice crisp brick. It was so easy she could not imagine why everyone was not doing it. When the bricks were dry she started to build a wall. To her great disappointment, one brick would not hold up another. They cracked and crumbled. She tried again with no better luck until Fred came by and pointed out that bricks needed straw. She let him do it. He used his bricks to turn the decaying caretaker's house in the backyard into a two-story building with a kitchen on top and a garage below. She had been right. She needed this man.

Willie didn't even try to buy his lot. Long ago in better times he had made a down-payment on sixteen acres of the old German resort on top of the mountain. Maggie and Peter had built themselves a house up there and he went up to visit them on weekends. He liked the quiet mountain air. "Someday I'll retire up here and build a vegetable garden," he promised. "Cool air, big tomatoes."

On Good Friday in 1936, Maggie, on the hill, got up early to clean house and bake a cake. Willie and his friends were coming up for Easter. She shook out the mats and was just setting the table when something caught her attention. She looked out the window and heard it again, the sharp whistle of an *iao* bird. How strange! These small wild creatures lived only in the forest, and here were six of them sitting in her lemon tree. She remembered hearing about the *iao* from her mother. Pele had always called them her *aitu* (spirit) birds. In her childhood Samoans identified some living creature as a personal totem and watched it for omens. Maggie still half-believed in it. Had Pele sent her the *iao* birds to tell Maggie something? A little frightened, she sat down in a chair, ears alert for any sound.

Suddenly she heard a human cry far off in the distance: *"Suga Meki! Suga Meki! Tope mai! Lou tama ua lavea i tai!"* (Maggie! Maggie! Come quick! Your father has been hurt down the hill!)

Her heart and feet leaped at the same time. Barely thinking, she grabbed two old sheets and a bottle of iodine and ran down the driveway. Two Samoan boys were standing on the main road, their eyes wide with fright. When they saw Maggie coming, they pointed downhill. She flew past them. Dad! Dad! Was he dead?

Half a mile further down, a knot of villagers gestured east towards the gorge. She didn't stop to ask any questions; she just veered off, following two tracks of flattened grass. A vehicle must have passed by recently. The tall weeds on either side tore at her skirt, but she plunged ahead clutching her sheets and bottle of iodine.

At the edge of the gorge a group of boys was trying to right an overturned truck. Willie was pinned underneath, bloodstained but still conscious. Maggie threw her arms around him, oblivious of the wheels teetering precariously over their heads. When the boys finally got him out, she sent one of them back to the road to stop a passing car. Meanwhile, she tore up the sheets and packed them around her father's injured chest. He did not even groan. He didn't say a word until she finally got him down to the hospital and they were taking him in on a stretcher.

Then he murmured, "Maggie, how can I repay you for all this?"

"By staying right here at the hospital until you get well!" she declared. But he wouldn't listen. As soon as he was bandaged, he insisted on being taken back to the chemist shop. His daughters took turns with the nursing. Maggie showed Faafete's daughter, Daisy, how to soften food for his broken teeth, and sewed him some silk pajamas and a dressing gown. But these could not repair his internal injuries. He died May 20, 1936, at the age of seventy-seven.

Willie had never made it into the Gentlemen's Club, but after forty-seven years of dispensing prescriptions on Beach Road, everyone knew him. Father Diehl conducted his funeral service, attended by Governor Turnbull, heads of government departments, and representatives of the business firms. Willie was buried beside Pele in the cemetery at Saleufi.

After the service, Maggie drove back to Afiomalu and stopped in front of her lemon tree. The six *iao* birds had vanished, but she now knew why they had come. Pele had sent them to welcome Willie home.

221

Aggie's old friend Bill Links, now managing Burns Philps grocery but still married, bought the chemist shop and land and moved in next door to her club. Like Olaf, Bill was a lonely man attracted by Aggie's warmth and laughter but unable to convince her to marry him. He too settled for joining her brood of bachelors. When she ladled out the evening stew for Charlie, Pele, Edward, Maureen, little Allan, Fred, and the other boarders, she always sent over a bowl for "Uncle Bill." Hadn't he brought her food when she was living in Trood's pasture?

Her kindness meant a lot to Bill, and he had his own way of reciprocating. When he won £50 at the races one Saturday, he presented it to Aggie in a sealed envelope with the message, "To help send young Edward to school in New Zealand." Now, how did he know how much she needed that?

In 1939, Aggie got a letter from Hauroa. Perhaps her little Peggy was graduating! Inside, however, was another clipping. The little girl with the golden curls, who had weathered the 'flu ship and later stayed on in New Zealand with Lyla to go to school, had died of TB like her father. She was only eighteen. Aggie was disconsolate at this second death among her children. This disease had haunted her too many times. Was it her fault for letting Peggy stay on with her father so long ago?

In her depression, Aggie began worrying about Pele Jr., who was fifteen and her mainstay in the busy household. Pele was a quiet, good-natured girl, reminiscent of the grandmother for whom she was named—not at all pugnacious like her mother. Her gift was a winsome innocence that caused the men in the bar to curb their words to protect her. Her skin was so fair she seemed almost fragile.

One day Pele complained of a sore throat. Aggie called a new doctor in town, and felt an immediate repugnance for the bald, pot-bellied gentleman who appeared. He reminded her of the banker in Hauroa.

After examining Pele the doctor shook his head. "This little lady is pre-consumptive," he declared, confirming Aggie's worst fears. Nothing could have upset her more. It must not happen again! She decided to build a small house for Pele in the backyard and have the doctor come see her every day regardless of the cost. But where would she get lumber?

Captain Dyke of a small merchant vessel in the harbor was in the bar at the time. "Aggie, if you have £3, you can have my surplus dunnage," he said.

Aggie sent a boy back out to the ship with the captain and he returned pulling a raft of timbers. "Two more coming," he puffed.

Old Paulo offered to do the carpentry, and soon transformed Dyke's dunnage into not one but two small cottages, so that Aggie could sleep close to her daughters. In deference to the treacherous Vaisigano, he raised them on posts above the marshy ground. Aggie named them "Pele's house" and "Maureen's house" in honor of her daughters.

Pele was moved into hers and the paunchy doctor visited her there every day, insisting that his treatment must be private. Such secretiveness bothered Aggie and she finally asked Pele what he was doing. When she discovered that his therapy involved a "breast massage," she met the doctor at the door next day, eyes and tongue blazing.

"Get out of here, you lecherous pig!" she screamed. "Never let me see your flabby face at this end of Beach Road again or I'll tell everybody what your 'treatments' consist of!" Practically everyone heard anyway as she chased him down the road towards town.

"A really terrifying woman!" he panted to his friends when he reached safety.

Next day, Aggie sailed for Tutuila with Pele. It was the first time she had been back since her unceremonious departure but she did not care. She trusted that hospital.

"No sign of TB in this young lady," the American doctor reported. "But she ought to have her tonsils out."

With two new cottages, Aggie would have liked to take in more boarders. But now that locals were filling more government posts and ships arrived only once a month, there were fewer homeless bachelors in town. She couldn't fill the rooms she had and prospects for expansion dimmed.

In April, 1940, Bill Links died. Aggie held his funeral in her parlor and he departed as he had always wanted, as part of her family. In death he reciprocated her thoughtfulness in a way she could never repay—he bequeathed to her Willie's land and chemist shop.

Chapter 19

The Yank Club and Hamburger Stand

(1940-1944)

POLITICAL WAVES generated in Europe usually reached Samoan beaches after several months, somewhat distorted by their trip around the world but still recognizable enough. So it was with Nazism.

The 538 Germans left in Samoa after World War I were a tight little sub-group within the European community, concentrated in engineering and plantation occupations. Half of the Reparation Estates managers and three-quarters of the public works officers were of German origin. Their social center was the old Concordia Verein. Most still thought of their homeland as the empire of the Kaiser. They scarcely noticed when Herr Matthes organized a small group called the Samoan Nazi Party and announced a free film entitled "Germany Awake!" Scarcely anyone in town read the small-print reports in the weekly paper about Japanese in China, Mussolini in Ethiopia, and Hitler in the Rhineland. Where were those places? The only world worth discussing was here in the middle of the Pacific.

Ernst Gebauer had been sent "home" for school and wrote that he had signed up for the Luftwaffe, but Apia was far more interested in his father, who had just reorganized the local symphony. It was giving its first concert in April! The only harbinger of war to command Apia's full attention was, of all people, Count Felix von Luckner, the dashing pirate who had kept the Pacific enthralled during World War I. When he suddenly reappeared, sailing into Apia Harbor on his little *Seeadler*, everyone came down to the wharf to greet him. Twenty years had not removed the spring from his six-foot frame or mellowed his gallantry. This time his sailing companion was a dainty blonde, so tiny he could lift her up in one hand. He assured the crowd that he had neither captured her from a merchant-ship nor rescued her from a deserted atoll. She was the daughter of a nobleman he had met in the Canaries in his youth, and she had waited for him faithfully for twenty years. Recently they had married, and he was now taking her around the world on a honeymoon. The only other person aboard was a photographer named Hans Gunther Oestereich, who had come to "take pictures of Samoan life."

Everyone settled for this romance except Governor Turnbull, who remembered this irrepressible count when he had been interned in New Zealand and didn't trust him an inch. The photographer was already pointing his camera towards the hulks of the old warships rusting in the harbor. Yes, German fascination with Samoa had pre-dated World War II. It might still be tempting them.

The count assured the local press that Samoa had noth-ing to fear from Germany. Japanese were the ones to watch! They were building military bases on the Marshalls just to the north, he said. One of these days, Samoa might beg the "German eagle" for protection. That interview did not reassure the governor, but what could he do? Britain and Germany were not at war and the count had the right of free speech.

Agent or not, the governor never discovered, but at least the count brought the possibility of war to Apia's attention. A few weeks after he had sailed, another German face appeared in town. It belonged to Herr Hess-man from Hamburg, who promptly set up a German-speaking school in Syddal's parlor. Thirty children of German descent were soon enrolled by parents who want-ed their children to learn the language, but they found him particularly eloquent about their "teutonic heritage." Local residents became sensitive to their origins again. When the government opened 689 acres of Reparation Es-tates land for thirty-acre leases, there was some complaint that twelve applicants were of German extraction. Who won the last war, anyway? A newspaper article warned residents of German descent that their admixture of Samoan blood might not endear them to the current Reich, in view of Hitler's racial theories.

Oblivious to the confusion he was causing in Apia,

Hitler kept right on marching. In September, 1938, he entered Czechoslovakia. The news drew muffled cheers at the Cor.cordia Verein, and Berking raised a swastika over his butcher shop. The British bootmaker next door retaliated by running his Union Jack even higher.[1] By now, Samoans felt they had to identify which side they were on. Alipia, speaker of the *Fono a Faipule*, assured the administrator of its loyalty by offering nine thousand warriors for the "defense of the British empire either here or abroad."

In December, 1938, Herr Raum, German Consul General in New Zealand, suddenly decided to visit Samoa for the first time. He assured Governor Turnbull that his interest was purely cultural. To his embarrassment, however, he was greeted at the wharf by Herr Matthes and Apia's Nazi party in uniform, giving a straight-arm salute. At the administrator's firm request, he asked his admirers to disband.

Hitler was not that obliging. In September, 1939, he invaded Poland and, two days later, France. Britain declared war against him and New Zealand immediately followed. That clarified things in Apia. Turnbull deported Herrs Matthes, Hessman, and a few other vocal Germans to New Zealand for safekeeping. The rest of the community demonstrated its loyalty in customary fashion by forming new clubs. They met each other now as the Red Cross, the local Defense League, the Ladies' Auxiliary, the Apia Patriotic Society, and the War Effort Committee, which raised £1,000 for a bomber to be christened *Western Samoa*.

Faafete's son Fred was the first *afakasi* to enlist for service overseas. He was soon joined by Bertie Mann, Harry Moors, and others. There was no longer any question as to which side Samoa was on.

Otherwise, life went on as usual. The war was somewhere else. In August, Maggie held a twenty-first-birthday party for her daughter Eileen, at which she announced her engagement to J.B. Wright, a New Zealand career officer in the Treasury. A third generation of Swanns was now coming to maturity in Apia and doing well. The administrator and all his department heads attended the wedding and Eileen wore a dress that rivaled Tongan Queen Salote's. Maggie had made it.

But these were difficult days for Mary. Her husband, Robert Croudace, had also done well. Arriving in Samoa in 1907 as an accountant for old H.J. Moors, he had become manager of Rothschild's, president of the British Club and the Chamber of Commerce, and an elected member of the Legislative Council. But now he was gravely ill and Mary, like Aggie, was forced to support her family. Like Aggie, her inclinations were social and her culinary skills a magnet for bachelors. By the time her husband passed away in 1940, she had eight boarders in her little house and needed a larger place.

Aggie had settled for the old British Club but Mary was tempted by an even larger relic, the old German Casino, whose inaugural ball Aggie had attended so long ago in Apia's first car. When DH&PG left, it had been taken over by the New Zealand Reparation Estates. Several capable women had tried to manage it as a hotel, but Apia was hardly a tourist mecca. Only a handful of overseas officers now huddled among the mahogany tables of the great dining hall and groped their way to bed along endless corridors of empty rooms. That clientele didn't justify repairing the toilets and cold basins at the end of each floor, much less making improvements. The previous manager had given up, and the position was up for tender.

Mary was an optimist. She didn't see the Casino's torn sofas, creaking floorboards, and peeling paint. She saw it in its bygone glory with groaning banquet tables, twinkling candelabra, and ruffle-clad ladies. Her bid was modest, but it won. Wiser heads gave her six months to discover she was dreaming.

Four years later Mary retired from the Casino with a fortune, having mounted weekly balls far gayer than had the Germans. It was not only that she was the right lady for the job, she managed to pick the best time in Samoan history for her enterprise. The Yanks were coming!

Count von Luckner had been right about one thing. The only attack Samoa experienced in World War II was mounted from a base in the Marshalls. Few Samoans had ever seen a Japanese except for a few shopkeepers like Shimasaki, who had settled down in American Samoa with Samoan wives and become part of the culture. Even the United States had underrated Nippon's interest in the

Pacific. The U.S. Navy had administered American Samoa since 1900, but did not begin to arm it until 1940, when twelve military planners suddenly appeared. They were followed by a marine battalion and a civilian construction crew which began improving the wharf and building houses for officers along the waterfront. Something more was coming!

On the morning of December 7, 1941, Japanese bombers from carriers near Midway suddenly descended on the unwary American fleet in Hawaii. Next day the United States declared war against the Axis powers. Overnight, the marine battalion and civilian crew in Pago Pago found themselves a very small, very forward outpost only a few hundred miles south of the Marshalls. Communications blacked out across the Pacific. Enemy vessels were loose and no one wanted his position known as he raced for a friendly harbor. Samoa was alone in a darkening sea!

Traditional villages had survived such isolation for two thousand years, but they were not U.S. Marines. "For Chris' sake," the Pago brigadier general told his supply officer in Pago Pago, "do somthin' quick. With the Jap fleet prowlin' around out there and our own shot to hell in Hawaii, we will have to surrender to the first damn sampan that floats in here unless we die of starvation first! This rock doesn't grow enough to feed Samoans, much less all of us. There ain't goin' to be no friendly ship comin' this way for months. Forget the ammo, boy, and start scroungin' for grub, anythin' you can buy, beg, borrow, or steal. And do it on the QT. All we need is a panic on this rock!"

Within a few minutes, the supply officer was conferring with his Navy counterpart and the chief customs officer. "We can't buy an apple from bush stores in Pago without prices shootin' through the ceiling. The shelves will be bare in an hour. It's too risky. Even if we took everythin' they got, it wouldn't last two weeks!"

"Cool down and listen to daddy," the customs officer told him. "I've lived here a lot longer than you have and I know how things are done. Did you ever meet that smiley, round-faced little fella' who brings in taro from Apia every week on the MV *Samoa?* The name's Fabricius—Emilio Fabricius. That guy's a caution, always standin' me to beers and tellin' me about the U.S. sailor in his family tree. He's always after a good deal. Ain't nothin' old Emilio wouldn't do for a customs officer! We could get him to buy what we want in Apia and bring it over with his taro."

At dawn the next day, two marine MPs met the MV *Samoa* as she docked and escorted a terrified Emilio to the customs office. Someone must have squealed on that last case of gin!

A few moments later, to his amazement, he found himself being offered a drink by three American officers. "Emilio," the customs officer confided, laying an arm around his shoulder, "you and I have been buddies so long I'm goin' to toss you the best damn deal of your life." Emilio's ears pricked up. "As soon as you get back to Apia tomorrow, I want you to buy up anything edible you can lay your hands on—cans, sacks, cases, anything. Fill the MV *Samoa* to the gunwales and don't bother about that customs officer over there. I'll take care of him. Here's $5,000 for your shopping spree and you'll get $5,000 more to keep if you bring her back full. Just don't go blabbing around about it, know what I mean?"

Emilio's eyes bulged and a grin spread from ear to ear. "No problem, no problem at all! I got a Yank in my family tree." They drank to this worthy ancestor.

As soon as he got back to Apia, Emilio picked out slow-moving stock from his own store and gave instructions to his clerks and family members to go shopping up and down Beach Road. "Emilio's got a big *faalavelave* (ceremonial obligation)," they explained to curious competitors. That was possible. He had chiefs as well as sailors in his family tree. Maybe Emilio was taking a big title and feasting a couple of villages.

By late afternoon, the purchases were safely aboard the MV *Samoa* and Emilio decided to make a last run up to Aggie's bar to celebrate his good fortune. She might even have a couple of extra bottles on hand. He could triple the price on something like that. Yanks liked their booze.

Aggie was sitting on her upstairs porch with a cup of tea. She sent Pele to make him a sandwich, since he looked a little pale. The sight of it reminded Emilio that he had forgotten to eat lunch in all the excitement. He was so grateful he told her the whole story. After all, they were cousins.

229

"Those Yanks are millionaires," he concluded. "Just think of my future!"

"Are you sure you've got a future?" Aggie asked quietly, gazing out at the harbor. "Isn't that the MV *Samoa* I see pulling away from the wharf?"

Emilio sprang to the railing. "Gawd Almighty!" he bawled on his way down the stairs. "Steffany's leavin' without me!"

By the time he reached the wharf, the little launch was out of sight with his future on board. The only craft left at the wharf was the pilot boat. Emilio jumped in, hot-wired the motor, and started off at full speed.

The pilot and his wife had just finished tea on the porch of their house at Pilot Point. "What's that going by so fast, dear?" she asked her husband, who was about to doze off. "It looks like your pilot boat."

He jumped to his feet. "It bloody well *is* my boat!" he shouted. "Some bastard's stealing it! Could be a Jap!" He ran for his car and careened towards the police station.

The chief of police soon ascertained that it was Emilio. Some trick to avoid customs, no doubt! By God, he'd nail him for it this time! He wired Pago to be waiting with a police escort. "Arrest that man as soon as he arrives. He's charged over here with piracy and smuggling!"

Back in the pilot boat, Emilio pulled out the throttle, but he was nearly at Falefa before he caught sight of the MV *Samoa* lumbering along through heavy seas. High time too; it was getting dark. He made several passes at the launch; trying to jump aboard. Finally, Steffany grabbed him by the wrists and pulled him over the rail. The pilot boat sped on alone into the darkness. "Why didn't you tell me you wanted to come so bad?" Steffany scolded. "I would have waited."

By the time the MV *Samoa* reached Pago Pago, a crowd of onlookers had gathered to see the "pirate." For once in his life, Emilio was glad to see a customs officer. His friend pushed forward and told the police he wanted to interrogate him about the cargo. The two supply officers were waiting in his office. They toasted a mission well done and paid Emilio off. He was a very happy man. A few hours later the New Zealand administrator in Apia got a call from the U.S. brigadier general in Pago, praising Emilio's contribution to the war effort. Charges were dropped.

It wasn't long before the business community in Apia realized what was happening. Merchants immediately stopped buying copra. Who knew when it could be shipped? At the same time, they tripled the prices of their overseas goods. Who knew when they could replace them. Samoans smiled at the furor and returned to their taro patches. A few more months of this and their *afakasi* relatives might be sitting on *their* steps for a change!

Even more alarming were wartime regulations. On December 14, 1941, the Apia newspaper carried an official announcement. Henceforth there would be no street lights. Each family could have a light under six candle-power, but only in a room with blankets over the windows. Air raids would be announced by a siren being erected in the middle of town. When it sounded, everyone was to leave his house and lie in the nearest ditch. Surface invasion would be heralded by four tolls of the cathedral bell, to be relayed by other church bells and log drums across the island. When they heard these, everyone was to grab a kit with bedding, clothes, knives, food, and kerosene; hike to the mountains; and build a shelter. All private vehicles would be commandeered by the police. At the end of these instructions, the weekly declared its own demise. It was out of newsprint!

Early on the morning of January 11, 1942, the Samoan Islands were attacked for the first (and only) time. A Japanese submarine surfaced silently off the north shore of Tutuila and lobbed eleven shells over the mountain towards Pago Pago. Ironically enough the first hit Shima-saki's store! The second fell on the Naval dispensary and third behind Centipede Row. The rest disappeared in the harbor. One Samoan guard and a lieutenant were injured by flying debris. That was all. No alarm was sounded, and few people realized what was happening. Before anyone could get around to surrendering, the submarine had slipped away and was never heard from again.

The only other attack was at sea a few weeks later. The wireless station in Apia picked up a distress call from an Allied plane, and the customs launch was dispatched with ten men and a doctor to pick up survivors. About a hundred miles out, they were raked by machine-gun fire from a Japanese bomber. Everyone jumped overboard to save his life, but the plane flew on and did not return. They climbed back into the launch and limped back to Apia with a damaged engine.

The war might not be moving in Samoa's direction, but it was still too close for comfort. New Zealand evacuated its officers' wives and children as soon as ships started moving again, and some local residents sailed with them. Aggie had already sent Maureen to join Edward at school "down under," but six-year-old Allan was still with her. She walked him to school every morning and called for him at noon, but what would happen if there were an air raid in the meantime? One day her apprehension was so vivid she returned to school at nine to get him. That made the sister so nervous she excused everyone for the day. But the Japanese never came. Instead there was an invasion of another sort.

On January 23, 1942, an American general appeared in Pago Bay with a contingent of Marines and Seabees. They were followed shortly by thousands of American GI's with an incredible amount of equipment: ships, planes, guns, jeeps, cigarettes, silk stockings, and candy bars. These Americans were prepared for love as well as war!

The first wave of Yanks came ashore on Tutuila, and before long that fifteen-mile-long island boasted more GI's than Samoans. Barracks, warehouses, and airfields soon covered every one of its few flat acres, and cement bunkers dotted the mountains. Yanks paid well, too! Samoan construction workers earned up to one dollar an hour and were only too happy to leave their taro patches. They even formed an American-Samoan Marine battalion. Soon money almost completely replaced subsistence. Everyone now relied on the ships for food.

And still the Yanks kept coming! It was soon clear that Tutuila simply did not have enough land to provide staging operations for battlefronts in Guadalcanal. In August, 1942, the bush wireless in Western Samoa carried word that New Zealand had given American forces permission to use their islands as well. The very next day, the first Yanks sailed into Apia Harbor.

Aggie watched from the door of her club as American LSTs disgorged a flood of "ducks." Some of these little landing craft began beaching on a wire mesh laid on the sand right across from her bar. Marines in olive drab leaped out and began unloading jerry cans of gasoline. The sun rose as they worked and soon it was blistering hot. She watched a sweltering major direct operations. His shirt was soaked. Feeling sorry for him, she got up from her bench in the arbor, crossed the road, and tapped him lightly on the shoulder. "Sir, could you use a cold beer?"

"A what?" he cried, spinning around as if she had shot him. "They told us this place was dry as a bone!"

"Not if you need medication," she smiled. "I keep mine on ice right across the road."

"Just show me that prescription lady!" he cried. "I think I'm dying! And my friend here's even sicker than I am. Can he come too?" With his foot he nudged an olive-drab figure bent over a packing case. "This is Dr. Beattie and I'm Major Hunt. Just call me Joe."

"I'm Aggie Grey," she smiled, shaking hands. "Welcome to Western Samoa."

She settled her new patients comfortably in a cool corner of the back porch and sent Pele for two beers and a bottle of whiskey. It was so cool and quiet here, with the sun filtering through the hibiscus and torch ginger, that the tired Americans recalled their long-lost visions of paradise. "Is it true what Margaret Mead wrote about girls here?" Hunt asked dreamily.

Aggie had never heard of Margaret Mead but she knew perfectly well what he wanted to hear. Yanks were apparently no different from the other lonely men she had mothered over the years. She was forty-five now and knew plenty of stories men liked to hear. By the time the three of them stopped chuckling, the sun was going down and Aggie's newest patients felt better than they had for many weeks.

"A day well spent," the major told the doctor as they ducked out under the arbor. "Now we have a friend where we need one." Aggie felt exactly the same way.

That night, Yanks were billeted all over town and in pup tents on the racetrack. Aggie put up nine Seabees in the storeroom under her back porch and invited them to take their meals with the family. They gladly contributed their K-rations to her kitchen and stayed for six weeks.

The following morning, one intrepid company marched twenty-five miles in the blazing sun to Mulifanua, seeking flat land for an airstrip. Major Hunt and Dr. Beattie set up offices in town and stopped in at Aggie's after work each day, bringing their friends. Soon Yanks almost completely replaced her local customers, who now found it more worthwhile to sell their "medicine" to Yanks than consume it themselves at Aggie's. Who wanted to drink pure gold!

"Just look at that!" Aggie laughed to Fred. "The Yanks have managed to do in a week what New Zealand has been trying to do for twenty years — turn us into teetotalers!"

"For $25 a bottle, I'd be anything," he replied. "Too bad our permits are so small. Isn't there anything else we can sell these Yanks?"

Beattie and Hunt told them there was. "Why don't you sell hamburgers?" they suggested. "GI's can't go to war without a 'burger' in each hand."

"What's a hamburger?" Aggie asked.

"Hard to explain," Hunt said. "It's an American art form. But if you find some beef, we'll show you."

Fred was not impressed with the idea of foreign foods in the house. Why couldn't GI's take tea and cucumber sandwiches like gentlemen? But when Hunt and Beattie arrived next day with three little camp stoves, he got caught up trying to pressurize all three at once from a single pump, and forgot his complaints. When he finally solved the problem, he rigged up a large griddle in the front room of the chemist shop. It even had a vent over it. Since Hunt insisted that the beef had to be ground, Fred resurrected a food mill without a handle and ran it with his electric drill. The grinder could handle a cow all right, but Fred explained it could only produce "mince." Major Hunt could not get over this kiwi obstinacy. To the American, "mince" meant something with raisins fit only for pies at Thanksgiving. They remained at loggerheads until Aggie discovered that British "mince" and American "hamburger" were one and the same thing. "Why don't these damn Yanks learn to speak English?" Fred growled.

Hamburgers required more than meat, however. For one thing, they had to be served in appropriate surroundings. Aggie covered the chemist shop counter and four borrowed tables with colorful oilcloth. After she set a flowerpot on each, the shop looked quite attractive. Even though she did have chairs by this time, Beattie and Hunt insisted on calling it a "hamburger stand." Americans were odd people.

Getting meat regularly was the real challenge.

Beef had disappeared entirely from the markets of Apia, but Aggie figured there might be some still on the hoof at the Reparation Estates. The day before the "stand" was to open, she went to see the Estates manager, Mr. Eden, with Fred's last bottle of gin. It was quite a sacrifice, but she did return with a heavy parcel wrapped in newspaper.

At the last moment, Hunt remembered two more vital pieces of information about hamburgers. They were never eaten directly from a plate. They had to be inserted in a big soft bun, accompanied by "ketchup." He sent over a Navy cook to show her how to make the buns but no one knew how to make ketchup. In desperation, she finally boiled up a batch of mango chutney.

The grand opening of "Aggie's Hamburger Stand" was set for Monday at 10 a.m., at which time Dr. Beattie felt that GI breakfast rations would have begun to wear off. Fred got up early to run the "mincer" with his drill. It had a way of flying off the table now and then, but it did work. Aggie rolled the ground meat into little balls and stacked them in a basin. Then she put on the coffee pot and set some bottles of cordial on the shelf.

Promptly at ten she opened the door. No one was in sight. Around eleven, a young Marine in his teens edged shyly through the door and stood in the middle of the floor. He looked as if he were about to run.

"Hungry, son?" Aggie asked cheerfully. "Why don't you come over and sit down?" He hitched himself uncertainly onto a stool at the counter.

"One burger and a pop to go," he whispered.

"A burger and a what to what?" she asked, bewildered. He identified the first "what" by pointing to a cordial. She nodded. The other "what" would have to wait.

She tossed one of the round balls onto Fred's griddle. "Ready for you in a minute!" she called over her shoulder;

"only Samoan hamburger in town!" She rolled it around vigorously until it began to burn.

"How the hell do you get this thing cooked in the middle?" she whispered desperately to Fred, who was watching. He only shrugged. That was female business.

The young Marine watched with surprise as she tossed out one black ball and started on another. Just then the door opened and a seaplane pilot stuck his head in the door, sniffing the air.

"Smells good in here," he said. "Gimme two burgers and a cup of coffee." He threw one of his long legs over a stool and sat down next to the young Marine.

"Just a minute," Aggie said, close to consternation. She threw on two more balls and began rolling them around as fast as she could.

The pilot watched with curiosity and finally asked, "Say, lady, are you havin' trouble?"

"What do you mean, trouble?" she countered defensively, trying to toss the steaks a bit.

"Maybe I can give you a hand," he said, jumping over the counter. He grabbed her spatula and pressed the balls flat. "That's how we do it in the States," he explained.

"Well, I'll be damned!" she said. "Here, let me put on four more, two for you and two for that poor little chap who has been waiting so long."

When the patties were done she slipped them into buns and onto plates, and proudly set them on the counter. The little Marine looked at his sadly and shook his head. Aggie felt like crying, until the pilot identified the other "what." "To go" meant "put them in a bag." Since she had no bags, Aggie wrapped them in newspapers.

"How much?" the young marine asked faintly, trying to recover from all he had been through.

"One and six," she said in a businesslike voice. "The second one's free, since you're my first customer."

By lunchtime, word had spread. Her tables filled and there was a line at the door. Fred pumped and ground; Aggie flattened and fried. She was so busy she lost track of the financial end. She just kept taking what was proffered, making the change requested and stuffing what was left in a jar under the counter. When business slackened in the afternoon she counted £8 in small change. Amazing! She had not made that much in a week at the bar. She grabbed Fred and led him in the first jig of his life.

"But you can't do it again tomorrow," he warned. "'Cause we're out of meat."

That hadn't occurred to her. She dumped the money into her bag and ran out, reaching the Reparation Estates store just as Mr. Eden was leaving. "No, Aggie!" he said before she could catch her breath. "You can't bring it back."

"I don't want to bring it back, sir," she puffed. "I just want a whole beast for tomorrow."

"What?" he shouted. "Didn't I sell you twenty-five pounds yesterday? Do you realize a whole beast weighs several hundred pounds? That could feed an army!"

"That's just what I'm doing," she assured him. "I'm making hamburgers for the GI's."

"Aren't they made of ham?" he asked skeptically.

"No, sir," she replied. "They're made of ground cow in a bun with raw onions and things."

He winced at the thought. "A whole beast would cost you £24 and you'd have to keep it refrigerated," he warned.

"Well, here's £8 we made today," she replied. "I'll give you the rest Wednesday."

He was leery of that, but the bottle of gin had indicated she must be onto something big. "I'll have the boys drop it off at your place in the morning," he sighed.

Fred spent the evening fixing an old refrigerator from Emilio's store, and got up early the next morning to grind the beast. Aggie ran over to get some cakes Johanson's wife wanted to sell at the store. When she returned she found a pile of mince by the grinder, but Fred was nowhere in sight. He must have gone out for a decent breakfast of spaghetti on toast. He hated hamburgers!

When she opened the door to a line of GI's at ten, Fred still hadn't returned. As soon as she was able, she left the work to Johanson's wife and ran out to look for him.

"Have you seen Fred?" she asked a boy chopping wood in the back.

"Not recently," he replied. "I saw him this morning, though, with his hand in a towel. He got into a car."

Aggie ran out and hailed a cab. "Hospital, quick," she told the driver. "Fred's been hurt!"

She found him pacing up and down the waiting room with his hand in the air. "What's wrong?" she cried, anxiously falling in beside him.

"Finger," he said laconically. "Damn mincer! Been waitin' here three hours already."

Aggie flushed with fury. She strode across the waiting room and flung open the door at the end, to reveal Dr. Monahan just raising a cup of tea to his lips. His eyes met her angry face. "Doctor Monahan!" she stormed. "How can you drink tea while Fred is bleeding to death out there? This hospital is a disgrace!"

"Who? Where?" he jumped up to avoid her volley of words and ran past her into the waiting room. "That woman's really frightening when she's angry!" he confided shakily to the nurse as they ushered Fred in.

As soon as the finger was properly bandaged, Aggie took Fred home. By now the shop was full of GI's on their afternoon break. Suddenly Aggie thought of something and the color drained from her face.

"What's the matter, Aggie?" the boys cried as she steadied herself on the counter. "You look like you seen a ghost!"

"Oh, no!" she breathed. "Maybe I should warn you! Fred cut off the end of his finger in the grinder this morning!"

There was a silence as the full significance of this sank in, then a long "oo-oo-oo" from her customers. They started coughing and spitting and making irreverent remarks,

"Extra lean!"

"Round ground finger sold here!"

"What's that scratchin' in my stomach!"

Aggie was about to burst into tears when she discovered that this was their way of laughing. GI's had a gruesome sense of humor, but she was beginning to appreciate them.

"Cordials and coffee on the house," she called, "so Fred's finger won't stick in your throat!" Instead of ruining her business, the incident made her famous. Boys came in asking for "finger-burgers." Some demanded to count Fred's digits before they ate. He did not find that a bit funny and took to mincing at night to avoid them.

The following Monday, Eden found Aggie in his office when he arrived. "No returns, Aggie," he said flatly. "All sales final!"

"Here's your £24 up front," Aggie said in a businesslike tone, ignoring the slur, "and a whiskey to boot. I want another beast."

"Another beast!" he yelled, slapping his hand on the desk. "You already took our whole quota for a week! You want me to get shot and made into mince myself?"

Out of deference to the whiskey, however, he risked one more beast. "After this," he said, "you will have to scour the countryside." Trucks loaded with GI's on their way back to the burgeoning airbase at Mulifanua thought nothing of sending the driver for "a dozen burgers to go," and she trained some boys and girls from Toamua to tend the shop.

One day Dr. Beattie insisted that Aggie needed a day off, and took her with him on a tour of the new base. She couldn't believe her eyes at what had happened out there. Tifitifi had disappeared! Miedicke's copra plantation was now an airstrip. The landscape all the way from Magia to Samea and back to the mountains resembled Los Angeles. Trucks, tanks, guns, quonset huts, hangars, and warehouses stood cheek by jowl. Near Leulumoega, Samoans in *lavalavas* were working with uniformed Yanks and huge bulldozers to build a road across the mountains to the south coast.

"Unbelievable!" she gasped. "How many GI's are in Samoa now?"

"About fifteen thousand," the doctor smiled, "if you count both the base and the outposts around the island. That's the Seventh Marines over there, training for an attack on Guadalcanal. Half will stay behind to supply them. Today we'll also be visiting the 147th Infantry, coming back from the Solomons. They're at the quarantine station. A lot of malaria, poor kids. War's not just fun and games, you know."

Presumably Uncle Sam was feeding his own, but that apparently did not fill the enormous craving for hamburgers. After she got used to their blunt mannerisms, Aggie enjoyed these boys; machine-crazy and a bit naive, but generous to a fault and surprisingly honest. She could issue "chitties" to lads from places she never heard of, setting off for places of "no return," and somehow the money would get back to her by way of a friend or a misspelled letter.

Sometimes, however, she paid for her fondness with great pain. After six weeks, the nine Seabees under her house were sent to the Solomons. Months later, one returned with their story. The company had been pinned down by heavy Japanese fire the moment they landed. They ran for cover into a nearby church. When a rescue party finally reached them two days later, only three were still alive. Aggie wept. She had lost part of her family!

If Yanks had a quirk besides hamburgers, it was laundry. American males apparently felt disgraced to be caught in the act. They were willing to pay almost any amount to have a woman do it for them. As soon as Aggie noticed this, she set out hampers for dirty clothes which old Paulo and his wife washed in the Vaisigano every afternoon. They returned it next morning with everything neatly pressed, and Aggie gave them the entire proceeds. The old man was so grateful to be included in the current wave of Yank prosperity that he planted a grove of coconuts in Aggie's backyard.

But hamburgers and clean laundry still left one GI problem — the lonely evening. Aggie reorganized activities on her upstairs porch. The old gramophone now ground out Tommy Dorsey and Bing Crosby. "Come up and join the fun!" she told the daughters of her friends and neighbors. "Who knows, you might find yourself a nice American boy!" She was an inveterate matchmaker. To her, romance was still as exciting as on the night of her first ball.

From his cot in the room behind the hamburger shop, seven-year-old Allan listened to the nightly revels, torn between love for his plucky mother and pain at not being able to capture more of her attention. She seemed to be everyone's "mom." He wanted one of his own. He was a quiet child, born in times of adversity. Well, perhaps she would notice him if he helped her with the work like Uncle Fred. He started collecting and washing bottles from the bar every morning, placing them back in their boxes, and pulling them down to the Burns Philps store, where they brought one shilling a case. His reward was not so much the shilling but a kiss from Aggie. She told him he had been essential to her enterprises ever since that raid the first month of his life. She was proud of him. But he was old enough now to go to New Zealand for an education. When Fred's sister offered to take in both Pele and Allan, Aggie bought them tickets, even though it meant losing two loyal assistants at once.

A few months after they left, Aggie had to buy a third ticket. For years, Charlie Grey had haunted her establishment, more like a wraith than a husband. He had never recovered from the depression, and the world had gone on without him. Aggie had mothered him along with everyone else. "Have you taken a supper tray to poor old Daddy?" she always asked the children.

But food could not repair the depredations of alcohol, and his liver finally rebelled completely. The doctor claimed it was critical this time, and ordered him to New Zealand for hospitalization. Aggie arranged for a friend to escort him and wrote the children to visit him every day. A few weeks later, when Allan stopped in to see him on his way to school, he found that the emaciated body had given up in the night. Gravely, he kissed his father goodby, feeling that now more than ever he must take care of his mother. He wrote that he wanted to come home, but Aggie would not hear of it. "If you really want to help me," she wrote, "stay and finish school."

The recipe for hamburger was not a military secret. Within a year many other "stands" sprang up around Apia. By now Aggie was so sick of scrounging, grinding, and frying that she was not unhappy to leave it to the competition. Why not try something else?

Down the road, Maggie had already discovered another Yank predilection. GI's seemed to keep in touch with their loved ones through an endless flow of souvenirs. Maggie supplied them with Indian bangles and carved ivory bracelets from Fiji. She even ordered a pearl which she sold for $50 to a lad who wanted to write his sweetheart about "diving into a crystal lagoon."

Why should Indians in Fiji reap all the profits when Samoans had crafts of their own? Aggie wondered. She remembered making baskets with the women at Vailima. Sitting around with them would be more fun than arguing with Eden about another beast. She reorganized her store into a curio shop, filling its shelves with beads, baskets, tapas, mats, fans, and tortoise-shell adornments. She soon found that GI tastes were limited. "Just what would I do with a thing like that?" one of them asked when she showed him a fine mat which required hundreds of hours to weave.

"Well, what are you going to do with five grass skirts?" she asked, wrapping up his order. "Isn't Minnesota cold for this sort of thing?"

"You'd be surprised how useful grass skirts can be," he winked. "Cold girl, warm heart, you know."

"Nothing about you Yanks surprises me any more," she laughed, putting the mat away. "You all have one-track minds." She therefore stocked what they wanted. As a shopkeeper her assets were the same as ever, a practical grasp of human needs and a liking for people.

Her bar continued to be popular. One late afternoon, an exhausted Navy officer dragged himself up the steps and slumped into a chair on the back porch. She went over and sat down beside him. "How about a whiskey and soda on me?" she suggested. "You look as if you had just come out of the jungle."

"I have!" he groaned. "The Apia jungle. Give me a good straight-shootin' Jap any time to these buddies of yours on Beach Road!"

He explained that he had leased Mac's old launch at an unheard-of-price as a lighter for American supply ships. It was the only one available. But whenever his ships came in, Mac's launch seemed to be "under repairs." Today it had happened again. The officer was forced to wave down a launch full of passengers from a steamer just to get himself ashore. No sooner had he climbed aboard than he realized the launch looked familiar. Old Mac was doubling · his money!

"I don't know what to do!" he sighed. "I've got a war to win and I can't seem to rely on you people."

Aggie shook her head sympathetically, forbearing to say that everyone in town was laying bets on how long old Mac could get away with that game. Her own money was on the Navy.

"Relax," she told the officer. "Maybe something can be done." She walked back to the laundry, where Fred was fixing her a washing machine. "You know, Fred, with all your talents you should be getting rich. Have you ever thought of unloading passengers? You always liked the sea."

"Got no boat!" he pointed out.

"Couldn't you build one?" she suggested sweetly. "We have some more of those kauri timbers. You said yourself they'd never rot."

"You don't know what you're talking about!" he said gruffly, but next morning he began assessing timbers.

A few months later, he took her for a ride in what he proudly called his "put-put." He told her he planned to bring in passengers for twenty-one shillings a head. That was a price Mac's big launch could not compete with, and he had to return to lightering supplies. For the rest of the war, Fred skimmed happily across the harbor with a business of his own. "You know what?" he told Aggie, surprised. "I'm really makin' money!"

But Mary was making a fortune. The Casino was no "hamburger stand." She had just finished repairing mattresses and making curtains for her 140 rooms when the Yanks splashed ashore. There stood the Casino—the biggest, best, and indeed only hotel in town. Who would presume to complain about one toilet and one cold-water basin at the end of each hall, when the alternative was a pup tent?

The first American to move in was General Price, head of the South Pacific command. She gave him a corner suite. Price was a firm believer in rest and recreation for morale. Nothing was too good for his boys! Supplies poured in— turkeys for Thanksgiving, hams for Christmas, and liquor all year round. He and Mary became the best of friends. She acted as hostess for his gala balls and invited all her friends' daughters. Sala, sister of Mataafa himself, was her top entertainer. The great hall of the Casino rocked again to music and laughter. Its mahogany tables groaned even louder than they had for the Germans. American celebrities entertained them. An admiral stopped by for a week with a party of ten, and Eddie Rickenbacker stayed with her to convalesce. All of them left calling their gay hostess "Auntie Mary."

Chapter 20

The Surplus Operation

(1944-1945)

NOT EVERYONE was enthusiastic about the prospering fortunes of the three Swann sisters. "Do you realize that about eighty per cent of Yank dancing, singing, and souveniring goes on with one of those three women?" one old-time merchant grumbled to another. "What can an honest trader do with Aggie at one end of Beach Road, Mary at the other, and Maggie in the middle! I can't really understand it; Willie was such an unassuming little fellow." There was only one possible explanation for successful female enterprise in his mind. Those women must be offering something no male could match. He retaliated with moral indignation.

Nelson's pain was deeper. He no longer felt at home on Aggie's back porch. The place was always overflowing with Yanks. He retreated to Tuaefu, but that aging mansion only depressed him. It was so big, so empty now that his daughters had married and gone. The billiard table no longer resounded to the click of balls and his proud silver service in the dining hall sat unpolished and unused on its mahogany sideboard. Chiefs seldom came to see him any more. Their interest had shifted from self-government to self-improvement.

He sat alone in his library at sunset with a lonely drink. Even this retreat had been shorn of meaning, its papers taken by the police and locked away somewhere in New Zealand. A year ago, twilight had been his favorite time of day, ensconced in his favorite chair on Aggie's back porch, pouring the day's adventures into her sympathetic ear. Now some brash American officer would be sitting in his place. How he disdained those callow youths! To them there was only one culture in the world—American. It handed them everything from Thanksgiving turkey to

244

world domination on a silver platter. He had to struggle for what he got! Somehow, they could never leave things alone. They couldn't even look at a Samoan village without planning a housing development, and everything they built looked like suburban Los Angeles. Yank dollars were a far greater threat to the Samoan way of life than Richardson's welfare programs had ever been, but they were not something that generated rebellion. Where were the proud *tamaaiga* and their warriors now? Down at the airstrip making money!

Olaf particularly disliked Major Hunt and Doctor Beattie. All they could see in a woman was either "mom" or "madam," a reflection of their own limited experiences. How could Aggie waste her time on men like that? This Yank invasion had deprived him not only of his cause but his favorite woman. He tried to fill the void with food and drink but only succeeded in making his body as heavy as his heart.

One evening he could stand it no longer. He felt tired and ill. Only one person could reverse this downward spiral. He drove over to Aggie's and sank heavily into a chair on her front porch to catch his breath. He could hear gay banter from the back and it annoyed him no end. Aggie was apparently teaching a couple of young officers to play *suipi* (casino). How could she waste her time like that when he needed her so much?

He leaned his aching head against the wall and his mind blurred into a dream. He was a giant planet encircled with golden rings. But his center was dying. Layers and layers of ice on his surface were slowly freezing his core! The sun with its warmth and light was now so far away its healing rays could barely reach him. Long, long ago it had flung him out there into orbit. He had circled out there helplessly ever since, unable to escape, unable to return to its fiery embrace. Around him in emptiness circled the lesser planets: Gordon, Charlie, Fred, Bill, Hunt, Beattie, and so many others, magnetized by a force they could feel but never understand. What was it?

He woke up thinking of an old Samoan song,[1]

Teine ma i e tauagafau,
Suamalie faatolo fualau,

245

Lololo pei o se popo.
Lau amio faagau loto!

(Girl who senses a man's pain,
You are sweet as the sugar cane,
Rich as the cream of the coconut.
Your tenderness soothes the heart!)

He needed her more than ever now. He was ill.

Swinging their battle jackets off their shoulders, the careless young Americans trooped across the front porch calling goodnight. None of them noticed the figure in the shadows. Inside, Aggie rose wearily and began collecting glasses. This club was becoming too much for her.

A familiar voice from the front porch startled her. "Aggie, come out here a minute and talk with me!"

"Sorry, Olaf," she called back wearily. "Not tonight. I'm just too beat and I still have to wash these glasses."

"Leave them, Aggie. It's important!" The urgent ring startled her. She set down her tray and ran out to the porch. She could see his heavy body filling her wicker chair. His face loomed up at her, glowing strangely white in the gloom.

Suddenly alert with concern, she sat down in the chair next to him and touched his hand. This strong man who had been part of her life so long looked as if he needed care, and she had been too busy to notice!

"Aggie," he said, as if each word were an effort, "my affairs are now in order but I am not. For seven years I have been waiting, hoping you would change your mind. Marry me now, Aggie, before it is too late! I feel so tired, so lonely! With you at my side I might recover."

His tortured plea shook her to the bone. Her prospering, flirtatious world was suddenly shattered by the very man who helped her build it. Love was not fun; it was agony, baring one's soul to existential questions. If she married him, he might indeed feel more comfortable the last few years of his life. She owed him that. But her motives would be misread by every hornet in town. His family would be torn asunder at the moment it most needed reconciliation; his children would feel betrayed, his epitaph would end in a snicker ("And what do you know, he ended up by running off with a barmaid!"). Aggie felt almost angry at him for forcing her to make a wrenching decision a second time. She wished she could run away and bury her head in a pillow.

Instead, she took a deep breath and answered him straight. "Olaf," she said, reaching for his hands and looking into his eyes, "you must trust my judgment now. I love you too much to do something that could only end in sorrow for us all. If you love me, Olaf, bring your family together and make peace with them and your reputation, and — take better care of yourself! Don't eat and drink so much. Otherwise, I'm so afraid of what might happen."

She broke off with a sob and ran to her room. Olaf watched her go. Then he rose numbly and lumbered to his car, feeling he had lost his last hope. After that he seldom rose from his bed. Rosabel and his daughters rallied to his side. He died in 1944 in the bosom of his family. Even Tuaefu revived its old glory for his funeral. The governor, department heads, members of the Legislative Council, and *Fono a Faipule* all attended. Mau and Malo gathered to pay their last respects to the hero of the Mau rebellion. News flashed around the South Seas, and the *Pacific Islands Monthly* mourned the loss of a prominent businessman.[2] Aggie sighed. She had not saved Olaf's life, but at least she had helped him die as everyone's champion!

Following tradition, guests brought fine mats and presented them to Olaf's family in the name of their relationship to the deceased. This was the Samoan way of revitalizing the threads that bind extended families and communities together: a public reiteration of their personal and historic connections.

Aggie felt she had to attend. Olaf was too much a part of her life to minimize their relationship. But how does "the other woman" announce her connection to the deceased at such an occasion? Discretion would suggest a quiet tear at home, but Aggie wanted everyone to know that, to her, Olaf had been more than a passing fancy. Under her mattress still lay the fine mat bequeathed to her at her mother's funeral. Pele had instructed Willie to save a good fine mat from that occasion for each of her daughters. When they married, it was to be presented to the groom's family in her name, to show his family this bride should be respected.

Since neither of Aggie's *palagi* husbands would have appreciated the significance of that mat, she had kept it under her mattress as a tie to her mother and her Samoan heritage. Now she realized that, while she had never married a great chief, she had indeed loved one. His funeral would be the proper occasion to present it to his family and so dignify the relationship. She rolled back her mattress and looked at it. Mats as old and fine as this were seldom seen these days. She lifted it to her cheek. It felt soft and smooth, like her mother's kiss. She dressed herself in stunning black and took a cab to Tuaefu, the fringe of Pele's fine mat drooping softly across her lap.

At the bottom of the hill below the mansion, she got out. Holding the mat under her arm, she walked proudly up the drive. After years of silence, the terraces were again alive with people. Heads turned sharply as she passed. Aggie was the one person in town no one expected to see at this occasion.

She crossed the stately portico and stood for a moment at the open door to get her bearings. She could see Olaf's body lying on a pile of mats at the far end of the room, his head towards the center. Near him sat the chief in charge of receiving fine-mat donations. After acknowledging the presentation, he passed the mats to some women in the corner, who duly noted the gifts in a book and laid them on a large pile. Around the side walls of the room sat the elite of Olaf's two worlds, grieving together.

Kneeling at the right side of the bier, Rosabel, dressed in black, was fanning the face of the deceased. From this position, she was the first person in the room to catch sight of Aggie at the door. Other eyes followed and mouths dropped open. What connection would she claim? She was not related by blood, marriage, political, or economic connection.

When she had everyone's full attention, Aggie seated herself with dignity on the floor and slowly opened her mat with the traditional greeting, "*Toulouna a le lagi* (greetings to this chiefly funeral)," followed by appropriate references to the titles of the dignitaries present. She ended her presentation with a simple reference to her own connection. "I have come to bid farewell to my dearest friend."

248

She rose and, lifting the corners of her mat high, walked slowly around the circle, sweeping its fringe lightly over the heads of the guests. A few women were too surprised to move, but the chiefs murmured as they always did when they saw a really good mat, *"Sa o faalale lei"* (how beautiful!). She had made her point. Olaf had belonged to her as truly as to any of them.

Bending down, she laid her mat before the chief in charge. He acknowledged it graciously and passed it to the girls behind. Aggie proceeded to the left of the bier to say goodby to Olaf. Leaning over, she kissed him full on the lips. The onlookers gasped, but Rosabel did not wince. Her eyes met Aggie's across the body just long enough to transmit a silent message. She understood what Aggie had done and the pain it had cost her. And she was grateful.

Not everyone had that much insight. As Aggie walked out the door, she could already hear sibilent whispers. "Did you see that?" "Right in front of his wife and children, too?" "The old man passed away in the nick of time; that woman was always after his money!"

Aggie's pride barely made it to the cab. Safely inside, she burst into tears. Their stings still hurt!

The whole thing was so unfair! As men made money, they automatically climbed Apia's ladder of respectability. With her it was just the opposite. The more successful she was, the more people gossiped. The doors of great homes were slammed by the wives of the very men who patronized her club. After Olaf's funeral, Aggie was more sensitive to hornet stings than ever. A woman with a bar was just too vulnerable. If she really wanted to gain respectability, she would have to choose a different business. Outright competition might not endear her to these merchants as much as pandering to their personal needs, but at least they would stop winking behind her back!

It was one thing to dream up an enterprise, but another to find the capital to give it birth. Banks did not lend to women, and Apia's gentlemen could hardly be expected to underwrite operations that might compete with their own. Aggie did not have a financial nest-egg of her own. How would she ever begin?

By 1944 the battles in the Solomons were over, and to the north of Samoa the islands of Micronesia were falling

249

to the Yanks one by one — the Marshalls in January, Saipan and Guam in July, Palau in September, and Leyte in October. By January, 1945, the front had moved west to Luzon, Iwo Jima, and Okinawa, too far away to use Samoa as a staging area. The Yanks now had closer islands from which to mount their final assault on Japan. Homesick GI's in Samoa were packing their gear, eager to get home — so eager, in fact, that they were abandoning much of their equipment.

The night they departed, Major Hunt and Dr. Beattie appraised Aggie of "a golden opportunity for someone who might like to start a taxi business." They gave the name of a sergeant anxious to sell two broken-down jeeps. "Don't ask him where they came from and don't offer him more than $35 each," they advised.

"Do the jeeps run?" Fred asked suspiciously.

"Who cares at that price?" Beattie retorted. "Can't you fix them? You can get any needed part at the transport dump in Pago."

Next morning, Aggie extracted $70 U.S. from her jar and walked a reluctant Fred over to the shed the American officers had described. A GI in a monkeysuit was asleep in front, with his back against a tree. Beside him were two derelict vehicles. No one else was in sight.

Aggie shook his arm and pointed to the jeeps. "How much?" she asked.

"$100 each," he mumbled, opening one eye.

"Forget it, Aggie," Fred broke in irritably as he lifted the hoods. "They wouldn't run anyway."

"Too bad!" she said slowly, peeking at the GI out of the corner of her eye, "I had only $35 anyway."

"They're yours, lady!" he cried suddenly, jumping up and holding out his hand. "I got better things to do than sit around here all day."

"That's certainly kind of you," she said, fingering the bills under his nose, "and I wish I could take you up on it, son. But unfortunately, if they don't run, I have no way to get them back to my place."

"All right, Aggie!" he sighed, recognizing defeat. "I'll drag them over to your place with my truck."

"I'll have a cold beer ready to drink to the deal," she smiled sweetly. "You've been so kind!"

Fred grumbled all afternoon about "those two pieces of junk you just bought," but he was already making a list of necessary parts, and the following evening she sailed for Pago with her money jar.

A few days later, she returned on a freighter with three more jeeps, as well as the parts. "Such a nice young man at the dump!" she told Fred. "When I bought the parts, he was so grateful he threw in three jeeps for good measure."

No one saw Fred for two weeks. Then he appeared with a fleet of five jeeps: one for a taxi, one for Aggie, one for himself, and two to sell. At this rate they would soon be able to take on Eugene Paul's Gold Star Transport, Ltd., with only an investment from Aggie's cookie jar. The gods must be on her side, Fred thought. He drove her personal vehicle proudly to the front door and honked its horn. "Hop in, Aggie! If you're going into the transport business, it's time you learned to drive."

If truth must be told, just the thought of sitting at the wheel terrified Aggie. She had had her ups and downs with that brick-making machine, and this jeep looked far more complicated. Fred showed her the starter, the brake, the clutch, and the gear shift, and demonstrated their use as he drove her across the bridge. At Apia Park he turned the car around and insisted she take the driver's seat. He perched anxiously beside her, his hand on the brake, and shouted instructions into her ear. That made her more nervous than ever. As they were about to pull up in front of the house, she suddenly applied the accelerator instead of the brake. Instinctively, Fred leaped for safety and Aggie and the jeep went bucking on down Beach Road alone.

From his Gold Star garage next to the fire station, Eugene Paul saw this apparition approaching and ran out to the road to watch. Just as Aggie reached him, she finally located the emergency brake and jolted to a halt.

"Good God, Aggie!" Eugene whistled through his teeth, "I thought for a moment you were going to kill me." She sat limply in the seat, unable to speak. He walked around the vehicle, examining it critically from every angle. Yes, it was just what he needed.

"How much do you want for this piece of junk, Aggie?" he asked casually, as he reached her side again. "I don't think it's safe enough for you to drive."

"Fred just fixed it up for me," she said crossly, "and it's not for sale."

"All right! All right!" he said walking around it again slowly to give her time to cool down. "But do you mind if I test it for you? Just a little spin is enough."

She slid over. That might be the easiest way to get it home. Eugene drove them out to Mulinuu, stopping now and then to test the brakes. The thing handled pretty well. Then he turned it around and drove back to his garage. Yes, it was in acceptable shape.

"I hope you found it safe," Aggie said with a touch of sarcasm as they came to a halt.

"Still a lot to be done," he replied, wondering what he should offer; "but I could probably fix it up." He suddenly lowered his voice, squinted his eye, and growled, "What would you take for it, Aggie?"

"$450 U.S.," she said, calmly looking away.

"What?" he shouted, his eyebrows leaping into his hairline. "That's highway robbery, Aggie! I can just imagine what *you* paid for it!"

"That's none of your business!" she retorted. "This is wartime and I'm just selling it to you as a favor. If you can't afford it, Eugene, please step out and let me go home!" She turned the key and shook the gear shift as if she intended to drive off.

"Don't, Aggie!" he cried in genuine alarm. When he followed this with a sigh and told her what a tough woman she was, she knew she had won. They walked to his office in silence and she watched carefully as he counted out $450.

"Thank you, sir," she said with exaggerated politeness as he handed her the money.

"Don't I deserve more than that?" he asked slyly, looking as if he expected a kiss as well.

"No," she said flatly, "a deal's a deal!" She turned on her heel and started walking down the street. She was going to enjoy her new business. It did not require flirting with the customers.

She decided to sell all five jeeps, the market was so good. A few weeks later she returned to Pago Pago for more. "Want some good tires, Aggie?" the officer asked as she was paying for the load. He had often visited her club.

"Sorry, Bob," she said. "Money's gone."

"Did I say anything about money?" he smiled. "Hop in my jeep, Aggie. I'll show you something."

He drove her to a corner of the wharf where a bulldozer was nudging a pile of tires into the ocean. Some of them looked almost new. "See, we're shoving them anyway. Take anything you want right now, before they're gone."

"Just tell that chap to stop the bulldozer!" she cried breathlessly, jumping out of the jeep. "I'll be back in a couple of minutes."

She ran to find the captain of the *Sulimoni*, which was sailing for Apia that night. "If you'll loan me your truck," she proposed, "I'll guarantee you a full hold."

At sailing time the crew was still tossing tires into the hold. "Two hundred! That's enough," the captain called. "Bolt the hatch."

"It's up to you to handle this thing with customs," he said, turning to Aggie. She nodded.

At three a.m. next morning, the *Sulimoni* pulled into the wharf at Apia. It was deserted. They waited half an hour before the customs officer arrived. With only five passengers aboard, he would have plenty of time to inspect cargo.

"Anything besides jeeps?" he asked Aggie, checking the manifest.

"I added some old tires at the last moment," she replied, wondering if she could handle the extra duty.

"How much did they cost?" he asked, his pencil poised.

"Nothing," she said truthfully. "Just navy discards."

He drew a line across the page and went home. She sent a boy to find Fred and sat down on the hatch like a mother hen. Fred finally arrived with a truck and some boys. By dawn the tires were neatly stacked along Aggie's back fence and her surplus business had a new line.

That evening, in the bar, the remaining Yanks gave three cheers for her newest endeavor, and she sat down to chat with a shy young chap who had just arrived from Tutuila. He told her that he was a war correspondent and his name was James Michener. Unfortunately, there wasn't much action to report from Samoa these days. He had heard that the best source of stories was her bar.

Aggie introduced him around, provided a few stories of her own, and invited him to come back any time. He hung around for a couple of weeks.

Not everyone approved of Aggie's new enterprise. Public opinion in Apia maintained that cars and tires were commodities better understood by men. Relaxing at the RSA (Returned Servicemen's Association) after a Chamber of Commerce meeting, several displaced members of the Gentlemen's Club discussed the matter.

"Aggie's lost her mind!"

"Used cars, my God! Did you ever see her drive?"

"But she's got a way with surplus officers that you and I could never match."

"Cheer up, boys! Yank surplus won't last forever. Before long, our Aggie will be back in the bar again!" They drank to that. But six months later they were still buying her jeeps, tires, and surplus parts. Her price was the best in town.

On one of her trips to Tutuila, Aggie found she had a competitor. An American salvage firm with political influence had sent down a representative, and he had priority on everything in sight. "Just cool it for a few days, Aggie," a friendly sergeant told her. "His contract requires that he get everything off the island within two weeks, and that ain't so easy. At the last moment he may be screamin' for you to give him a hand."

She walked down Centipede Row from the wharf to Goat Island, looking for the man in question, and stopped at a beach near the oil dock to examine a good-sized tug pulled up on some rails. She walked around it slowly, admiring its varnished wood and bright brass fittings. If she only had something like that, she could give Mac's old launch a run for its money! She could see it now. Fred would be engineer and she would handle the bookings. They would offer a price that would beat anyone in town and style as well.

Her daydreams were interrupted by an American who was not in uniform. He had also stopped to look at the tug. "Good day, sir," she said brightly to initiate conversation. "I wonder who owns this thing."

"Me!" he said gloomily, "and I just can't figure out how to get her off this beach. If the beach isn't cleared in three days, I lose my surplus contract."

"That's too bad!" she said sympathetically, "this doesn't look like an easy thing to move."

"It isn't," he sighed. "I thought I had the problem licked this morning. A Samoan kid came by and agreed to take it off my hands, but he hasn't come back."

"How much did you ask for it?" she asked innocently.

"I told him he could have it for a twelve-volt battery," the salvage man replied. "I need one of those badly to start my truck."

"A what?" she asked surprised.

"A twelve-volt battery," he repeated. "Some creep from Western Samoa came over a few weeks ago and bought every one they had! If I can't even start my truck, how in the hell do they think I can get my stuff out? Pardon my language, lady!"

"Well, I know someone who has a twelve-volt battery," Aggie volunteered sweetly, thinking of the load she had brought back to Fred last time. "Did you want some money too?"

"No money," he said. "It was part of a package deal and I can't get it back to the States anyway. Just tell your friend to bring me the battery and I'll give him the papers. But warn him he'll have to get it off this beach in three days or he'll have a suit on his hands."

On her way back to town, Aggie visualized herself on a varnished deck with Fred at the wheel, riding triumphantly into Apia Harbor. Brass fittings, no less! Wouldn't her gentlemen be surprised!

She ran into the little radio station near the wharf to send Fred a telegram. "Emergency!" she explained breathlessly to speed things along. The operator nodded sympathetically and tapped out: COME WITH PITA AND GASCOYNE BRING 12 VOLT BATTERY ON SULIMONI TONIGHT STOP DESPERATE. AGGIE
She must have a cardiac problem or something, the operator thought.

Next morning Aggie met Fred and the boys at the wharf in a jeep she had borrowed from the sergeant. "Don't ask any questions now, Fred," she said as he opened his mouth. "Just put that battery in the back and hop in. I have something to show you that could keep us in business even when the surplus is gone."

When they reached the beach, Fred didn't even notice the brass fittings. He headed straight for the rear of the tug and peeked inside. Aggie ran after him, anxious to hear his verdict.

"My Gawd, Aggie," he bawled, "this damn thing doesn't have an engine! If you think all it requires is a twelve-volt battery!" He couldn't even find words to describe her appalling ignorance.

"That's not what the battery's for," she said coldly. "That's what I'm using to buy the tug."

He stared at her incredulous. "You mean no money?"

"No money," she said. "All I had to promise was that you would get it out of here by day after tomorrow."

"No problem at all," he retorted sarcastically, "if you'll get me a bulldozer, a winch, a quarter-mile of cable, and a marine engine by this afternoon!"

"Fred grouses about every little thing," she thought sourly to herself as they drove the battery over to the salvage man. But she was in no position to argue with his requirements.

"Did you bring my battery?" the anxious American asked as soon as he saw her. "Well then, my dear, you and your friend here have got yourselves a real bargain. That tug's worth thousands. They only dragged her up there to fix a crack in the propeller shaft. Somebody backed her into the wharf or something. Otherwise she's good as new. Sure you can get her off by day after tomorrow?"

"No problem," Aggie said, reassuringly, "if you will loan us a bulldozer, a winch, and a piece of cable."

The American was about to remind her that they were not part of the bargain, when he recalled that his own contract was also at stake. He shrugged helplessly and led her out the back door to his dump. Everything imaginable was piled up helter skelter. "Help yourself to anything you can find," he said. "Just bring it back when you're finished."

Fred and the boys spent the rest of the afternoon extricating what they needed. Next morning they worked the cables under the tug, trying a variety of hitches until Fred was satisfied. Curious onlookers gathered, asking questions, but he refused to look up. "What a grouch!" they mumbled, but he didn't hear. The problem was too absorbing.

Late in the afternoon a captain appeared. "Time to get her movin,'" he said. Fred obediently climbed up on the seat of the bulldozer.

The operation was a bit complicated. It involved heading the bulldozer inland in order to pull the tug seaward. Gascoyne tested every hitch before he finally lowered his hand with a shout. Fred's bulldozer rammed forward; cables twanged, planks shrieked, the crowd roared, and the tug suddenly leaped backward into the sea in a shower of foam. The crowd cheered as it righted itself, and the captain ran forward to congratulate Fred. But he had disappeared. He hated crowds.

The captain congratulated Aggie instead. What was she going to do with it, now it was afloat? His question suddenly startled her. She had been so busy with the launching problem that she had not thought of the next step. She looked seaward. The tug was gently floating down the bay, no one aboard and no engine!

Jumping into the captain's jeep, she raced towards the wharf, where she found Fred talking with Steffany. He made them an offer, and in less than an hour the MV *Samoa* had the tug in tow and was heading for a small dock at Loaloa.

It took several days to fix the crack near the propeller shaft. That gave Aggie more time to look around. Here the dock area was cluttered with old barracks equipment. "Help yourself, ma'am," the sergeant said; "otherwise it'll just go to Davy Jones. Your tug will ride better with something inside, you know."

By the time the patch was finished, Aggie had the hold full of metal chairs, benches, beds, tables, and sea chests. She felt like Emma Coe, returning with her marble altar and the trappings of "paradise."

Again in tow by the MV *Samoa*, they started towards Apia. With all this metal furniture, they were riding pretty low in the water, but there was no danger of turning over. Off Aleipata, Fred noticed they were deeper than ever. Jumping down into the hold he found himself knee-deep in water. Unattached from its engine, the propeller shaft was working loose, and the crack was beginning to open again.

He shouted to Steffany to speed up the MV *Samoa* and grabbed a hand pump. He and the boys kept pumping all night, but the water still kept rising in the hold. Despite its best efforts, the MV *Samoa* kept going slower and slower.

As the sky began to brighten, the two overburdened boats finally dragged around Pilot Point. The water was now too deep for pumping and the tug was almost awash. Survival was up to the MV *Samoa*, straining every cylinder to reach the wharf before her burden went down. She failed. The tug settled with a final gurgle on the reef near the bones of the *Adler* and its passengers were offloaded ignominiously in a rowboat.

As the sun rose, firemen in the station across Beach Road rubbed their eyes in surprise. A little tug was cuddling up beside the rusty old warship!

"Maybe she spawned in the night," someone suggested. "You never know about those old warships." They set off in their whaleboat to investigate.

When they returned, they found Aggie watching them anxiously from the beach. "That tug out there is mine," she explained. "Could you please help? She's very important to me."

"Don't worry, Aggie," they reassured her. "Her bottom's intact. If Fred can patch the stern, we'll pump her out for you and she'll lift herself off on the next tide."

Members of the Gentlemen's Club noticed the newcomer a little later as they drove by towards their offices. "Whose tug is that?" they asked a busy fireman.

"Aggie's sir. She's got the papers."

The firemen were as good as their word. On the next tide the little tug lifted herself up enough so that the MV *Samoa* could nudge her over to the wharf. Half the town dropped by after work to take a closer look at Aggie's newest investment. "Look at those brass fittings!" they said. "She'd be posh to ride in."

When he had fixed a more permanent seal, Fred pulled the tug across the harbor with his "put-put" and moored it near the mouth of the Vaisigano, where they could watch it until he mastered the next problem—an engine.

"I'll have to run up those emergency sails of hers or they might mildew," Fred told Aggie one afternoon. "If it's clear tonight, they should be dry by morning." They stood side by side that evening watching their treasure bowing and dipping on the ripples in the sunset.

That night the wind rose. Next morning, rain whipped across Aggie's face as she opened her window to look out. She suddenly gasped and shouted for Fred. Powered by its sails, the tug had dragged its chain and was banging itself against the reef across the road. It looked as if it wanted to sail right in her front door!

"My Gawd!" Fred exclaimed when he saw what was happening. "We've got to get her off that reef bloody quick or she'll beat herself to matchsticks! Call a launch."

Steffany had gone. Aggie called every firm in town that had a craft—Mac's, Nelson's, Carruthers', Meredith's, and the rest down the line. But their responses were all alike: "Sorry, Aggie, it's out . . . under repair . . . crew's on leave." The message was quite clear. None of the gentlemen were going to raise a finger to help her.

"Those bastards!" Aggie wailed. "They want me back serving their drinks again!"

Some boys from Vaiala village waded out in the surf to try to hold the tug away from the rocks, but this did no good. All of them watched helplessly as the tug's sides cracked open. About noon, their best investment gave a final groan and sank before their eyes. Only the tip of her mast remained visible, just beyond the rocks, to mark her grave.

When the storm had passed, Fred went out in the "putt-putt" and dived for the brass fittings. Aggie polished them lovingly in remembrance of her dream. When she held them in the sun, they shone like gold. An Indian came by from Fiji and bought them up by the pound.

Chapter 21

Birth of a Nation and Aggie's Hotel

(1945-1962)

YANKEE DOLLARS had kept both Samoans and *afakasi* so busy during the war years that they had almost forgotten the question posed by the Mau. What was Samoa going to be after a century of contact with the West? A society of extended family groups struggling to elevate their titles up a hierarchy towards two great "crowns," or a nation of independent individuals trying to improve their standard of living?

The answer was not clear. Thanks to Western-type schools and jobs, almost every young Samoan was now suffering the cultural dilemmas once confined to *afakasi*. Some, like Olaf, tried to advance in both cultures at once — and ended in frustration. Others, like Aggie, pursued advancement in one but kept the other in reserve for times of crisis. Some oscillated erratically to make the most of every situation; others firmly proclaimed themselves one but secretly wept at losing the other. More and more went overseas to make their fortunes, but sent money back to cover their family obligations. Both communities favored independence for Western Samoa, but for different reasons.

Nelson's mantle as leader of the business community fell on Eugene Paul. As owner of Gold Star transport enterprise, he favored self-government because he believed local residents could handle public services more efficiently than newcomers from overseas. Expatriates were expensive, unversed in local culture, prone to manipulation, and unable to speak Samoan. He envisioned a few modest services like public works, police, and education, which would in no way interfere with private enterprise. *Afakasi* with business experience and two languages would be ideal for such jobs.

260

Nelson's mantle as spokesman for the Samoan community fell on the shoulders of two current *tamaaiga*, Malietoa Tanumafili II and Tamasese Meaole, who were serving as advisers *(fautua)* on the Legislative Council. The latter had been leader of the Mau and had married Nelson's daughter. Independence was the major commitment of his life because he considered it essential to the survival of Samoan culture.

Like Nelson, this Tamasese had been educated in Apia's Marist schools and apprenticed as an accountant on Beach Road. But wealth had never intrigued him. He spoke English as fluently as Samoan and read avidly about other countries emerging from colonialism. He had considerably more knowledge about the outside world than his titled predecessors. He was aware that the Samoan way of life, practiced by a hundred thousand souls in a world of five billion, was hardly in a good bargaining position. He was suspicious of "goodwill" in international relations. Stronger nations were not apt to do something for nothing. If they were not thinking of Samoa as potential colony, they were thinking of it as market or a military base, all equally threatening to its traditional culture.

If they hoped to maintain any independence at all, Samoan families would have to stop feuding about "crowns" and present a united front. Otherwise they would continue to self-destruct, trying to gain favors from every warship in the harbor. To avoid stirring up Samoa's traditional factions, Tamasese made no move towards acquiring *papa* titles. Independence was a better goal to unite his people.

Even before the end of the war, Tamasese urged the *Fono a Faipule* to make it clear that Samoa would expect more than "goodwill" from New Zealand this time. When the kiwi prime minister visited Samoa in 1944, the *faipule* presented him with a formal petition for self-government. He promised to discuss it with his cabinet, but there was no reply. On October 30, 1946, Samoa's current administrator, Colonel Voelcker, announced to the Legislative Council that he could finally let them see a draft of New Zealand's proposal to the Trusteeship Council about Samoa's future. "You will be happy to hear," he smiled, "that we are suggesting the status of Western Samoa be changed from a

Class C mandate to a trusteeship in training for eventual self-government."

Tamasese's face reddened with anger. Despite the Mau, the Atlantic Charter, and the Goodwill Mission, New Zealand still treated Samoans like children. This proposal had been drafted without consulting a single Samoan and submitted to an international body with no Samoan on it. How would New Zealanders feel if Great Britain dictated their future like that?

He was too good a politician, however, to burst directly into words. Instead, he requested a temporary adjournment of the Legislative Council to allow the *fautua* and local members to discuss the offer. They returned with a unanimous statement of dissatisfaction and a request that New Zealand submit an important topic like its future to a meeting of All Samoa.

Colonel Voelcker was shaken. He had been warned that, despite his quiet demeanor, this Tamasese was a potential troublemaker.

Wary of another Mau, however, New Zealand's minister of external affairs acceded to the request and even came to Samoa himself to explain the New Zealand proposal to "All Samoa." To satisfy everyone, that body was now defined as including representatives not only of the traditional districts, *tumua, pule,* and *tamaaiga,* but from modern electoral districts and the business community as well. Malietoa and Tamasese acted as its co-chairmen.

In the week of oratory that followed, Tamasese began to realize that his main problem was not New Zealand but the Samoan penchant for politics. Each faction had an opinion of its own and took such pride in maneuvering it to success that it was difficult to get agreement on anything at all. But they finally settled on two requests: immediate independence and unification of American and Western Samoa.

Since the proposals it received from New Zealand and Samoa were so different, the Trusteeship Council sent a mission to Samoa in June, 1947, to see what was going on. Its members were somewhat unnerved to be greeted by Samoans in Mau uniform and presented with a proposal for two heads of state, a house of "princes" and a house of chiefs. All for a country with the population of 120,000.

But the chiefs insisted that they needed it to incorporate all the dignitaries of the *faa Samoa*.

The Trusteeship Council eventually decreed a series of developmental tasks to be completed before Samoa could be given its independence.

1. Change the position of New Zealand administrator to "high commissioner," with less and less supervision from External Affairs.

2. Transform the administrator's Legislative Council into a Legislative Assembly by adding eleven representatives from the *Fono a Faipule*, and gradually increase its powers as it gained experience. An elected Leader of Government Business (a sort of prime-minister-in-trading) would eventually replace the high commissioner as chairman.

3. Provide bright young Samoans and *afakasi* with scholarships to New Zealand and bond them to return and serve in the Samoan public service.

4. Draft a constitution acceptable both to the Trusteeship Council and the Samoan people.

Progress along this route would be monitored by periodic inspection teams from the Trusteeship Council. At the end of a decade or so of the training, Samoa would presumably emerge as a reasonable facsimile of a parliamentary democracy, worthy of independence. Nothing could have been more intelligently designed, if that was what they really wanted to be.

Malietoa and Tamasese agreed that it was a better route to independence than fighting another Mau war. The *faa Samoa* had been able to take new shapes before. The people spent the next decade trying to explain chiefs and overseas officers to each other as they tried to accomplish these tasks. Collisions continued to occur, but visibility between the two worlds greatly improved.

"Just don't make waves," Tamasese advised the chiefs on the constitutional drafting committee. "Put in as much of the *faa Samoa* in this document as you can and leave the rest vague. After we are independent, we can change it anyway."

Economically Samoa was also doing well. There was no 'flu epidemic after World War II and copra and cocoa were bringing a good price. Samoans laid off at the airport were able to satisfy their new cravings for foreign goods by shipping cases of bananas on the fortnightly freighter, and Apia's merchants thrived.

Only wartime clubs and hotels languished. Now the Navy ships and planes had gone home, the only way to reach the islands was by freighter, a mode that did not appeal to many tourists. Only a handful of overseas officers wandered the lonely corridors of the aging Casino and huddled around a few tables in its cavernous dining hall. Even they expected to soon be displaced. To a general's former hostess, the prospect was very depressing. Mary bid a low figure when her management lease came up—and lost. Annie McFagan, of the original Gentlemen's Club, replaced her at the Casino.

Sadly, Mary packed her sheets, towels, and plates. She could think of nowhere to take them. Her departure was already two months' overdue when Aggie suggested, "Why not bring them over to my place, Mary, along with any of the bachelors over there who'd miss your cooking. I have only Fred and old McDonald here, so two bedrooms and both white cottages are free. Fix them up any way you like. I'm going to Tutuila for a couple of weeks' vacation."

That sounded great to Mary, who loved to "fix things up." She installed a few more beds, set four little dining tables on Aggie's back porch, trained two girls, and brought over her eight "boys" from the Casino. The result was not much more than a glorified boardinghouse, but for everyone's morale she called it a "hotel." Its personal and relaxed atmosphere would have fitted any tourist's dream of South Sea living, but unfortunately no one outside Samoa had ever heard of it and would have had trouble getting there even if they did. Her beds were never full. This "hotel" had no future.

When General Price wrote asking Mary to chaperone a nun to the States, she leaped at the chance. It would enable her to attend the wedding of her only daughter in Texas and look around for employment more challenging to her entrepreneurial talents. She sold her furniture, plates, linens, and five acres on the mountain to Aggie at a bargain price, and set off to seek her fortune. She was gone for ten years.

Aggie was philosophical about her sleepy little "hotel."

At least Apia's "gentlemen" had returned to her for their afternoon "happy hour." She served their drinks and chatted with them on her back porch just as she had in pre-war days.

The relaxed pace also gave her more time to go visiting. "Maybe it's memories of Toamua," she told Fred. "I enjoy village life. Hospitality isn't a business out there—it just comes naturally. Parties aren't planned; they happen on the spur of the moment whenever people get together." She illustrated her point from a recent experience when coming back from Tutuila.

The MV *Samoa* had experienced engine trouble and put into Aleipata for the night. Aggie, an elderly Samoan lady, and her buxom granddaughter of sixteen were the only women on board. The high chief of the village had invited them and Captain Steffany to spend the night at his *fale*. As usual, the other chiefs of the village came over to greet them.

After the flowery welcome speeches, Aggie, acting as orator for the visiting party, introduced Steffany as their "distinguished captain," the old woman as "wife of a great chief," and her granddaughter as their *taupou* (ceremonial maiden). The host and his village would be pleased to find they had such important guests. After everyone's dignity had been established, they celebrated the pleasure at meeting each other in a round of kava, and the host provided a feast worthy of such an occasion. The young people of the village were then called for an evening of entertainment.

GI's required a few beers to work themselves into the proper mood, but not the youth of Aleipata. They filed in quietly and sat down shoulder to shoulder on the floor. Suddenly they bent their heads in unison, and there was a moment of electric silence as they felt their togetherness. Then their leader suddenly leaped into the air with a yell. They responded with two sharp claps before his feet touched the ground and burst into song *fortissimo*. He encouraged them by prancing around making faces and soon had them under such perfect control that he could start and stop their song with a twitch of his body.

The excitement was catching. Two girls jumped up, bowed with open arms, and began to sway in the restrained and graceful motions of the *siva*. As if to mock them, two old crones rushed out from the audience, tossing their pendulous breasts and throwing themselves underfoot with lewd and ridiculous gestures. The onlookers rocked with laughter. A group of male jesters followed, re-enacting a thinly disguised version of the latest village scandal. Any venom that might have been lurking around the village dissolved in mirth.

A rhythmic clapping began, and as it speeded up Aggie could feel her heart beat faster. The antics were becoming more arousing. She couldn't help jumping up herself to join the dancers; the mood was on her. Soon everyone in the house was on his feet, swinging and swaying in unison. Even at midnight, Aggie's bar could not boast a bonding like this. In their enthusiasm, three young men swung themselves into the rafters, their *lavalavas* flying open in glorious abandon. Aggie felt as if she too were flying!

Suddenly an awful thought stopped her feet dead. My God! What had she done? In an excess of politeness, she had introduced the buxom granddaughter as *taupou* of the visiting party. No wonder the boys were swinging in the rafters! This was not a moral problem; it was a question of dignity. She had unwittingly exposed their party to a risk that was becoming ever more imminent. If one of those exuberant boys should manage to "capture" their *taupou* after the entertainment tonight, both the visitors and the host would be disgraced. Word would soon spread through the district that they had been unable to protect their maiden from the charmers of Aleipata!

The buxom girl in question would certainly be of no help in averting this problem. She was even now performing the final dance *(taualuga)* with a fine mat around her waist, with a playful smile upon her lips and limbs glistening with scented coconut oil. A plume of red feathers bounced joyously on her heavy hair, and garlands of flowers danced upon her breasts. She was transported with delight at her unprecedented popularity. The young men who were not in the rafters were rolling at her feet. Her grandmother would be of no assistance either. That old crone was nodding proudly. Who, after all, had attached those feathered plumes and anointed those shining limbs?

Steffany was down at the beach fixing the engine. It was up to Aggie to preserve the reputation of the *MV*

Samoa. She could think of only one possible ally, their host. He too would feel humiliated for not protecting his guests.

Aggie found him standing just outside the house, as apprehensive as herself, and they agreed on a plan of action. As soon as the young people left, he would hang a large tapa across one end of the *fale* to provide privacy for the three ladies. But he gave Aggie his walking stick and promised to remain awake and alert all night on the other side of the tapa. All she had to do was call.

As the three women prepared to lie down on their sleeping mats, Aggie instructed the girl to lie in the middle. Then she turned down the kerosene lamp to a glimmer, only too aware that they were separated from the moonlit night only by a string of coconut-frond blinds *(pola)* flapping loosely against the posts.

No sooner had her head touched the pillow than she heard stealthy movements on the pebbles outside. A beckoning hand on a smooth brown arm slipped between the *pola.* Aggie gave it a sharp crack with her walking stick. There was a surprised grunt of pain and the arm was abruptly withdrawn. A few moments later the blinds on the other side parted slightly and a bright eye peeked in. Aggie let out a sharp exclamation and the chief's voice responded promptly from beyond the tapa. The blind fell. Neither Aggie nor her host slept a wink that night, continually amazed at the persistence and ingenuity of the young men of Aleipata.

Next morning the *taupou* awoke refreshed and as virginal as the night before. Everyone else looked haggard. The young men who carried their bags to the boat were tired and out of sorts. But, at least, Aggie noted with satisfaction, they still treated the visiting party with respect.

"I don't need to tour the world like Mary," she confided to Fred. "There's excitement enough for me just between here and Aleipata."

Not all the excitement was traditional. In 1946, Air New Zealand introduced a flying-boat service between Fiji and Samoa. This amazing plane had pontoons instead of wheels. It splashed to rest on the waves off the old Yankee airstrip now lost in the weeds, and disgorged a few brave passengers into a rubber boat. These early visitors considered themselves adventurers rather than tourists. They expected to put up with hardships exploring remote parts of the world and were delighted to rest up for a few days at Aggie's sleepy little hotel.

Apia's cultural life revived. After ten years of silence, a weekly newspaper, the *Samoa Bulletin*, appeared on the streets again. It was half in English, half in Samoan, and boasted two things its predecessors never had—illustrations and serialized stories of sheiks and princesses. The high commissioner had copies distributed free to the villages, hoping to put them in touch with the town. Educational institutions grew into intermediate and high schools. The Marist Brothers' School on the Mulivai expanded its nine grades to twelve; the LMS opened an intermediate school for four hundred at Malua Fou; and the Mormons began a secondary program at Pesega. In 1953 the government opened its own secondary school, Samoa College. Educated youngsters would soon be needed for an independent country. There were economic developments, too. New stores blossomed along Vaea Road, thanks to the children of the former Chinese plantation workers. Morris Hedstrom became a department store to rival Burns Philps. Even public services improved. The wharf and Vaisigano Bridge were rebuilt, and a new hydroelectric plant at Fuluasou brightened Apia's flickering globes.

One afternoon in 1951, Aggie and Eugene Paul were chatting on her back porch. He had worried for years that Samoa would gain self-government at just about the time it lost its ability to support itself. New sources of income were growing far slower than the taste for foreign goods. But this particular afternoon he had good news.

"You'd better start restocking your craft shop, Aggie," he confided. "I hear Union Steamship is going to put more than a million pounds into refitting the old *Tofua* for passengers. Think of that! Seventy-three first-class visitors once a fortnight, looking for your souvenirs in my taxis!"

"I just wish you had news like that for my empty beds," Aggie sighed; "they'll still sleep aboard."

Two weeks later he did. "Aggie! There's a rumor that TEAL (Tasman Empire Airways, Ltd.) is considering a three-day package flight from Suva to Samoa, the Cooks, and Tahiti twice a week! They're going to call it the Coral Route. Tourists will take off in a Solent flying boat from Laucala Bay and land at the wharf near the airport. They'll spend the night and have supper and breakfast in Apia, then take off again. I've got the van. You've got the hotel. All we need is a TEAL contract!"

That really was good news! Aggie started counting her beds even before he finished speaking. A Solent would hold fifty people, counting its crew. Where would she put them all?

A few weeks later the whole Pacific seemed to be cracking open! Pan American applied for a flight from Hawaii to American Samoa. "American tourists will certainly want to come on over here!" Eugene exclaimed. "What is there to see in Pago Pago?"

"How many would be interested enough to risk eight hours of seasickness on the MV *Samoa?*" Aggie asked.

"That's where we come in," he laughed. "Let's start an inter-island airplane of our own!"

He didn't have to tip off Aggie twice. The day he described the anticipated Coral Route, she went straight to TEAL and signed a contract for housing and feeding half their passengers. Even twenty-five guests would require considerable expansion.

Fortunately, the Coral Route was slow in starting. A couple of months later, Aggie came into Fred's workshop to inspect his eighth bed. "Where would you put twenty-five beds even if you had them?" he asked. "Out on the sidewalk?"

"Don't be nasty, Fred," she said. "It's easy. We'll divide the cottages and each of the four bedrooms upstairs into two, and make two new rooms downstairs where the bar used to be. You can count on at least some of them wanting to sleep together."

"But one of those upstairs bedrooms is mine!" Fred protested. "You can't have mine!"

"I know you better than you know yourself, my dear," she responded affectionately. "You couldn't sleep a wink up there with all those noisy tourists. I'm thinking of a nice quiet little room for you down under the kitchen, where you won't be disturbed.

He appreciated her concern and undertook the job of building cubicles with louvred partitions and swinging doors. This solution allowed plenty of air and sociability as well. A guest could chat with his neighbor without leaving his bed. Bathroom facilities also retained a South Sea touch—a wooden tank on the wall flushed by a long chain, a cold-water shower from directly overhead, and a sink with a single tap, which coughed up tiny shrimps in tea-colored water when it rained.

Fred widened the left side of the back porch to hold more dining tables, and Aggie hung ferns around the eaves. It was a charming place to eat on sunny days. But the same could not be said in a downpour. Waiters had to run from the kitchen across a flooding backyard with food on an open tray. Aggie solved this problem by hiring King King, the Chinese carpenter, to build a covered bridge from the kitchen above the caretaker's cottage over to the porch. Painted white, the sunny passageway proved to be a perfect place to ripen bananas.

A bar and a few boarders had kept them busy enough before; but the logistics of satisfying twenty-five luxury-loving tourists boggled her imagination. Fred might be a genius at mechanics, but handling reservations, counting linens, planning meals, keeping accounts, and buying supplies were not his thing. Aggie herself preferred the role of hostess. What they needed now was a business manager who could quietly take care of all those details. Pele Jr. was no longer available. She had married and settled in New Zealand.

Allan had just completed secondary school and matriculated at the university. In 1951 he returned home for Christmas. Aggie was overjoyed to see him. He was sixteen now, but looked so young as he stepped out of the airport van that an elderly guest mistook him for a bellboy and sent him upstairs with the luggage. Allan quietly obliged and Aggie burst out laughing. He was still as serious as the seven-year-old who had once collected empty bottles in his little red wagon.

By the end of Allan's six week vacation, Aggie wondered how she could manage without him. He had developed an accounting procedure, established a paging system, and organized a storeroom with an inventory. She

270

couldn't figure out where he had learned to do such things. Allan had also discovered that he liked this kind of work. If hotel-keeping were to be his future, what better place to learn? They did not teach such things at the university. He offered to stay, but Aggie would not hear of it, insisting that she wanted a university graduate in the family. On the morning of his departure, she kept her dismay well in check. It was Allan who broke down. "Please, mum, please let me stay! I feel so homesick every time I go back."

Aggie threw her arms around his neck and burst into tears. That was permission enough. He promptly took his bags back to his room and unpacked.

From that moment on, Allan, Aggie, and Fred were an inseparable team. It was not that they always agreed— they were always arguing. It was simply that they couldn't get along without each other. "How did you ever come by a son like that?" Maggie was to ask enviously. "I wish he was mine."

Aggie's cubicles were, however, still waiting for Coral Route passengers six months later. The hotel might have died at birth except for an unexpected event. In March, 1952, the *Samoa Bulletin* announced that Gary Cooper and Roberta Haines had selected Western Samoa for their first overseas film, "Return to Paradise," based on a story by James Michener. The film director and leading lady were to arrive in May and Gary Cooper in July. The other actors would be recruited locally. Auditions would take place at the Tivoli movie house.

By the time Gary Cooper arrived, Samoa's most beautiful village, Lefaga, had been selected as the setting; Beach Road's prettiest adolescent, Moira MacDonald, had been chosen as his daughter; and every one of Aggie's twenty-five beds was occupied. She could have filled twice as many. Allan was managing accommodations and meals; Aggie was rehearsing a local dance team and teaching Roberta Haines to *siva*. Fred went out to Lefaga to help install a twelve-ton generator and erect a mess hall, shower, office, and sheds. Movie people were even more generous than GI's, Apia discovered. So much money was suddenly running around that the cost of living rose 11.5%.[1]

When everything was ready, the *Maria Ines* steamed

into Apia with 120 tons of camera equipment. The beach at Lefaga was soon littered with cables, arc lights, cameras, and reflectors. Sound men caught Gary Cooper's every breath in microphones mounted on long poles; cameramen recorded his every motion with lenses on wheels. The confusion came to a climax on September 12, when eighty dugout canoes rushed out to sea in a fake rainstorm to "rescue" the crew of a flaming plane that had just "crashed" in Lefaga Bay. Samoa could talk of nothing else.

Then the make-believe vanished even faster than it had appeared. By September 27, Roberta, the cameras, the technicians, the money, and the great man himself had gone. All that remained was Gary Cooper's shack, standing in Aggie's garden. He had given it to her, saying it might hold two more customers; but her cubicles were empty again. "Don't worry, mum," Allan reassured her. "As soon as Americans see Moira dancing on Lefaga beach in a sarong, they'll come pounding on our door."

As it turned out, they didn't have to wait for her movie fans. In October, the long-awaited TEAL flights began. Eugene Paul flew to Suva and came back with the first load of VIPs. The four-engine Solent swooped down gracefully onto the wavelets in a plume of foam; and these harbingers of mass wanderlust transferred from the launch into Paul's limousine for a welcoming party at Aggie's. Samoa's tourist industry had begun!

Four weeks later, Aggie's newest guests got up one morning and stared out to sea in amazement. The harbor had gone dry and the skeleton of the *Adler* lay rusting in the sun. Gleeful children ran around the reef to pick up stranded shellfish and baby sharks.

Aggie had seen that kind of thing before. She raced to the sea wall, waving her arms at the children and shouting, "Come back! Come back!"

Just as they scrambled back up the bank, a huge tidal wave surged into the harbor. It crashed against the sea wall, flooded across Beach Road, tore back up the Vaisigano, and swirled around into Aggie's backyard. Her house girls dashed out of their room below the kitchen. The posts of Gary Cooper's house trembled, and frightened tourists waded in from the two white cottages in the garden.

"Good thing old Paulo put stilts under those little

houses," Aggie observed as she directed rescue operations from the porch. "And think what dinner would be like tonight if we hadn't built that passageway! Everytime something happens to the Vaisigano, we end up with a lake in our backyard."

She turned and looked towards the chemist shop. It still stood high and dry. "You know, Fred," she said, "maybe we should fill in the whole backyard. I remember how Dad did it. He dug holes four feet deep and dumped rocks in them to make a foundation." Fred shook his head emphatically. That was asking too much.

Weakened by the flood, Gary Cooper's shack blew down the following year. Aggie was determined to replace it with something equally magnetizing to tourists. What better than a swimming pool? Fred and Allan pointed out that there was a beach right across the road but could not dissuade her.

"You just don't understand," she said, thinking of her beloved pool at the house on the hill. "There's something about a pool that makes people feel they have 'arrived.' They like to write their friends they are 'sitting at poolside' even if they wouldn't be caught dead inside one. Now Gary Cooper's shack is gone, we need something to make our guests feel we are special. The Casino doesn't have a pool."

"They're a pain in the ass to clean!" Fred groused. "The only thing that can be said for a pool is that it won't blow down." He built her one anyway.

Fred's creation was hardly Olympian in size, but it was sturdy. Because of the high water-table in the backyard, the pool's thick concrete walls rose four feet above the garden to allow a six-foot plunge at the deep end. Aggie held a christening party the day it was filled. The whole TEAL crew jumped in and declared it "smashing."

Next morning, Aggie rose early to take a quiet dip herself. The garden sparkled with dew in the speckled sunlight. She climbed the wall to dive in and stopped dead in surprise. No water! Just a few dry leaves blowing across the bottom. For a moment she thought she was dreaming; then she shouted for Fred. He rushed out and peered over the edge.

"I'll be damned!" he declared, jumping inside to examine the drain. It had collapsed downward, and the floor was hopelessly cracked. "This ground is too porous to hold a pool, Aggie. You'll just have to give up the whole idea."

"I won't give up on something my guests consider 'smashing'," she retorted, marching off across the grass. "I'll think of something."

Fred looked after her, shaking his head. What a stubborn woman! Disasters never phased her; they only roused her dander. What in the world was she after, anyway? Not money for herself — she actually had rather frugal habits. Not men — God knew how many had offered to make her happy. Maybe she was just trying to prove something to the "hornets" who were still buzzing.

In 1954, Eugene felt that the time for Samoa to start its own airline had arrived. Air New Zealand was proposing to restore part of the old Yank airport and connect Samoa to the big cross-Pacific routes. Why shouldn't a small local plane take care of the lesser hops?

"I've got my eyes on Savaii, Tonga, and the Cooks," he told Aggie, "and especially American Samoa. Those Yank tourists are still dying to get over here." She could see a really big future in that scheme, and became a charter investor in Western Samoa's Polynesian Airlines.

But it would mean more beds. "One more cubicle," Fred declared, "and no one will be able to open his door."

"Who said anything about cubicles?" Aggie asked. "I'm thinking of another cluster of white cottages in the garden around a swimming pool."

"I told you pools were out," Fred said flatly. "But the guests could swim in for meals whenever their cottages flood."

"That's why we've got to hire someone to do the fill I was talking about," she smiled sweetly.

Allan designed three cinderblock cottages, but warned her that such improvements could never be financed from her cookie jar. They would have to get a loan. Jackson, the solicitor, told them that the bank would be interested only if they were incorporated.

Giving birth to a corporation was more complicated than any of them had dreamed. But the following year, a tiny new corporate entity was added to the roster on Beach Road. Its full name was "Aggie Grey Hotel, Ltd." but of course everyone called it "Aggie's."

The Bank of New Zealand honored the event with a loan of £25,000 and Aggie's team put that right to use. By 1955, three cinderblock cottages boasting six modern hotel rooms stood high and dry in Aggie's side yard, around a brand-new swimming pool. Each had a carved "tiki" at its door to welcome guests.

Unfortunately, the six *tiki* waited for Polynesian Airlines passengers until 1959. The tiny new airline had become tangled in an international intrigue worthy of the era of the three consuls.[2] While Polynesian was still shopping for a plane, a DC3 suddenly set down on a new airport with passengers from Pago Pago. American Samoa had beat them to it, with an airline of its own. New Zealand stood loyally behind Polynesian by refusing to give this American upstart a regular landing permit until Polynesian could get into the air. But the dispute took two years while Aggie's investment languished. She tried to calm her nerves by taking a vacation in New Zealand. Allan was twenty-two now and perfectly capable of running the hotel in her absence. He was not a "wild one." No girl had ever captured his imagination.

"Just keep it that way, son," Aggie said as she kissed him goodby. "Promise you won't get married until you're twenty-five, anyway, and know what you want." He laughed and they shook hands on it. Well, she wouldn't have to worry about Allan while she was gone.

In Auckland three months later Aggie suddenly received a telegram from him: MUM PLEASE LET ME OFF THAT PROMISE AND CATCH THE NEXT PLANE HOME FOR MY WEDDING. Now, who in the world had managed to do that? Aggie flew home next day to find out.

Marina Thompson was eighteen, the daughter of a Danish father and a Tokelauan mother. Her fair skin, blue eyes, and fine features made it hard to believe that she had been born and raised in Samoa. Like Allan she was a quiet, gentle person. At the wedding Aggie wondered how this shy and beautiful creature would ever get along in the hurlyburly of a tourist hotel.

For the next two years, Marina reminded Aggie of a porcelain doll, calmly watching the rest of them race and roar through the day. But apparently that was just her way of learning. As soon as Marina felt she knew what was going on, she got up and joined the rest of them as competently and energetically as if she had been doing it all her life. Aggie now had four strong members on her team. Her new daughter-in-law even showed a streak of enterprise. She tore down the wall between the grocery and craft shop and set up a dress shop, featuring soft scarves, notions, and hand-painted Samoan dresses *(puletasi)* laced with coconut rings. Though she was not partial to belly-laugh stories like her mother-in-law, Marina loved to entertain. She proposed a buffet night once a week and trained dancers for the show. Surprisingly enough, she could soon be as tough as any of them when it came to collecting bills and counting linens.

In 1957, Polynesian finally got its long-awaited Percival Prince plane from Australia. New Zealand released the promised permit for American Samoa's DC3 and both airlines scrambled for the skies. But not for long. There was barely enough traffic for one airline. Washington evened the old score by denying the Percival Prince to land in Tutuila. Polynesian investors watched in despair as the American Samoa's DC3 made daily flights. Bankruptcy seemed imminent.

At the last moment, chance intervened. The DC3 was damaged and the Percival Prince soared into the breach. By the time the DC3 could be repaired, its one-year New Zealand landing permit had run out, and a new one just never did arrive. American Samoa's line expired instead.

Aggie was now so busy with hotels and airlines that local hornets found little to buzz about for several years. Gossip might have died of starvation except for the arrival of a freelance writer named Willard Price, who was scouring the world for "adventures." What he could not find in fact, he invented and clothed in breathless prose. He had already published one book on the South Seas which climaxed in a giant squid hunt. Now he was writing a sequel.[3]

Aggie assigned him an upstairs cubicle which might well have proved an adventure in itself. But he insisted on Pele's garden and at a cut rate. "I need peace and quiet and a place to cook my meals," he insisted.

Aggie explained that the cottage had already been booked by a honeymoon couple who also wanted peace and were willing to pay the full price for it. That made the writer angry. This woman obviously had no feeling for the arts! But he could not change her mind.

A few months later, he rewarded her via a prominent American newspaper. In a nine-inch column edged in eye-catching black, he suggested that Aggie had been James Michener's prototype for Bloody Mary in his Pulitzer-Prize book *Tales of the South Pacific*. Price's theory was beautifully timed. The book had just been made into a musical film, "South Pacific," which was about to be released all over the world.

Never having read Michener's story, Aggie was at first irritated only at having her name associated with the taboo word "bloody." But when Allan explained Bloody Mary's role in the plot, Aggie was inconsolable. This was the worst sting a hornet had ever given her. In the case of the Happy Hour, the attorney general had at least listened to her side. Unfortunately for Aggie, the movie was a sensation and no one who had ever been to Samoa could resist passing along "inside information" about "good old Aggie" with a knowing wink. It brought out the hornet in everyone. Guests she had never laid eyes on began greeting her with glowing eyes and the information that they had come "half-way around the world to meet the *real* Bloody Mary!"

Allan assured her it was doing wonders for business. How else could they have obtained free, worldwide advertising? But to Aggie it was a personal disaster. This was one time she could not laugh off the ignominy. In distress she wrote to Michener to ask who Bloody Mary really was. He replied that the charming madam of his book was a figment of his imagination, a fictional compilation of various "Marys" he had encountered in his wartime travels. But Aggie's hornets preferred Price's version.

To take her mind off the topic, Allan suggested that she expand her craft business. Aggie enjoyed tortoise-shell jewelry inlaid with silver, delicate strands of seeds, pert little baskets, and feathered fans. Touching them relaxed her, and they didn't pass rumors. She examined closely each new piece a villager brought in, turning it over and over. If it struck her fancy, she stroked it like a baby, took it to her room for safekeeping, and appeared wearing it next day. "Women! Women!" Fred used to say, but he was the same with his own tools.

Aggie needed help finding overseas markets. When Fred went to Christchurch for dental work, she tucked some pretty baskets in his bag and asked him to see if he could find a buyer. On his return he told her that an elderly wholesaler had offered to take as many as she could send for sixpence each.

"What?" she exclaimed. "It takes a woman days to find and dry pandanus and weave one of these." Instead of turning the buyer down, however, she asked the weavers to add a strong handle, woven around the bottom. She sent the new improved basket with a note: "As you can see, sir, these are not ordinary baskets. Their handles do not pull out. I know what they would sell for in New Zealand and you can well afford to pay my price, which is two shillings each when I deliver them at the Apia Post Office." He sent an order by return mail and they did business for years.

Tapa cloth was a popular item overseas, but it posed a different problem. Village women usually came in with pieces that were shabby and torn. They kept their good ones for family ceremonies. Aggie soon had a pile that wouldn't sell.

When her friend Mary Pritchard, queen of Samoa's tapa makers, dropped by from Tutuila, Aggie asked her how to clean, patch, and repaint the bark cloth. Mary gave her and the girls a demonstration, and even took them into the bush to look for natural dyes: the red *loa* berry, the brown *'o'a*, and black *'ele* clay. She tapped another tree for a clear sap. "Never buy dyes from the stores," she said. "They fade."

Next day she set up her tracing board in Aggie's garden and showed them how to paint the repaired tapa pieces. When varnished with the clear sap, they were unusually bright and shiny. One of the girls enjoyed tapa restoring so much that she decided to work on it full time. Both she and Aggie made money.

But even her prospering craft business failed to keep Aggie's mind off Bloody Mary. She couldn't sleep at night, and Allan feared she might have a nervous breakdown. "Why don't you take a vacation? Go to the States this time," he urged. "You've never been there. By the time you

278

get back, you'll be able to laugh at the whole thing."

Unfortunately, the first American to greet Aggie on the dock in San Francisco was a reporter. "Aggie!" he cried, thrusting a mike in her face. "We have heard so much about you! Tell us how it feels to be Bloody Mary!"

She had certainly come to the wrong place! She felt not only angry but homesick. She cut her vacation short and bought a ticket home on an Australian cruise ship, the *Oronsay*.

As soon as she stepped aboard that liner, she began to feel better. Ships were so romantic! The deck chairs reminded her of the delirious week with Charlie when she was fleeing the lecherous banker. She sank into the nearest one and hid herself in a blanket. Maybe someone else would come along.

When Aggie peeked out, however, her eye fell, not on a man, but on a small woman huddled miserably in the next chair. She looked as if she had been crying. "What's wrong?" Aggie asked, concerned, and found that her neighbor was seasick. She had been assigned to a hot little cubicle down in the hold and was afraid she would never survive the trip.

Aggie remembered the hold of the *Talune* and offered the steward a five-pound-note if he would let her friend sleep on the couch in her own large, airy cabin, which opened right onto the deck.

From that moment on Aggie and Flo were inseparable. That evening two shipboard "bachelors" asked if they might join them at table. Flo was a little flustered, but Aggie immediately asked them to sit down. In a few moments the four of them were laughing like old chums. With those bachelors for company, every day was a romp and every night a ball. Well after midnight, Flo and Aggie would sit on Aggie's couch reliving their adventures. They tucked their toes under them and giggled like schoolgirls. The effect on both of them was wonderful. Flo came out of her shell and Aggie was exuberant. It was years since she had had such fun.

The climax of the voyage was a "Shipwreck Ball" and dance contest. "Go on up, Aggie!" Flo and the bachelors urged. "The honor of our table is at stake!"

When she tried to demur, they plied her with whiskey

until she admitted that she had been dying to dance all along. She trotted up to the stage, a red hibiscus bobbing over her left ear. In her bright *puletasi*, with a garland of flowers around her neck and a tiny basket in her hand, she looked like a Polynesian poster. Without even asking, the band struck up "Isa Lei."[2]

"Faster! Faster!" she whispered to them, tapping her foot and snapping her fingers until they caught the beat. Then she launched herself on the waves of sound. Suddenly she was back in the *fale* at Aleipata. As the music speeded, so did her heart and her feet. The audience tapped and clapped and whistled. She felt as if she were flying through the rafters!

As the last note faded, she spread her arms to the audience and dropped in a low bow. Then she ran back to her table half-laughing, half-crying. The crowd cheered again and again but she refused to return.

At midnight the ship's captain appeared on the stage waving an envelope, and the passengers fell silent, listening for the winner. He called Aggie forward, but when she arrived beside him he held the envelope teasingly over her head. "Aggie, you have won the prize, but you can't have it until you pay your penalty."

"Penalty?" she asked, surprised.

"You have to dance again," he laughed, "because I wasn't here to see you the first time.

The band struck up "Isa Lei" once more, and she sailed off like a bird. Her reward was not only the envelope but a kiss from the captain.

It wasn't a big prize, only £2/10/0 Australian. She used it to buy something from the ship's store that had been attracting her, a curious little cork that played a few notes of "Isa Lei" when she tipped its bottle and got it wet. It reminded her of something important she had learned on this trip. Why waste time on Bloody Mary? It was too much fun being Aggie.

While Aggie and her team were trying to prod their unique little hotel to its feet and coordinate its shaky parts, Tamasese and his mentors were trying to do the same with the government of their unusual islands. Nothing ever turned out quite as expected, and the process required persistence, imagination, and considerable faith.

Samoa's training for independence reached a climax with the drafting of its new constitution. Was it possible to design anything that would be acceptable to the British, the Trusteeship Council, and Samoan sensibilities? Even if such a government could be designed, would it work?

Two conventions of "All-Samoa" and some very tense compromises resulted in a parliamentary democracy unlike any other on earth. Two *tamaaiga* were designated joint heads of state. The third settled for prime minister. Only chiefs could vote, and members of parliament could be elected either by traditional consensus or modern secret ballot. Since no one could decide how to incorporate the *pule* and *tumua* without outranking everyone else, they were left out for the time being.

The Trusteeship Council was so leery of chiefly suffrage that it insisted on a universal plebisicte to see if untitled family members really wanted to disenfranchise themselves. On May 9, 1960, for the first time in Samoan history, all adults—not just titleholders—were invited to the polls to indicate whether they wanted this constitution. Of these 83% voted yes.

At midnight on January 1, 1962, Western Samoa became the first fully independent Polynesian nation in modern times.[2] Every church in the islands rang its bell or pounded its log drum for joy. Colonial administrators were going home. Samoa's own chiefs would be at the helm again!

In a special mass at the Catholic Cathedral, Tamasese gave a prayer of gratitude. His brother's blood had not been spilled in vain. After sixty-two years, his people were free again!

Aggie gave an independence party. What a relief! No longer would she have to worry about who was Mau or Malo, and tiptoe around political discussions at parties. Both communities had united behind this new creation. After this, she no longer identified herself as an *afakasi;* she told her guests with pride, "I am a Samoan."

Up at Vailima, New Zealand's high commissioner, Sir Guy Powles, congratulated his expatriate officers. He had encouraged and shepherded this progress every step of the way. After forty-eight painful years, New Zealand was free of this burden!

Chapter 22

Development

(1963-1970)

THE NEW ship of state took off under full sail with Samoans at the helm. Now, in addition to traditional and church hierarchies, it had a full set of government rankings as well, from messengers and filing clerks to cabinet members and heads of state. Its more energetic citizens held positions in all three hierarchies at once. The new island nation was better designed than ever for people who liked a feeling of status.

But how about those who preferred wealth to rank? This particular aspiration was no longer confined to the merchants on Beach Road. Many young Samoans also liked to hear a jingle in their pockets when they came to town, something they could spend for themselves.

United Nations experts were concerned about keeping the new government solvent. With so many dignitaries on board, would there be any money left for roads, schools, and hospitals? Fewer Samoans settled for subsistence these days. Commercial life would have to be developed.

Almost every country on earth sent some form of economic assistance: Dutch ferry, German brewery, New Zealand hospital, Japanese fishery, Danish furniture designers, Australian engineers, and Chinese acrobats. The United States dispatched its Peace Corps. Only one prediction could be made when grafting their western technologies onto Samoan institutions—nothing would turn out as planned.

One afternoon a friendly young Peace Corpsman appeared at the grocery counter in Aggie's store. How different these young Americans were from their GI fathers, Aggie thought as she greeted him—no tanks, no rifles, no money. He wore a *lavalava* instead of a uniform and spoke passable Samoan. What had happened to the Yanks?

"Do you carry chicken feed?" he asked politely.

"Chicken feed!" Aggie exclaimed. "I thought Americans ate hamburgers!"

He shook his head and told her his story. He was living with the pastor's family in Papa Village at the far end of Savaii. He loved the place and was determined to help it prosper. Development required considerable ingenuity, however, because the Peace Corps had dropped him off there with nothing but his backpack and a feeling of goodwill. Two days later he found himself dreaming of a tender piece of crunchy Kentucky fried chicken. These village chickens must have survived a trip on the first sailing canoe. They were a tough and scrawny lot, scratching around in the sand for a livelihood and laying clutches of tiny eggs in the forest like wild birds.

To demonstrate a "real" chicken, he went to Apia and traded his transistor radio for a pair of genuine Rhode Island Reds. Returning to Papa, he built a coop for them beside the pastor's house. Everyone in Papa was impressed with their eggs—so big! so brown! so often! Following instructions in a Peace Corps manual, he hatched them in a box hung with strips of cloth.

By the end of his first two-year tour, his chicken project was feeding the family. He was now selling eggs and buying commercial feed instead of scraping coconuts, and was about to make a profit. Since that was not allowed in the Peace Corps, he gave the project to the pastor's wife before he went home on leave.

"Eat the old hens," he told her, "but keep the layers and sell their eggs. If you always save enough to buy the next bag of feed, you'll find yourself getting rich like Europeans." She was grateful indeed to know the secret of their success.

When he returned from the States for his second tour of duty, he was delighted to find that she was doing well. The family had baked chicken twice a week; her eggs were in demand; and she had purchased another bag of feed. There was only one problem. She was feeling very unpopular. Asking for money in return for her eggs was damaging to her reputation as a pastor's wife. Surprised that her eggs were not offered to them as a gift, her neighbors whispered sneeringly, *"Fia palagi"* (aping a European), which was tantamount to being called a selfish bitch. She did not feel like a Samoan anymore, and wanted to quit the world of business.

The young American pondered this anomaly. The Peace Corps had enjoined him to maintain local custom, but it had also assigned him to economic development. Suddenly a solution occurred to him. Why not give the chicken project to the village Women's Committee? No one would feel selfish if they all owned the enterprise. He was so thrilled at discovering the key to Samoan development that he offered to pay for their first bag of feed from his own allowance.

"That's why I'm here looking for chicken feed," he smiled ingenuously at Aggie. "And I sure hope you've got some. The other stores are out."

She could have kissed him. He was so young — so eager, as much in love with his village as Willie had been with Pele. Why did Samoans and *palagi* fascinate each other so much? She only hoped this new romance would not end in pain. She sold him the feed.

A week later, she ran across the young man again, not in the grocery but in the bar, drinking up the last of his allowance. She went over and sat down beside him. "Hello, son. How's the Papa chicken project?"

He did not look up. He did not even smile. "I'm quittin' the Peace Corps!" he mumbled to his glass.

"But why?" she asked. "Didn't you just sign up again?"

After another drink, he explained that when he returned to Papa last week with his bag of feed, he had discovered a community celebration in progress. The Women's Committee was giving the village a feast in honor of its new chicken project. Every one of his Rhode Island Reds was baking in the oven!

Economic development was more apt to happen in Apia. The 1964 Parliament approved a project to deepen its harbor and build a new wharf at Pilot Point so that freighters could unload directly on the dock. Dredgings were to be used to add sixteen acres to the town by filling the shallow reef across Beach Road and give the bones of the old *Adler* a decent burial. Undertakings of this sort were beyond the local treasury. Most of the money had to be borrowed from overseas, although local merchants did their bit by subscribing to a £25,000 National Development Loan. Many considered it a patriotic but risky investment. The wharf could end up as an anvil around their necks if local agricultural production did not increase enough to keep it busy.

With a foreign debt to repay, development was no longer optional. Parliament hired Andy Gerakas, an expert from Hawaii, on small business, to organize an Economic Development Department and propose a five-year plan for increasing production.

Aggie's team generated its own development plans. Every step involved landfill. As their first increment, they envisioned a row of motel rooms running from the kitchen into the coconut grove.

Work on the new wing slowed down briefly when Marina produced a blond, blue-eyed baby. Without a moment of hesitation, she named the little girl Aggie Jr. A few months later, the baby had trouble with her formula. She became listless and looked at her grandmother with solemn eyes that reminded Aggie of Ian, the baby she had lost so long ago. She insisted that Allan and Marina take her namesake to New Zealand immediately for medical care.

"You know what we should do while they're gone?" Aggie asked Fred a few days later, as they were sitting in the store. "This place has been a chemist shop, a hamburger stand, a craft shop, and now a grocery and dress shop, but we could do even more. How about a second-story apartment? I could live up there to watch over things and free my present room for guests."

"That's a great idea, Aggie," he replied. "Let's suggest it to Allan as soon as he gets back."

"Nonsense!" Aggie retorted. "I was building houses before he was born. I'll do it myself and surprise him."

Second-story construction proved to be an even greater surprise to Aggie. Unlike the house in the pasture and her brown-paper bar, it involved drafting plans, borrowing money, hiring carpenters, and buying materials. She began to realize how much she had depended on Allan to handle such things. She hired some carpenters and cajoled, pushed, and bribed them along, but when Allan and Marina returned with a healthy baby four months later,

285

the apartment was not finished and Aggie certainly was. "You carry on from here, son!" she said, with a sigh of relief, handing him the keys. She hobbled back to her old room and stayed in bed for a week.

After that she confined her activities to public relations and new inspirations. Allan went ahead and completed not only her apartment and the line of rooms behind the kitchen, but also a two-story house for his own family behind the store. By that time, Aggie was ready with her next idea, a second line of rooms along the river. Since the lot was almost full by now, Aggie suggested a second story to the line of rooms behind the kitchen. By the time he finished this project, Allan was exhausted. Keeping up with Mum's inspirations was no picnic.

But her timing was perfect. These additions were completed just in time to welcome the "overseas experts" and eager businessmen who flooded the island after independence. The back porch could not hold enough tables for them as well as for an increasing number of tourists. But where would they put a bigger dining room? The team decided to eliminate the sunny passageway with its bunches of bananas and expand the left side of the porch right across to the upstairs kitchen. That would also provide space underneath for a bigger bar, and leave the right side of the porch free for a lounge.

Aggie painted her downstairs bar in a *tapa* motif and added a border of seashells she and the girls picked up on the beach. With pots of ferns and hanging plants, it looked like a grotto in a corner of her garden and could accommodate tourists, experts, overseas businessmen, and Peace Corps workers, as well as her former gentlemen, without any trouble. The growth rate of Aggie's Hotel astonished the rest of Beach Road.

In 1965, Parliament finally passed Andy Gerakas' economic incentives bill, providing duty and tax relief to budding enterprises. It also set up a development bank to provide local entrepreneurs with loans. Polynesian Airlines promptly purchased another plane and expanded its service to Tonga and Fiji, and Eugene Paul assured them the economy was finally "taking off."

Unfortunately, however, the cost of living "took off" first. Work on the wharf lured young Samoans out of their banana patches and into town, so that agricultural exports actually declined. The price of food skyrocketed. In February, 1965, another parade of angry Samoans marched down Beach Road. This time they were protesting not foreign rule but the high cost of living.

Even Nature refused to cooperate. On January 19, 1966, Samoa experienced its worst hurricane since 1889. Wind tore fronds away from the food palms, flattened banana plantations, and blew the roof off Vailima. For the next six months, Apia's new wharf was covered not with exports going out but relief supplies coming in. Tourists shied away.

In June, another disaster discouraged tourists. Polynesian Airline's new DC3 disintegrated in mid-air, killing eight souls. Aggie invited Anna Stancil, widow of its chief navigator, to start a tour service for her guests.

Samoa was obviously not going to turn into another Hong Kong or Singapore, but the experts kept on trying. The United Nations opened a regional office in one corner of the old Casino and hired a Polish planner to draft a beautification plan for Apia's reclaimed waterfront. Unfortunately, no one could afford to implement it. Negotiations began with America's Potlach Corporation for a ten-million-dollar hardwood mill in western Savaii. The airport was enlarged; the soap factory expanded; and a new wharf was built in Salelologo. Four Peace Corps architects designed a new Parliament building for Mulinuu, round like a *fale* but equipped with air-conditioning, a simultaneous translation system, and a panoramic window. In 1967, Parliament approved another five-year development plan, budgeting £35,000 of its own and borrowing £1,498,000 from overseas. About half was to be used for agricultural development. The rest was earmarked for public works and tourism.

Despite this newest onslaught of Western ideas and experts, traditional aspirations still lingered in many Samoan hearts. Fifteen months after independence, Meaole died and the Tamasese title was given to Lealofi IV, son of the hero who fell in the Mau rebellion. He was a quiet and personable medical practitioner at Apia Hospital and popular with the Safenunuivao political family. They felt that now their country was independent, it was time to start filling up the traditional hierarchy again. They would begin by collecting *papa* titles for their favorite *tamaaiga*. Who knew? Some day they might be able to surmount Samoa's hierarchy with a Tupua "crown"!

There was a rustle of excitement in Atua district as the Safenunuivao began collecting fine mats, reviewing genealogies, renewing family alliances, and drilling their long-dormant war group, the *Manu Samoa*. The *tumua* orators of Lufilufi were overjoyed. The new constitution had not enshrined them, but it could not remove them from the hearts of their people. Now they would have a function again. The last time they had formally bequeathed their Tui Atua *papa* title was to Mataafa Iosefo in 1888, but they still knew exactly how to do the task. Their roles and perquisites had come down to them in the greetings to their titles.

Before daybreak on Coronation Day, the red-turbaned warriors of the Safenunuivao's *Manu Samoa* slipped in around Lufilufi, wielding axes and knives and prepared to protect their *tamaaiga*. This was by no means a formality. The new prime minister in Apia was also a legitimate candidate for the Tui Atua, and his Salevalagi political family might well have objected. Some feared he might call out Apia's police as his war group, but he refrained.

As the sun rose, supporters from the Satuala family in Aana and the Mavaega family in Savaii arrived with fine mats. No mention of the occasion had been made in the Apia press, but the bush wireless had been working overtime. The thousands of mats presented to the *tumua* that day on the *malae* indicated that this new Tamasese also had wide support. One mat in particular sent a shudder through the onlookers. It was stained with the blood of Lealofi's father! The family had kept it hidden since Black Saturday. That was enough for the *tumua*. They lighted their ritual fires and for the first time in eighty years annointed a Tui Atua again. Would he go on to try for the *tafaifa*?" Samoa's kingship game was still alive despite Europe's best efforts to end it.

The Tui Atua ceremony was not put on for tourists. No guest at Aggie's even heard of it. Her overseas experts would probably have bewailed seeing two thousand Samoans miss a working day. Actually, Tamasese Meaole

288

never supported tourism. Tempting tourist dollars might subvert the real function of Samoan ceremonies, and cruise-day hawkers with begging children were a hazard to Samoan dignity. But the hard-pressed overseas experts saw tourism as one of the quickest ways to get this faltering economy on its feet. According to their estimates, twenty thousand tourists a year would respond to the lure of quaint villages, sunny beaches, and swaying *siva* dancers.

In 1965, the Pacific Area Tour Association (PATA) was organized to spread word in the West about the South Seas' virginal charms. Its first conference was to be held in Western Samoa. Agents from around the world were invited to sample paradise for themselves. That, of course, would require air-conditioned hotel rooms for them.

Overseas investors were only too eager to build hotels on South Sea island beaches, but, like the Peace Corpsman, they had encountered unexpected problems in Samoa. It wasn't that the villages didn't want hotels. Enthusiastic negotiations went on for several years between Lefaga (whose beach had already been immortalized by Gary Cooper) and a gung-ho American millionaire. But even elementary questions like "Who owns the beach?" proved unanswerable and so threatening to local peace that nothing happened. Except for Aggie's, no new rooms were being built, and Andy Gerakas was desperate. How would he even house the two hundred tour agents coming to the PATA conference, to say nothing of the twenty thousand tourists to follow?

He finally came to Allan, suggesting "a big expansion quick." Thanks to the new incentives act, he was now able to offer duty exemptions, loans, and tax holidays. Aggie's team was tempted. The only drawback was space. Their yard was already full. Fate again intervened on Aggie's behalf.

In 1965, there was another hurricane, and the unpredictable Vaisigano shifted its course to the east, exposing a new sand bar on Aggie's side. She and the government argued for months about who owned it, and Gerakas' urgency finally gave her the leverage she needed. Within weeks the government offered the area to her for £2,500, and she settled.

Allan returned to his drawing board and came up with

an L-shaped wing of forty-four rooms designed to connect the line along the river with the row behind the kitchen. That would bring their total to eighty-six. Aggie took his pencil and added a pool in the courtyard. This one would be big enough to hold an island with one palm tree. She was so enchanted that she drew a thatched *fale* beside the pool. "That's all those agents will probably ever get to see of Samoa," she said.

Allan estimated the cost of this expansion at £140,000. Thanks to Gerakas, the manager of the Bank of Western Samoa did not blink an eye this time. "You can draw £60,000 now and the rest whenever you need it," he said.

Since they promised Gerakas that half the rooms would be ready for the PATA conference in May, 1967, there was no time to waste. Allan contracted with Samoa's best local carpenter, Joe Shick, to do the job. He liked Joe's idea of grooving concrete to look like stone.

By January, 1967, the basic structure was up and Joe was finishing off about twelve rooms a month. Each member of Aggie's team had a role in the undertaking. Allan purchased supplies, Fred checked the work, and Marina produced three kinds of meals three times a day—one for European guests, one for Indian salesmen from Fiji, and still another for Samoan carpenters.

Aggie was responsible for her *fale* being built by the pool. It would have to be large enough to seat two hundred PATA delegates, but she was also determined that it would be authentic. She hired a group of traditional Samoan craftsmen *(tufuga)* and kept their spirits up with traditional oratory, *kava*, fine mats, and feasts. In keeping with its authenticity, the *fale* was soon hopelessly behind schedule. A month before the conference, Aggie yielded to the inevitable and hired the house on Pilot Point for PATA meetings.

Fortunately, Allan's rooms in the new wing were finishing on time. By May 25, he had only one more critical job to perform before the tour agents arrived next day—installing the air-conditioners. Releasing his sixty appliances on the wharf would require the balance of his loan. Allan stopped at the bank on his way to the wharf to pick up a check. To his dismay, he was turned down flat! The new manager, anxious to add a wing on the bank, had been incensed when Allan had hired Joe Shick away from him. This was too good a chance to get even!

Allan was now the desperate one. How would he explain hot and humid rooms to two hundred tour promoters tomorrow? He rushed to Morris Hedstrom to pick up the lumber he had ordered for the job. His order was ready, but as he was driving it out of the yard an accountant called from the window that his credit was no longer good. Someone must have told him. Allan had to offload the lumber.

In small societies, personal enemies loom larger and friends are vital. Allan went over to see Vernon McKenzie, from whom he had been purchasing supplies for years. When his friend heard the problem, he cabled Norge to release the conditioners and co-signed for them himself. Joe Shick's crew worked all night and staggered home to bed just as the first delegates arrived.

The PATA conference met at Pilot Point in all-day sessions while Aggie's crew bussed over lunch and tea supplies. The delegates emerged with a proposal to ease entry permits, provide training courses for hotel workers, and run tourist promotions. Aggie's team emerged with enough to pay for the air-conditioners and complete their new expansion. The only problem now would be keeping all those rooms full.

A month later, Samoa celebrated its fifth year of independence, and so many guests appeared for the festivities that Allan had to put them three in a room. After that, Aggie's Hotel had to begin promotions. Its first advertisement appeared in the *Samoa Times* in August, 1967:[1] "In Samoa, stay at Aggie's Hotel. Leisurely comfort combined with gracious and typically Samoan hospitality and cuisine. No visa for up to 3-day visits. 78 rooms now available for tourists and guests or Pago Pago holiday makers. Handy to Apia yet quiet and secluded."

Mary returned from her long sojourn in the United States and took over management of the Casino again. She and Aggie became fierce competitors. Mary's rooms with meals started at £2/2/0 and Aggie's at £3/0/0. Even with this edge, the musty Casino could not lure enough visitors away from Aggie's pool with an island in it. Western Samoan Trust Estates (WESTEC) finally tore the old Casino down and replaced it with a modern 118-room hotel called the Tusitala, whose lounge and dining room, built like two enormous *fale,* looked out on a swimming pool.

Mary moved just up Beach Road and opened a place of her own, the Apian Way, right next to another new hotel, the Tiafau. Aggie herself became one of several investors in the Hideaway Hotel on the other side of the island. Hadley, an American developer,[2] filled in a swamp near Moataa, hoping to erect a Samoan version of the Royal Hawaiian. But unfortunately for all of them, Samoa never did get the twenty thousand annual visitors the experts had predicted. Samoa's hotels were seldom full, though Aggie's usually had the biggest share. Who else had a host of loyal GIs bringing their wives and children back to meet "Auntie Aggie"? Who else could find a proprietress with a worldwide reputation as Bloody Mary?

Counting the small courtyard, and eighty housekeeping apartments added in 1970, Aggie now had 120 rooms. Allan kissed his mother with relief. "Well, this is it, Mum; our lot can't hold another thing. Promise me you won't have any more inspirations! Your partners are killing themselves just taking care of your old ones!"

She smiled at him tenderly but refused to shake on it. She had been expanding ever since she opened her brown-paper bar in 1935, and it was hard to stop now. How about a little "village" of small houses in the garden, a launch to take guests on a sunset cruise, extensions in Fiji, or even New Zealand? But Allan had good reason to be concerned; he had to manage her inspirations and had long ago discovered that the last nail was only the first headache. Crises were inevitable the moment a busload of tourists seeking "paradise" were greeted by a staff of young Samoans longing for the comforts of the Western world. The hosts and hostesses proferred smiles and flower leis; the guests usually responded, "We just *love* your customs!"

After that anything could happen. Allan and Marina stood between their two Never-never Lands, trying to forestall mutual disenchantment. A university education wasn't as critical as quick thinking, patience, and a sense of humor. The staff spent sixteen-hour days handling distress calls like these:

"You call this food? Get me something I dare put in my mouth!" "But, sir, my cousin made that raw fish herself!"

"I hate to bring this up, but the blouse I gave you to wash has never come back." "Sorry, ma'am—thought it was a present, and gave it to my niece."

"You've got to do something about these nightly black-outs. Can't you see I've got to finish my letters?" "I already did, ma'am. There's a candle in your drawer."

"Your water gives me the trots!" "It must be your stomach, sir. Mine's OK!"

Allan and Marina had to soothe, translate, scold, improvise, and cover for both sides, shifting instantly between English and Samoan. They floundered around a bit when the guests were German or Japanese.

Breakfast for Aggie's original boarders had been easy —spaghetti on toast for Fred and Amby Gilboy, taro with coconut cream *(faalifu talo)* for everyone else. Now the Japanese clients required sausage and rice, the Indians curry, and the Americans bacon and eggs. One of the most difficult problems was the American yen at lunch for salads with raw vegetables. Juicy red Marglobe tomatoes, blanched celery, and iceburg lettuce grew several thousand miles away and could not be shipped frozen or in cans. Air-freighting them in from New Zealand cost Allan more than £500 a month.

"Why don't you just raise vegetables here?" guests often suggested. "With summer all year round, it should be easy." But it wasn't. Those particular plants preferred a temperate climate and a less virile insect population. Finally, Aggie recalled the land Willie had once bought on top of the mountain. It was cool up there. He had left five acres to each daughter, and Aggie had bought Mary's when she left. Why not try raising vegetables up there?

Samoans were not vegetable farmers, but Aggie did locate one "green thumb," belonging to a boy named Pita, who had been working for Frank Moors. She gave him a free hand, a tractor, and a cabin on her mountain lot. Within one year, Pita was sending down tomatoes, beans, and cucumbers and experimenting with celery. Before long, they had so much left over that Marina contracted to provide flight meals for New Zealand Airlines.

Aggie's team now supervised a staff of 118: receptionists, bookkeepers, waiters, cooks, chambermaids, seamstresses, laundresses, drivers, shopgirls, and handymen. They worked in shifts around the clock. By 1970, thousands of village boys and girls were flocking to town, eager to replace the monotony of subsistence living with the excitement of karate moves and a pocketful of cash. It was quite easy enough to find strong bodies and broad smiles, but quite another to find workers with precise habits, a penchant for anonymity, and sufficient self-discipline to resist lifting a hotel towel.

Aggie's relationship to her staff was very Samoan. She looked at them not as employees but as members of her own extended family. Many of them really were her kin. Toamua families often sent their daughters to town to live with Aggie, much as Pepe had sent Pele to live with Seumanutafa almost a century before. Though Aggie held no title, they thought of her as the chief of this large household. She assigned jobs, gave instructions, inspected progress, and scolded malingerers. She made very clear what she expected and was by no means easy to please.

Argument did not pay. But in return she provided more than wages. She acted like a parent, designing their clothes, sticking flowers over their ears, and dabbing her "daughters" with perfume. She advised them about sex and helped find spouses. When they were sick she nursed them; when they were in trouble she stuck by them; and when they had *faa lavelave* (Samoan obligations) she was generous. The relationship was directive but personal.

Since they needed a strong mother in the confusion of these times, they responded with surprising loyalty. Some remained with her for decades, perfecting their skills along with the team as the operation grew. Soaga, who had helped raise Allan, was still on hand fifty years later, making uniforms for his staff. Safata, who had once waited on New Zealand governors at Vailima, now ran Aggie's kitchen. Mega and Lama made salads and desserts for decades and trained their children and grandchildren to succeed them. These loyal co-workers referred to the hotel as "ours," not "theirs," and rightly so. It could never have grown up without them.

"How do you manage to keep your staff, Aggie?" a distraught New Zealand manager at the Tusitala once asked her.

"By acting like a Samoan," she answered. That relationship was hard for a *palagi* to duplicate.

By now, Aggie's Hotel was as secure on Beach Road as Burns Philps or Morris Hedstrom. Its assets were valued at more than £1,500,000! The overseas experts were elated that at least one indigenous enterprise had "taken off," and blessed it as one of Samoa's major sources of foreign exchange. The government was so grateful for its taxes that Aggie's face soon smiled from a ten-cent postage stamp. No one laughed at her at Chamber of Commerce meetings any more; in fact, she was unanimously selected to represent the business community at a formal dinner on the royal yacht when the Queen of England came to visit.

Her name was familiar now not only in the South Pacific but in Europe and America as well. More disembarking tourists asked for directions to Aggie's than to Robert Louis Stevenson's grave, and it was her photograph they were more apt to take home to show their friends.

Despite her newfound wealth and prominence, Aggie still went on greeting guests, counting linens, having inspirations, and performing the last dance at Marina's show. Fred continued to wonder at all this energy. What *was* she after?

The large fale and pool of Aggie's hotel.

The 1967 expansion of Aggie's hotel.

PART VI

MATURITY

Chapter 23

Transition

(1970-1977)

OLD AGE creeps up on a busy life so imperceptibly that it may not be noticed at all until an unexpected event forces one to view life from a radically different perspective. Two events triggered the transition for Aggie: her health and the completion of the hotel.

In seventy-three years of responding to personal relations, Aggie had often been forced to cope with sickness and death. But she had been so busy and robust herself that it never occurred to her that she too was mortal. She toasted and feasted and enjoyed the small hours as if they charged no toll. It was therefore a surprise to her in 1962 when her own insides rebelled. She consulted a doctor on her next trip to New Zealand.

After examining her closely, he shook his head. "It's your liver, Aggie," he said gravely. "You've got to stop drinking and start losing weight or I won't be able to attend your eightieth birthday party."

The word "liver" frightened her. Willie, Charlie, Olaf! Was it possible hers too could succumb to such ailments?

"I'll stop drinking," she assured him hastily, "but I do have to eat, you know."

He didn't disagree. He only said, "Aggie, pick up that box over there and carry it across the room." The box surprised her, it was so heavy.

"It weighs two stone (twenty-eight pounds)," he told her. "That's about as much as the excess weight you're carrying around on you every day. You've got to reduce that load, Aggie. Don't spread your butter on so thick."

His illustration and her own fright were so vivid that Aggie stopped eating entirely. By the time she reached Fiji on the boat trip home, she had lost thirty pounds. Her friend Nan Brownly came down to the dock to greet her

299

and was so shocked at this haggard version of Aggie that she took her home and put her to bed. It was weeks before Aggie recovered her strength, and she never felt oblivious of her body again. Her heart bothered her, she had less energy, and her joints were painful.

She emerged from the experience with a new lifestyle: no alcohol, light food, afternoon naps, and a three-month vacation in New Zealand during the hot season. But there was one indulgence she absolutely refused to give up despite the pain. She would not stop dancing the final *siva* in Marina's show. Too much of her life would go with it.

The completion of the last courtyard in 1970 did not stem Aggie's entrepreneurial inspirations, though Allan did his best to keep them under control. She went right ahead filling her garden with little oval *fale* until it resembled a village hidden among the torch ginger. She named each one for an important person in her life. "That's enough, Mum," Allan finally decreed; "to honor everyone you know would take a city."

She returned to her nautical interests. Think how guests would enjoy a moonlight cruise! No other hotel offered such an outing. She bought an old boat and even some brass fittings in memory of the departed tug. "Just fix it up in your spare time," she told Fred and Allan.

But they *had* no spare time. It took every waking moment just to keep the guests fed and the plumbing working. Aggie's boat bobbed forlornly under the bridge until her next trip to New Zealand, when Allan chopped it up and fed it into the kitchen stove. When she returned, she was furious. He had been so obedient before! For a week the members of the team did not speak to each other. Then they shook hands on a promise, "No more boats."

No more *fale*, no more boats; she had to do something with her energy. On subsequent trips to New Zealand she turned to real estate, buying an apartment here, a house there, until she owned a town. She intended to give them to Allan. He would appreciate investments like that for his growing family.

He did not. "Aggie's destruction company!" he called her latest operation. By "destruction" he doubtless referred to himself. He didn't want more income; all he wanted was a rest! In fact, he would have been glad to sell the hotel and everything else in favor of a quiet life with Marina, Aggie Jr., and now Tanya and little Fred. Before Aggie's next trip he made her shake his weary hand and promise no more *fale*, no more boats, no more real estate — nothing! This time she could see he meant it. The shock was like losing the House on the Hill or the Happy Hour. Even worse, because this time she could not throw her head back in defiance and press on again.

Fate was so ironic! After giving her a lifetime of hard knocks and bruises, it had suddenly made her rich and then asked, "What are you going to do with it all?" She could no longer invest it. She could not take it with her. Even people to bequeath it to were passing on. In 1973 she received an urgent phone call from New Zealand. Pele Jr., her soft-spoken helper of the lean years, was dying of throat cancer! Aggie was beside herself at the injustice of it all. Why not herself instead of Pele? Her husbands were gone and her children grown. She was seventy-six now, and her enterprises concluded. Pele had suffered as much as she did in getting the hotel started, and would now be unable to reap her reward!

Aggie rushed out to buy a ticket. She must get to Pele's side to say goodby. Fate only leered at her again. All planes were grounded by a storm. No money in the world would get her there. By the time she reached New Zealand three days later, Pele was dead. In the black hours of mourning Aggie relived her past: her mother, Ian, Gordon, Willie, Olaf, Charlie, and now Pele Jr. Wealth made no difference at all to the basic nature of life. Success was irrelevant. Why in the world had she worked so hard?

When she returned to the hotel this time, strangers seemed to swirl about her. Every limousine from the airport brought more hands to shake, every mail more invitations to meaningless cocktail parties and balls. Phone calls, interviews, photographers passed by in an endless blur — "one more smile, Aggie!" After an hour of these once enthralling activities, she now fled to her room above the store and sank into a chair, her face in a frozen grin and all her joints aching. She longed for real friends and enemies again. Fate had dealt its final blow. These were strangers, only strangers!

In a panic she padded off to find Fred. There he was in

his shop under the stairs, grumbling about hair in the swimming pool drain. They had a first-class fight over the pros and cons of bathing caps and she slammed the door and tramped upstairs feeling much better. Yes, she was still Aggie. How she loved that grouchy little man!

She lowered herself into her chair again to ponder the situation. If she hadn't changed, maybe the hotel had: too many rooms, too many people, too big to know everyone. It was paying off in money rather than relationships.

Life was such a belly laugh! Here she, a woman, had struggled to the top of Apia's ladder, only to discover what Samoans had known all along: keep your eyes on people, not just their pocketbooks.

Now that Allan frowned on financial inspirations, Aggie reverted to discovering more Samoan qualities in herself. One was her natural and rather pragmatic sense of compassion. She found that people in trouble often came to her now—particularly, of all things, women. No longer a rival in the sexual arena, she learned she had surprising empathy for the problems that girls face in a small, ingrown, low-income community. Gossip, double standards, big families, domestic violence, poverty, and limited opportunities had once been part of her life too. Such things did not surprise or frighten her. Instead, she had developed some canny defenses and used these to help others when she could.

One afternoon, a sixteen-year-old girl dashed up the steps to her apartment and slammed and bolted the door. Aggie was resting in her bedroom and the noise woke her up. She rolled over towards her window just in time to see a man's head appear over the gutter. As she watched, he slithered up her slippery roof and put one leg over her windowsill. He was so close she could smell his redolent breath. He had been drinking.

"Just where do you think you're going, young man?" she challenged sharply, sitting up in bed. He was as surprised as she was.

"That girl winked at me," he said lamely. "I thought she wanted me to come up."

"Well, you should have known better when she bolted the door in your face," Aggie replied, unmoved. "Now climb right back down the way you came, before I push you out!"

"But the roof's slippery," he whined. "I might fall." In his condition, that was a definite possibility.

"You should have thought of that before you came up this way!" she retorted unsympathetically. "Now get out!"

The girl was badly frightened. He had been harassing her for weeks. Since she was afraid to go out, Aggie hired her to help in the apartment. The man did not reappear. He had seen enough of Aggie to keep his distance.

On another occasion she was dozing in the living room and woke to find a young mother kneeling beside her chair. The girl sobbed out a woeful tale. Her husband had disappeared with someone else, leaving her with their four small children. His family no longer felt obliged to support them and her own refused to take her back. The children were hungry. She didn't know what to do. Aggie recalled hungry days of her own in the pasture and gave the girl a job in the hotel kitchen, where she could get food to take home.

The new girl worked out well but a few months later was kneeling beside Aggie's chair again. Her problem was not yet resolved. She was still living with her errant husband's family, and one of his brothers was making unwanted advances. She did not feel safe. Aggie remembered being grabbed by her husband's brother in New Zealand and invited the girl and her children to move into a *fale* in her garden. Guests should see some real Samoans in her "village" now and then.

Needy elderly people also caught her attention. Western Samoa could not afford a public-welfare system. Old people were supported by their extended families and were usually treated with respect. That made it even harder for the few that found themselves adrift, unable or unwilling to attach themselves to a family group. Maggie, now in her eighties and crochety as ever, was one of these. Her husband had long since died; her daughter had settled abroad, and her son was a problem to her. She lived alone above the Surfside Club, always complaining about the noise but stoutly refusing a *fale* in Aggie's garden. Aggie sent her a hot meal every evening. But other unattached elderly folk were not as fortunate. Aggie became a prime mover in Samoa's first home for the elderly, named *Mapu i Fagalele* (rest at Fagalele).[1] The title came from a proverb about weary travelers arriving in the calm waters of Falealupo Bay after a stormy boat trip around Puava Point. Aggie often sent fifty meals at once over to the home, most of whose residents were now younger than herself. Inspirations, she discovered, did not have to make a profit to be worthwhile.

She also relearned the pleasures of simpler living. Now that she was no longer bedazzled by Apia's social life, she realized how much Toamua, Tifitifi, Fagaloa, and the hut in the pasture had meant to her. There was a sort of steadiness out there, a closeness to people and to nature that relaxed and revived her. On her next trip to New Zealand, she spent her time looking for sea urchins instead of real estate, and came home feeling better. So did Allan. Mum was finally letting go.

Another compensation of aging was being able to look at things in a broader time perspective. Her children claimed that "her memory was getting short," but she knew better. It was getting longer. If she couldn't always focus on the present, it was only because she needed the time to piece together so many recollections. When she did manage to link a chain of thought across the century, amazing things happened. Her vision suddenly leaped into a stereographic retrospect, allowing her to view things younger people could not.

One afternoon she plodded down the steps of her apartment and sat down slowly on a bench in front of the store. A breath of air with the smell of the sea wafted her gently back to 1912. Suddenly there was no shop behind her, only a marsh. Her family had just moved into that crumbling old "slate" house next door, fresh from Tifitifi. In an instant, she was an eager adolescent sitting on its mossy stoop beside her father. A barefoot woman in a torn *lavalava*, crouched behind them, was inquiring about "salts" for her fretful baby but no one else was in sight. Aggie's eyes followed down the shady dirt lane towards town. It was lined with hitching posts, coconut trees, and white picket fences. In the distance she could see a buggy with one horse turning into the LMS Mission compound behind the *talie* tree.

She turned and looked in the other direction. There stood Heatherington's spanking white British Club across the grass. Two fine gentlemen in waistcoats sat on its front porch smoking cigars, their feet propped on the railing. She wanted to run over and peek inside at their exciting realm, but Willie strictly forbade it. Clubs were no place for a fifteen-year-old girl.

Beyond the Club a flimsy wooden bridge stretched over the Vaisigano. Two naked boys teetered precariously on the railing for a moment. Then they grabbed each other, shrieking with delight as their brown bodies plummeted into the water.

The sound of an automobile horn snapped her back to 1977. She opened her eyes and sat incredulous at the scene before her. An endless line of frustrated pick-ups and buses honked their way down a three-lane highway, trying to avoid unaccountable little "traffic islands." Cards on the bus windows indicated that they were heading back to almost every village on the island. Shoppers and commuters inside were stacked on each other's laps. It was as if those remote villages, once reached only by boat or trail, had suddenly become suburbs of Apia!

Office girls, workmen, school children, and tourists jostled each other on the sidewalks. Apia had suddenly exploded with people, and they looked much different now. Torn and faded *lavalava* and bare feet were rare. Instead, workmen in blue jeans, tourists in shorts, and office girls in brilliant *puletasi* jostled. Children in varicolored school uniforms. So many different schools! Every youngster must attend these days. Only the naked boys jumping from the bridge still looked the same.

To her left, the curve of the harbor was now packed tight with buildings. Down by the clock tower, an eight-story office building had replaced the Central Hotel. To her right, she could still see the kauri timbers of the old British Club, but its sign had changed to "Aggie Grey's Hotel". No guests sat on its front porch now; they were all relaxing in the garden around a swimming pool.

Her eye passed across the Vaisigano Bridge and stopped short at the other end. About twenty young men from Moataa village were leaning on the far post or sitting on the rail. They had been gathering all afternoon, and the sight troubled her. Several thousand lads like these had flocked to town in the last few years. Those who could not find work spent their time at karate movies or just "cruising." Allan had even found some of them under the bridge brewing a "tea" composed of Coca Cola and "Magic mushrooms."

In her childhood, lads like these had wielded the nets, bush knives, and digging sticks that fed the village families. For excitement they had wound turbans around their heads, blackened their faces, flung stones, and brandished axes to defend the virtue of their sisters or promote the glory of their *tamaaiga*. They could survive in the rain forest or frighten Europeans on Beach Road into barricading themselves in upstairs apartments.

Nowadays, they spent their childhood in schoolrooms learning the ways of the West and their youth wandering the streets of Apia looking for jobs that were not there. Not one in a hundred understood the words *tafaifa* or *pule* and *tumua*. They had to resort to karate, "magic mushrooms," and gang rumbles to prove their manhood.

Who was left back in the village, she wondered, to plant the taro and paddle the fishing canoe? Who were now the arms and legs that fed the family? Food was so expensive now. A bunch of green bananas once given free to any stranger now cost $5 in the marketplace. Small wonder there was stealing! Before the war, a farmer could pile his cocoa pods under a tree and leave them there for weeks. Now he had to guard his produce with a gun. Sometimes, Aggie was glad that she was almost eighty and would not witness the next century. What would happen when current village elders, schooled in tradition and motivated by family dignity, released control of the great families to youths brought up in the streets of Apia?

As the shadows deepened, Aggie saw the figures on the bridge merge and move stealthily towards town. The young men of Moataa were coming to challenge the young men of Apia village to a rumble. That was not new, but now for the first time she was afraid. Until a few years ago, pastors and chiefs had been able to control such confrontations by threatening the "wrath of the Lord" or warning the delinquents not to "disgrace their mothers' stomachs." Last year had been different. The boys had thrown rocks at the LMS pastor and broken Aggie's shop windows. When Seumanutafa tried to run out to stop them, his family had held him back, fearing for his life. Were chiefs and pastors losing their control?

Aggie retreated painfully up the stairs and bolted her door. Panic and confusion swept over her again—not for herself this time, but for the two communities in which she had her roots. Nothing seemed stable anymore. Was the *faa palagi* destroying the *faa Samoa?* Had she and her hotel, surely as Weber and his eagle, helped speed the process? The question shook her heart. She buried her face in her hands.

Presently, a night breeze from the mountain caressed her tear-stained cheek. She looked up. Tapuitea, the evening star, shimmered in the iridescent sky, so brilliant and close that she could almost touch it. At least the star had not changed. It winked at her just as it had over Fagaloa Bay so long ago, inviting her to examine memories again. That time, too, she had though her world was at an end. The house on the hill was gone. But, actually, the apparent loss had not been an end at all, only retraining for a bigger world.

Maybe it would be like that for Samoa. Turmoil in the streets of Apia might not signal that the Samoan way of life was over, only that it was being redesigned. Perhaps the hierarchy of the two great "crowns," with all its ornate rankings, was no more immortal than her house on the hill, but just one elegant design to fit one era of their history. What did the old proverb say? *"O le vaa o Samoa fau po fau ao"* (the Samoan boat is being built on, night and day).

As long as it was continually reshaped to fit their own purposes, it could not help but be Samoan. The *faa Samoa* wasn't a set of ancient institutions; it was a national yearning to build a place where everyone felt recognized and knew where he belonged.

307

Chapter 24

Eighty Red Roses

(October 31, 1977)

AGGIE'S New Zealand doctor got his wish — an invitation to her eightieth-birthday party. Hundreds of people — guests from the hotel, the elite of Beach Road, government officials, village chiefs, tapa makers, basket weavers, airline executives, friends from Fiji, Australia, America and, even England — came to celebrate the occasion. They crossed the back porch and crowded down the steps into her garden.

It was a beautiful evening. A full moon silvered the palm fronds and flickered across the thatches of the *fale* in the garden. Torches lighted the pathway towards the pool. Sharp eyes could even discern a fisherman in the shadows beyond its island, a solitary figure holding a long pole. That must be Fred hunting leaves in the pool.

The big *fale* by the pool buzzed like a beehive. As the partygoers ducked under its thatches, they noticed a small sign on a table explaining that Aggie had no need for birthday presents, but would welcome contributions to *Mapu i Fagalele*, Samoa's home for the elderly.

The underside of the great leashed dome glowed in a pinkish light, shed upwards from giant clam shells along its rim. At the west end of the room, a huge fan chair faced down the aisle past rows of canvas chairs towards a raised stage at the rear. Guests jostled their way around knots of laughing friends to a bar at the back and returned, gingerly threading their way towards an empty canvas chair or a place at one of the little white tables beside the pool. The room was a clash of colors and cultures: Samoan chiefs in fitted *lavalava* and red pandanus necklaces; Tongans girdled with *titi*; Fijians with great round hairdo's; Beach Road gentlemen in dress suits and their wives in off-the-shoulder *puletasi*.

An impressive chord from the band brought everyone to attention. As the audience stood and turned to the rear, Allan stepped under the thatch with a silver-haired lady on his arm. Aggie was dressed in a shimmering *puletasi* and stood solemn as a queen while everyone sang the Samoan national anthem. Then Allan led his mother to the fan chair, her slight shuffle only accentuating a regal gait. She turned in front of the chair, completely self-possessed, and bowed stiffly in each direction. There was a burst of applause.

It took several minutes for Peter Paul, master of ceremonies, to bring the noise under control. "Eugene's son," Aggie thought, recalling her departed crony. "Without his help, I would not be sitting at this throne tonight."

"Ladies and gentlemen," Peter shouted, "you may have thought you were coming to a birthday party; actually you are attending a coronation. In the past, Samoa has produced two queens. One was Queen Salamasina, who, with the help of the goddess Nafanua, managed to acquire all four *papa* titles and become our first *tafaifa*. The second was Queen Emma, Apia's famous *afakasi* lady who amassed a fortune buccaneering in the southern seas. Now, I am proud to say, Samoa has produced a third great lady. Since the title of queen is no longer in fashion, I will bestow upon our Aggie a more modern designation — First Lady of the South Pacific! Aggie, you may ascend your throne."

The din was deafening. Allan lowered his mother into the fan chair and waiters passed champagne.

"Now, let us raise our glasses in a toast," Peter continued, as the room quieted, "To our Aggie, First Lady of the South Pacific! To her beauty, her brains, and her way with men! Long may they continue to brighten our lives!"

Aggie did not hear the cheers. The words of the toast had suddenly made her think of Willie. She wasn't sure quite why, but his face was suddenly as clear as if he were looking into her eyes. He was smiling as if he had just won a wager.

Her attention reverted to the present as the guests sat down. Peter stepped to the mike again and intoned, "To officially greet our first lady, I want to present a person known to all of us as the leader of our new government. Ladies and gentlemen, let me present — the prime minister of the independent state of Western Samoa!"

Everyone clapped again as a smiling young man not much older than Allan took the mike. Aggie gazed at him fondly, not listening to a word he said. Yes, it was Efi, Tamasese's son, Olaf's grandson. She felt as proud of him of him as if he were her own. There was so much to remember.

She returned to the present in time to catch his last words. " . . . I don't know quite why," he was saying, "but I always felt that Aggie took a special interest in me, almost like that of a mother." He jumped down from the podium, strode to the fan chair, and gave her a kiss.

The crowd loved that. When they finally turned their attention to the microphone again, Peter said: "Now let us proceed to the testimonial. Fred was supposed to give it, but no one can find him." There was a roar of laughter. Everyone knew Fred.

In the shadows beyond the pool, Fred stood half-hidden behind a fern, with the pool rake in his hand. He was listening to the noise in the happy house across the moonlit water. He could see Aggie in her glittering gown, seated on the throne, the focus of attention. There she sat, ramrod-straight, staring off into space, her face a mask. How ridiculous! Is this what she had wanted all these years? Not men, not money, but public adulation? He shook his head, grunting something that sounded like, "She's not that crazy!"

Actually, her regal posture had a simpler explanation. Back in the fan chair, Aggie was saying to herself, "My damn knees are killing me! How can I ever do the last dance? I'm apt to fall on my face!"

She could almost hear the audience snicker. "There goes Aggie, playing the fool again!" She held her body tighter and tighter to still the pain of memories she had never been able to shake off.

Without moving her head, her eyes roved sideways, seeking some way to escape the worrisome crowd. Suddenly, they fell on Fred's familiar figure standing in the shadows beyond the swimming pool. He looked so much like a solitary fisherman, she almost laughed. How like Fred! Always himself. Whispers never bothered him; he probably never heard them. All he cared about was his contraptions—and her. His loyalty never faded. Even if she danced like a robot tonight, it would make no difference to him! Her panic subsided.

She could hear the MC talking again. ". . . since Fred has disappeared," he was saying, "Allen Pavitt has offered to give the testimonial instead. I think he has a story to tell." Aggie watched with tenderness as an elderly man pushed his way through the chairs and went up to the mike. He had been one of the "boys" at her old brown-paper bar.

"You all think of me now as the 'Fruit Distributor' man," Pavitt began, referring to the job from which he had recently retired; "so that you may be surprised to hear that in my younger days I was known instead as 'a very gay blade.' I arrived in Samoa in 1932, during what we called the Great Depression, and finally found a job out at Muli-fanua Plantation which paid me £16/13/4 a month. That wasn't much, but I made the most of it at Aggie's little club. All she had in those days was a sagging little bar up front, decorated in brown wrapping paper. We sat on benzene crates and sang our blues away. Beer didn't flow in those days, it only dripped; but Aggie knew where to find those drops.

"Because I had so far to come, I could not make it to town till after midnight every Friday. But Aggie always got up to get me a sandwich and a blanket. Saturday was my night to howl. She would wind up the old gramophone on her upstairs porch and let us dance. You may not believe it, but all the girls were after me in those days! I was always in hot water.

"One night Aggie came down on me for my wild wild ways. 'Allen,' she said, 'you seem to have no sense. The reason you're in trouble all the time is that you always go for the wrong kind of girl. Now let me introduce you to someone who will keep you on the straight and narrow.' That's how I met Paese here, who grew up with Aggie. I married her and have had to toe the line ever since. Thanks to her, I became your Fruit Distributor man."

He returned to his table and put his arm around his seventy-year-old wife amid shouts of "Bravo, Paese!" Aggie found herself cheering too. Paese was the niece Faafete had brought to live with them![3] Her daughter was

311

now Aggie's receptionist.

Over in the corner, Aggie caught sight of a chief from Toamua, asleep in a chair. She was surprised that he could nap through all the noise. He had arrived early this morning with some nice fresh fish for her feast. Though far younger than herself, he always called her "daughter" because he was now the Pepe titleholder of her mother's family.

Her reveries were interrupted by Toluono, a distinguished white-haired *pule* from Savaii who had stopped by to shake her hand. His daughter, Alofa, was now a member of Aggie's "family" at the hotel. Everyone here tonight was part of her life.

Peter Paul stood up again to offer the presentations. "You may have noticed Aggie's request that we direct our presents to the old people's home, but some gifts have appeared in kind, and I want to present them now."

As he spoke a gigantic basket of red roses began moving down the aisle as if on legs of its own. It came to rest in front of the stage next to a huge birthday cake.

"Eighty red roses!" Peter shouted, as if he had just finished counting them, "One for each year of Aggie's life! Now who do you suppose would give her a bouquet like that?"

"Must be an ardent admirer," someone called from the audience.

"We all know she still has plenty of them," Peter called back. "But with this particular one, it's been an on-again, off-again affair for twenty years. We'll all be relieved to know if things are finally settling down. Ladies and gentlemen, the card reads, 'With best wishes, Air New Zealand!'"

The second presentation was by the four tall ladies with distinguished round coiffeurs. They came down the aisle with an enormous tapa and a fine mat. Nothing of this size was produced in Samoa! *"Sa o faalalelei"* (how beautiful!) the audience murmured. The ladies placed their gifts beside the roses and the room stirred with whispers. Who were these strangers? Why were they here? Aggie knew. She had almost as many relatives and friends in Fiji, the home of her father and grandfather, as she had here in Samoa.

The third presentation was by Marina and the young

people who worked in the hotel. They had created some special songs and dances for the lady in whose family they felt at home. Feathers bobbed on thick black hair, dark eyes and brown skin glistened—except for the dancer in the middle of the front row. Her hair was blond, her eyes were blue, and her vivacity stole the show. "That's her grand-daughter, Aggie Jr.," the guests explained to each other. "Look's like she's going to carry the torch for the family!"

As their numbers drew to a close, Aggie grew nervous again. Her dance was next! How could she do it with every joint aching?

"Ladies and gentlemen," Peter called through the mike, "this is the moment we have all been waiting for! Our first lady will grace us with the dance of honor. Come on, Aggie! We want *you* for our *taualuga!*" Everyone stood and clapped.

Aggie placed her palms resolutely on the arms of her chair, refusing to let Allan help her rise. She balanced herself momentarily, pushed her aching legs down the aisle, and slowly mounted the stage. She turned and spread her arms as if in supplication. If only her limbs would un-freeze and let her go! Raising her head, she looked at her audience in surprise. They were not hornets. Everyone was related to her somehow! By some miracle the *faa Samoa* had captured the *faa palagi!* Within her own lifetime, it had shaped a bunch of drifters from many lands into an ex-tended family. True, they had erected their own ladder and played their own game, throwing each other off the rungs as they scrambled for the top. Tifitifi, the auction, the Happy Hour, Olaf's funeral, the tug, and Bloody Mary —she knew what it was to be cast out. She had struggled with them her entire life and never felt quite secure.

But meanwhile some magic must have been at work, weaving them all imperceptibly into this island net, pa-tiently crossing their bloodlines and catching them into its web of social and economic obligations. Aggie herself had provided ceaseless fingers and a prime location. In her bars, her porches, her bedrooms, thousands of these little knots had been tried and tested.

Now here they all were tonight, proudly calling them-selves Samoan, greeting, feasting, titling, and maneuver-ing each other in the best ceremonial tradition—so bound by their inter-relationships they could not possibly push anyone out.

If she stumbled and fell tonight, they would all rally to hold her up. She was finally secure!

Her stiff knees loosened with relief. The band struck up "Isa Lei" and she sailed off into the performance — laughing, swaying, winking, flirting outrageously, just being our Aggie!

Front entrance — Aggie's hotel.

EPILOGUE

A noted travel writer visiting Apia in 1984 reported that the main attractions of the town were Robert Louis Stevenson and Aggie Grey. She arrived for an interview wearing a red-flowered dress and a large necklace of corals and shells. She was now eighty-seven years old and frail, but smiled as she extended her hand.

"When did you come to realize that you were famous out here in the South Pacific?" was the final question.

"Oh, that!" was the reply. "Well, when the government put my picture on a stamp, I guess that's when I felt I was pretty well known."

Samoa celebrated in 1987 its twenty-fifth year of independence and Aggie her ninetieth birthday. The former was a full-dress occasion with visiting warships, twenty-one-gun salutes, American fireworks, Chinese acrobats, longboat races, a government ball, and triumphal arches all the way to its brand-new airport. Samoa was thriving on international attention. Aggie's party this time was a quiet affair, attended only by family and a few close friends in deference to her frail condition. Human beings can challenge fate but only for so long.

Beginning in 1984 she suffered a series of mild strokes which progressively took their toll on her eyesight, her hearing, her memory, and her mobility. She danced her last dance in 1985, when to everyone's surprise she suddenly rose from her wheelchair and performed a *taualuga* (farewell dance) for her guests. Her last trip to Auckland was to meet James A. Michener, who was himself making a final tour of the islands that brought him fame. They sang the old barroom songs together and laughed about Bloody Mary. "I only got the good parts of her character from you," he explained.

These days, Aggie's travels are confined to a trip downstairs to spend a few pleasant hours in her favorite spot, a wheelchair in the garage under the old chemist shop. She does not recognize many of the people who walk over to greet her, and seldom talks. But when she does, guests

315

are often taken by surprise. Her jokes are still as robust as her heart, which still plugs valiently on. Maggie has died and Mary is ill, but Fred still gets around at eighty-five, tinkering with pipes and fussing about the swimming pool. There is little to fight about now, and Aggie finally seems content just to be at home.

The Vaisigano has provided no new land, but the hotel has managed to keep on growing anyway. Allan and Marina have added a final row of fales along the river in the back of the tract, and are now planning a modern three-story complex to replace the old house in front. Its kauri timbers, which first arrived as ballast on an old sailing ship and were later rescued from the International Hotel fire to build the British Club, are not, alas, as immortal as reputed.

Aggie Junior married in 1985 and now has two daughters, Tamarina and Tanya. That number gives Aggie a current total of sixteen grandchildren and twenty-one great-grandchildren. She can indeed now rest content. The Swann family saga will still go on.

Aggie Grey died peacefully at 8:30 p.m. on the night of June 26, 1988.

APPENDICES

APPENDIX A-1. BIBLIOGRAPHY

Ala'ilima, Fay C. and Ala'ilima, Vaiao J., "The Samoan Traditional System." Unpublished manuscript. Pacific Collection, Hamilton Library. University of Hawaii, 1965.

Bier, James A. *Samoa*. University of Hawaii Press, 1980. (map)

Braisby, Alfred L. *A Documentary Record and History of the Lauati Rebellion in Samoa*. 3 vols. Wellington: Dept. of Island Territories, 1909.

Davidson, James W. *Pacific Island Portraits*. Canberra: Australian National University Press, 1973, Chapter 12.

_____. *Samoa mo Samoa*. Melbourne: Oxford University Press, 1967.

Derrick, Ronald A. *A History of Fiji*. Suva: Government Press, 1946.

Dutton, Geoffrey. *Queen Emma of the South Seas*. South Melbourne: Macmillan, 1976.

Eustis, Nelson. *Aggie Grey of Western Samoa*, Adelaide: Hobby Investments, 1979.

Fijian Weekly News and Planters Journal, Vol. #1, Nos. 1-13. Levuka, August 8, to Nov. 21, 1868.

Fiji Times. Obituary of James B. Swann, May 25, 1901, p. 2.

_____. Obituary of Sir Charles St. Julian, Dec. 5, 1874, p. 4.

Fleur Maps. Lands and Survey Dept., Government of Western Samoa, Apia.

Gilson, Richard P. *Samoa, 1830-1900*. Melbourne: Oxford University Press, 1970.

Gray, John A. *Amerika Samoa: A History of American Samoa and its U.S. Naval Administration*. Annapolis: U.S. Naval Institute, 1960.

Jetaway: Air New Zealand In-Flight Magazine #36, April-June 1978, p. 14. (Description of Aggie's eightieth birthday and story of "witch")

Kennedy, Paul M. *The Samoan Tangle*. St. Lucia, Queensland: University of Queensland Press, 1974.

Kramer, Augustin. *Die Samoa Inseln.* Vol. I. Stuttgart: Schweitzerbartsche Verlagsbuchhandlung, 1903.

"The Making of a Tui Atua." 16-mm. color film of the installation of Tamasese Lealofi IV as Tui Atua, November 25, 1965. Taken by Dr. Sixten Haroldson and edited by Fay Ala'ilima.

Martin, John R. *Representative Institutions in Western Samoa during the Mandate.* Master's thesis, Victoria University College, 1959.

Milner, G.B. *Samoan Dictionary.* London: Oxford University Press, 1966.

Moors, H.J. "Some Recollections of Early Samoa," *Samoa Times,* June 13, 20, 24, 27, 1924; February 6, 13, 27, 30, 1925; March 6, 13, 20, 27, 1925; April 3, 10, 1925; August 14, 21, 28, 1925; September 11, 25, 1925; October 2, 9, 16, 23, 30, 1925; November 6, 20, 27, 1925; December 4, 11, 1925; January 1, 8, 15, 29, 1926; February 5, 12, 19, 1926; March 5, 12, 19, 1926; April 2, 1926 (Moors' death).

Nelson, O.F. Correspondence, Jan. 16, 1928-Apr. 21, 1933. Pacific Manuscript Bureau (PMB), Microfilm #712.

Nelson Papers. New Zealand Archives. IT 1/23/0, 1/23/1, 1/23/6, 1/23/8bc (5-23), 1/23/20 (1-2).

O le Tusi Fa'alupega. p. 152. Malua, W. Samoa: Samoan Church Press, 1958.

"Obituary James B. Swann," *Samoanische Zeitung,* June 22, 1901, p. 3.

"Obituary O.F. Nelson," *Pacific Islands Monthly,* March 20, 1944, p. 10.

"Obituary William J. Swann," *Pacific Islands Monthly,* June 16, 1936, and *Western Samoa Mail,* May 29, 1936.

Pacific Islands Monthly, Sydney: Pacific Publications. Aug. 30, 1930-present (used 1940-1950).

Robson, Robert W. *Queen Emma: The Samoan-American Girl Who Founded an Empire.* Sydney: Pacific Publications, 1973.

Ryden, George H. *Foreign Policy of the United States in Relation To Samoa.* New Haven: Yale University Press, 1928.

Samoa Bulletin. Weekly newspaper. Apia, Western Samoa. Nov. 3, 1950, to May 25, 1967.

Samoa Guardian. Weekly newspaper. Apia, Western Samoa. May 26, 1927, to February 27, 1930.

Samoa Herald. Weekly newspaper. Apia, Western Samoa. March 7, 1930, to December 31, 1931.

Samoa Times. Weekly newspaper. Apia, Western Samoa. 1915 to February 21, 1930. (microfilm).

Samoanische Zeitung. Weekly newspaper. Apia, Western Samoa. Apr. 6, 1901 to 1915. (microfilm).

Smith, Stephen J. *The Samoa (NZ) Expeditionary Force*. Wellington: Ferguson & Osborn, 1924.

Stevenson, Robert L. *A Footnote to History*. New York: Scribners, 1892.

Thomas, Lowell, *The Sea Devil*. London: W. Heinemann, 1928.

Westbrook, G.E.L. "New Years' Day in Apia, 1899." *Samoa Times*, January 5, 1923, p. 6.

——————————. "The Samoa (NZ) Expeditionary Force," *Samoa Times*, April 3, 1925, p. 3.

Western Samoa Mail. Weekly newspaper. Apia, Western Samoa, January, 1940, to March 28, 1942.

APPENDIX A-2. INTERVIEWS

Note: All interviews were taped unless otherwise indicated.

Annandale, Ted. June 9, 1978.

Carruthers, Dick (storekeeper and friend). May 4, 1978.

Croudace, Mary Swann (Aggie's younger sister). April 26, 1978; June 18, 1978; July 5, 1978 (trip to Toamua).

Eteuati, Sisilia. June 23, 1979. Tape of Suani song.

Fabricius, Margaret Swann (Aggie's older sister). March 22, 1978; March, 1978; April 4, 1978; April 17, 1978; June 7, 1978; June 15, 1978; July 8, 1978.

Grey, Aggie Swann. June 5, 1978; June 9, 1978; June 17, 1978; June 19, 1978; June 23, 1978; June 28, 1978; July 6, 1978; July 12, 1978.

Grey, Allan (Aggie's son) March 18, 1978; June 5, 1979 (notes only).

Jackson, Reginald (attorney and friend). March 23, 1978.

Kneubuhl, John (Lena's son). June, 1979, and June, 1985 (notes only).

McKenzie, Vernon (storekeeper). July 11, 1979. Recollections of Beach Road (notes only).

Nuusa, Repeka (former employee). August 7, 1980.

Paul, Flo (Eugene Paul's wife and friend). April 19, 1978.

Pavitt, Allen (friend). May 11, 1978.

Pavitt, Paese (childhood family member and friend). May 11, 1978; May 20, 1978.

Phinneas, Herbert. July 12, 1979. Recollections of Beach Road.

Seumanutafa, Pogai (high chief Apia village). June 12, 1979; June 19, 1979; June 22, 1979; June 26, 1979; July 3, 1979.

Taylor, Enid Meidicke (friend). June 13, 1978.

APPENDIX A-3. NOTES

Chapter 1. The Warship and the Village
1. *Fiji Times*, Levuka, June 1, 1872, p. 8.
2. Ryden, *Foreign Policy of the United States in Relation to Samoa*, pp. 312-15 (Commander Day's account).
3. Gilson, *Samoa: 1830-1900*, p. 287.

Chapter 2. Meeting
1. *Samoa Times*, June 13, 1924-April 6, 1925. "Recollections of Early Samoa," series by H.J. Moors/describing his arrival at Beach Road and conditions in Samoa *circa* 1876.
2. Now Aggie Grey's hotel.
3. "Slates" were prefabricated panels of fiber and cement, used in early Beach Road stores and houses.
4. Now the Central Office.
5. Now the NPF Building.

Chapter 4. Winning and Trapped
1. This song about "Suani" was widely known in the early 1900's. The Manono version given here was sung by Sisilia Eteuati and taped on June 14, 1979.
2. Stevenson, *A Footnote to History*.
3. Gilson, *Samoa: 1830-1900*, p. 404.

Chapter 6. Flight of the Wild Bird
1. The Treaty of Berlin in 1899 awarded Germany the

larger Samoan islands of Upolu and Savaii, which together with the small islands between them are known today as Western Samoa. The United States was given Tutuila, Manua, and Rose Islands, which are still called American Samoa. Great Britain settled for the Solomons.

2. Market Hall was a large structure with an iron frame, located where the fire station and Old Market parking lot are now. It was the site for balls, community meetings, and early movies, and was then purchased by Eugene Paul and eventually torn down.

3. This school was at Malifa. It became a public primary school during the New Zealand administration.

4. *Samoanische Zeitung,* December 20, 1902, p. 9.

Chapter 7. Rebels
1. *Samoanische Zeitung,* August 22, 1908, p. 7.
2. Governor Solf to the German Colonial Office. September 4, 1900, DRI, 15-19. "The further aim of the Government will be to find ways and means to render ineffectual as a political factor, and eventually do away with, the institution of *tumua* and *pule.*" Davidson, *Samoa mo Samoa,* p. 80.
3. Davidson, *Samoa mo Samoa,* p. 83.
4. Lauati was released by the New Zealand administration in 1915 but died en route home.

Chapter 8. Tifitifi
1. Olaf Fredrick (O.F.) Nelson was usually called "Fred." In this book he is referred to as "Olaf" to prevent confusion with another Fred.
2. A Samoan game played on the *malae* on moonlit nights between two teams of children. Someone throws a *nonu* (hard inedible fruit) onto the grass between the teams. The child who finds it earns a point for his team.

Chapter 10. Age of Innocence
1. A "heavy supper" served at Samoan entertainments often includes: taro, boiled banana, *palusami,* corned beef, roast pig, baked fish or chicken, and potato salad. It is served late in the evening.
2. For a description of "slates" see Note 2, Chapter 2.
3. *Samoanische Zeitung,* September 13, 1913, p. 1. "Marriage of Margaret Swann."

Chapter 11. Age of Revelation
1. *Samoa Times,* September 26, 1914, supplement.
2. The flightless kiwi is New Zealand's national bird and the term is often used to refer to a New Zealander. Not derogatory.
3. *Samoa Times,* June 30, 1917, p. 4.
4. *Ibid.,* February 16, 1918, pp. 3, 4.

Chapter 12. The Grim Reaper
1. *Samoa Times,* March 9, 1918, p. 4.
2. *Ibid.,* June 8, 1918, p. 3. The Alcazar was later towed across the bay to its present site at Matautu.
3. *Ibid.,* September 28, 1918, p. 4.
4. *Ibid.,* June 21, 1919, p. 4. "Girls at Papauta School."
5. *Ibid.,* December 21, 1918. Obituaries.
6. *Ibid.,* April 5, 1919, p. 4. "The Native Petition."
7. *Ibid.,* June 21, 1919. p. 5. "Mortality Returns."

Chapter 13. Bereaved
1. New Zealand National Archives, IT 1/32. "Report by Colonel Tate on the Administration of Samoa."
2. *Samoa Times,* December 19, 1924, p. 4.

Chapter 15. The Mau Rebellion
1. *Samoa Times,* March 25, 1927. p. 6. The Native Affairs Ordinance.
2. New Zealand Archives.
3. *Samoa Times,* November 19, 1926. p. 7.
4. Nelson Papers. NZ Archives. IT 1/23/8bc.
5. *Ibid.*
6. *Samoa Times,* August 24, 1928, p. 7. "Report of the Mandates Commission."
7. Nelson Papers, New Zealand Archives, IT 1/23/8BC.
8. *Ibid.*
9. *Ibid.*
10. *Ibid.*
11. *Ibid.,* 1/23/8 (20), March 25, 1931. Administrator to External Affairs, p. 93.
12. Nelson Papers, New Zealand Archives, *op.cit.*

Chapter 16. The Great Depression
1. *Samoa Herald.* January 2, 1931. p. 4.

2. *Ibid.*, auction announcements: March 6, 1931, p. 4 and March 13, 1931, p. 1.

3. *Ibid.*, December 22, 1933, p. 4.

4. The "Fish Tree" refers to one near the customs office,

Chapter 16. The Great Depression

1. *Samoa Herald*. January 2, 1931. p. 4.

2. *Ibid.*, auction announcements: March 6, 1931., p. 4 and March 13, 1931, p. 1.

3. *Ibid.*, December 22, 1933, p. 4.

4. The "Fish Tree" refers to one near the customs office, where fishermen hung their catch to sell.

5. Nelson Papers, New Zealand Archives, *op.cit.*

6. *Ibid.*

7. New Zealand Archives, 1/23/20, August 6, 1934, p. 192. Nelson to Family.

Chapter 19. Yank Club and Hamburger Stand

1. For a photograph of this see *Pacific Islands Monthly,* November 15, 1938, p. 62.

Chapter 20. The Surplus Operation

1. A song recalled by Leiataua Amituanai Vaiago Alailima as reminding him of Aggie.

2. See "Obituary: O.F. Nelson," *Pacific Islands Monthly,* March 20, 1944, p. 10.

Chapter 21. Birth of a Nation and Aggie's Hotel

1. *Samoa Bulletin*. June 20, 1952, p. 1.

2. For a more detailed account of the rival local airlines see: Eustis, *Aggie Grey of Samoa,* pp. 149-152.

3. Willard Price's book *South Sea Adventure* (1952) is an adventure story for children. The book he was working on at this time was probably *Adventures in Paradise: Tahiti and Beyond.* On p. 237 he refers to Aggie as Michener's prototype for Bloody Mary.

Chapter 22. Development

1. *Samoa Bulletin,* August 10, 1967, p. 12, and also in subsequent issues.

2. A developer named Hadley cleared and filled the area with the intention of building a Royal Samoan Hotel.

The project was not completed.

Chapter 23. Transition
1. *Mapu i Fagalele,* the name of the old people's home, is derived from an old saying *"Lutia i Puava 'ae mapu i Faga-lele"* (Suffer the rough water rounding Puava Point but rest calmly in Fagalel Bay).

APPENDIX B-1. GLOSSARY

Note. This list includes proper names and words from the text for which the reader may want pronunciation or more explanation. In Western Samoa the glottal stop is not entered except where needed to differentiate two similar words. This practice is used in the text. In this glossary, however, the orthographic marks (taken from Biers and Milner) are included as an aid to pronunciation.

Introduction to Samoan pronunciation. Vowels are usually prounounced: a (ah), e (ay), i (ee), o (oh), u (oo). A macron elongates them. Consonants are the same as English except for 'g' (pronounced 'ng' as in 'tongue'). The glottal stop is a constriction of the glottis at the back of the throat (as in the pause in exclamation 'oh! oh!' or the negative 'unh! unh!').

Āʻana. Westernmost of Upolu's three traditional districts. See Appendix C.
ʻafakasi. Part-Samoan; of mixed blood; half-caste (not derogatory)
ʻāiga. Samoan family. Used more broadly than in English to cover not only nuclear and extended family groups but also families of related titles and family alliances (e.g., ʻĀiga Mavaega, ʻĀiga o Maletoa, ʻĀiga Tupu).
ʻĀiga i le Tai (lit. "family in the sea"). A traditional district covering Apolima, Manono, and Mulifanua. It is an ʻĀiga of Malietoa.
aitu. A spirit or ghost, often malevolent.

ali'i. Samoan titles are of two types: chief *(ali'i)* and orator *(faipule)*. The highest chief in a council (e.g., village, district) is known as its *"ali'i sili."*

aloe. (Engl.) Plant with fleshy leaves, whose sap is used to treat burns.

'āmene. Amen.

Apia. Capital of Western Samoa, on north coast of Upolu.

Apolima. Small island between Upolu and Savai'i.

Aso Sā o Tamaiti (lit. "Children's Sunday"). Also called "White Sunday." A Sunday in October on which children give renditions in church and are presented with white clothes and a feast by their families.

Ātua. Traditional district in eastern Upolu. See Appendix C.

'ava. Kava; roots and stem of *piper methysticum* plant, used to make a ceremonial drink.

Black Saturday. December 29, 1929; day on which New Zealand police clashed with a Mau parade, killing Tamasese Lealofi III.

'Crown.' Here refers to the two top titles or positions in the Samoan hierarchy: the Malietoa and Tafa'ifā ("Tupua Crown").

DH&PG. Deutsches Handels und Plantagen Gesellschaft. A German corporation based in Hamburg, which owned the largest plantation in Samoa until World War I.

'ele. Clay used for the reddish color in tapa designs.

'Elena. Ellen; here the wife of Pele's brother Misi.

'Ele'ele Sā. (lit. "forbidden soil") Specifically the European protected area around Apia governed by British, American, and German consuls from 1879 to 1899.

fa'alavelave. A meeting or ceremony to which a Samoan feels obligated to contribute.

fa'alupega. A listing or roster of village titles showing their traditional relationships and functions.

fa'amasino (lit. "to clarify"). A judge; here specifically a Samoan judge in the Lands and Titles Court.

fa'apālagi (also *faapapalagi*). In the Western way; according to *palagi* (Western) custom.

fa'a Sāmoa. In the Samoan way; according to Samoan custom.

fagota. To go fishing.

faipule. Orator type of titleholder; also legislative representative.

fale (pron. fah-lay). Samoan thatched house with rounded ends and open sides. A *fale vaa* is a boatshed.

Faleālili. An Atua sub-district on the south coast of Upolu.

Faleata. The Tuamasaga sub-district in which Lepea and Toamua are located.

Falefā. Village on the north coast of Upolu west of Fagaloa Bay.

Fale'ula (lit. "red house"). Village seven miles west of Apia, where Methodist mission schools and headquarters are located.

fau. Type of hibiscus whose inner bark is used for strainers and lashing material.

Faumuinā. Highest title of Lepea village.

fautua. Advice; adviser; here specifically the positions given Malietoa and Tamasese during the negotiations for independence.

fia pālagi. Acting like a *palagi* (usually derogatory).

filaria. A parasitic worm transmitted by mosquitoes which can cause swelling of the extremities.

fine mat (Samoan, *ie toga*). A finely woven mat of soft pandanus. A highly regarded type of mat presented at ceremonies and worn in special dances. The number of fine mats presented at a ceremony is indicative of its importance.

fofō. A Samoan healer; also a massage.

Fono a Faipule. Council of rulers; specifically the chiefly advisory bodies set up by colonial administrators and the modern parliament.

fue (pron. foo-ay). Switch of sennit fibers bound to a stick, which is carried by orators.

'iao (lit. "dawn crier"). Wattled honeyeater, a forest bird.

Isalei. Title of a well-known Fijian farewell song.

Kala. Name of an unmarried relative who lived with Aggie's grandparents and took care of her as a child.

Kauri. A New Zealand hardwood whose timber does not rot.

328

lagi (pron. lah-ngi). A chiefly funeral ceremony; also, sky.

Laupepa. Son of Malietoa Moli, whose descendants are a lineage of the Malietoa title.

lavalava. A length of cloth wound around the waist and tucked in. Common garment for both men and women.

Lauati. From a Tongan title *(Lauaki);* Lauati Namulau'ulu was a famous orator who led the rebellion against the Germans.

Lega (pron. leh-nga). Yellow powder made from the root of the *ago.*

Legislative Council (LEGCO). Here refers to a body established by New Zealand to advise its Samoan administrator. It consisted of five expatriate department heads and three local European representatives. The two *fautua* were later included.

lieder (German). Pl. songs.

loa. "Lipstick plant" *(anatto).* Seeds are used for red dye.

local European. A full or part Caucasian who resides in Samoa but not under a Samoan family titleholder.

    loli. Edible black sea cucumber.

London Missionary Society (LMS). Originally an ecumenical mission of British Protestant churches. Later considered a denomination. Recently renamed the Congregational Church.

Lotopa. Area southwest of Apia just inland of Pēsega. Site of Willie's original plantation.

lumane. Edible sea anemone.

Mafui'e. Mythical Samoan god who is said to cause earthquakes by shaking the pillars of his cave.

malae. Meeting ground; often a grassy area in the center of a village.

malaga (pron. mah-langa). A trip; also a visiting party.

Malie. Village west of Apia. Traditional seat of Malietoa.

Mālietoa. One of the two top Samoan titles; originally given to the family which led the expulsion of the Tongans.

Mālifa. Section of Apia where the central primary and intermediate schools are located.

Mālo. Victor; government; also the pro-government faction during the Mau rebellion against New Zealand.

Mālōlōlelei (lit. "rest well"). A German resort built at Afiomalu on top of the mountain above Apia, where Aggie's garden is now.

Mālua. A Congregational (LMS) seminary. Malua Fou is a Congregational intermediate school in Apia.

Mana. Supernatural power to foretell the future, heal, or control natural events.

Manu'a. Three small islands east of Tutuila in American Samoa.

Maota. Residence of a chief.

Mapu i Fagalele. Name of the old people's home near Apia. Derived from a proverb: *"Lutia i Puava 'ae mapu i Fagalele"* (suffer in the rough water off Puava but rest in Fagalele Bay).

Matāafa. A prominent *tamaaiga* title. M. Iosefo led the One-Day War, and a recent incumbent was Samoa's first prime minister.

matai. Family titleholder.

Matāutu. The peninsula and village on the west side of Apia harbor.

Mau (lit. "belief or "viewpoint"). Specifically the Samoan uprisings against Germany and New Zealand.

Mauga Mū (pron. mau-nga moo). Name of a crater in Savai'i which erupted in 1905.

māvaega. Last will and testament of a chief; also the name of a political family which supports Tamasese *tamaaiga*.

Mē. May (the month); also the annual church collection.

Mea'ole. Birth name of the Tamasese who succeeded Lealofi III and was active in drafting the 1962 constitution.

milo (pron. mee-low) Seashore tree whose bark is used to make a tonic.

Misi. Brother of Aggie's mother; also the Samoan word for missionary and miss, e.g., Misi Meki (Miss Maggie).

Mulinu'u. Long peninsula east of Apia harbor. Site of Tiafau (the traditional *malae* of all Samoa) and the present legislature.

mūmū lele (lit. "flying redness"). A fever which progresses up the limbs towards the brain.

Niuē. An island south of Samoa in the Cook group; also the area of Apia village granted to Niueans.

Nuʻuuli. Village west of Pago Pago in American Samoa.

ʻoʻa. The *bishoffia javanica* tree, whose bark is used for brown dye.

Pāʻese. Faafete's niece, who lived with the Swanns as a girl and later married Allen Pavitt.

pālagi (also *papalagi*) (Pron. pah-langi). (Lit. "burst from heaven") formerly referred to any non-Samoan, including Chinese; now only Caucasians.

palolo. Threadlike reproductive segment of the sea annelid which detaches at dawn once a year and is collected as a delicacy.

palusami. Coconut cream and sea water cupped in taro leaves and baked in an earth oven.

paopao. Small dugout canoe with one outrigger.

pāpā (lit. bedrock). Specifically the four titles of Upolu's traditional districts (Tui Aana, Tui Atua, Gatoaitele, and Tamasoalii), which make up the *Tafaifa*. See Appendix B-2.

pareu (Tahitian). Flowered cotton cloth often used for *lavalavas*.

peleue. Suit coat. White coats are commonly worn by Protestant missionaries and Samoan preachers.

Pēsega (pron. peh-senga). Area on the western side of Apia where the Mormon Church College is located.

pola. Woven coconut frond which serve as blinds around a Samoan fale.

political family. Here used to refer to related lineage, family, or village groups which have organized to support candidates *(tamaaiga)* for either the Malietoa or *papa* titles.

poumuli. Hardwood tree used for houseposts.

puʻa. Tree whose seeds are used for marbles.

pule (pron. poo-lay). Authority; also one who has authority; specifically, the six top orator positions of Savaii.

puletasi. A Samoan garment consisting of a short dress over a matching ankle-length lavalava.

Sāfata. Village on the south coast of Upolu.

331

Sāfenunuivao. A political family from the villages of Salani and Falefa, which supports *tamaaiga* from the Tamasese family.

Sala'ilua. Village on the south central coast of Savaii.

Salamāsina. First *tafa'ifa* (a woman); also name of the sister of the current Malietoa.

Sāmoa. Chain of small south Pacific islands located north of Fiji. Divided since 1900 into American and Western Samoa.

Sāmoa 'Ātoa (Lit. "All Samoa"). Specifically a call *(faalupega)*, which includes all major elements of the Samoan hierarchy; also gatherings at which all these elements are represented. See Appendix B-2.

Sāmoa mo Sāmoa. Samoa for Samoans. Slogan used during the Mau uprising against New Zealand.

Sāmoa Tūla'i. "Samoans, Arise!", the Samoan national anthem.

Savai'i. Largest and westernmost island of Western Samoa.

sega (pron. seh-nga). A parakeet whose red feathers are used to decorate fine mats.

Sei 'Aute. Hibiscus flower worn over the ear; specifically, a ladies' club to which Aggie once belonged.

sennit. Coconut husk fiber braided into twine and used for lashing.

Seumanutafa. Highest title of Apia village.

Siapo. Tapa; material made from the bark of the paper mulberry.

Si'umu. Village on the south coast of Upolu opposite Apia.

siva. (both noun and verb) Samoan dance.

sua. Ceremonial food presentation, usually including a packet of taro, a pierced drinking nut, a cooked chicken, a roast pig, and a fine mat.

Suani. Swann (proper name).

ta'alolo. A formal gift-giving ceremony.

tafa'i (lit. "stand beside"). A pair of title orators who sit on either side of a high chief to advise him.

Tafa'ifa (lit. "four *tafa'i*") Someone who has acquired the four *papa* titles and is thus recognized islandwide. See Appendix B-2.

Ta'imua. A council of seven high chiefs, originally established in 1873 as a provisional government for Samoans. Expanded to fourteen by Steinberger. Abolished by Solf in favor of a geographically representative Fono a Faipule.

Ta'isi. Title which originated with the son of Galumalemana.

Talavou. Son of Malietoa Vaiinupo, whose descendants form a lineage of the Malietoa title.

Talie. A tropical almond of the *terrinalia catappa* species; specifically, the tree in front of the LMS Mission on Beach Road.

Tama'āiga (lit. "child of the family"). Specifically a candidate or title supported by a political family for one or more of the four *papa* titles.

Tamasese. A *tamaaiga* title whose incumbents are supported by the Safununuivao and Aiga Mavaega political families. T. Lealofi III led the Mau. T. Meaole was a head of state. T. Lealofi IV acquired the *Tui Atua* title, served a term as prime minister, and later was deputy head of state.

Tanu (short for Tanumafili). Tanumafili I was the son of Malietoa Laupepa and figured in the One-Day War. Tanumafili II is current head of state.

taualuga. The last dance of an entertainment. Considered a special honor to the dancer.

taupou. Ceremonial maiden. Some titles carry the right to entitle a special girl to play ceremonial roles such as mixing kava and entertaining guests. Aggie's mother had a *taupou* title.

tautua. Voluntary service rendered especially to one's family and titleholder.

ti. A plant of the *cordyline* species used for decoration and relieving headaches; also refers to "tea," (the British drink and afternoon meal).

tifaga. Movies.

Tifitifi. Village formerly located near the seaplane landing in Western Samoa where Willie briefly managed a bush store.

Tiki. Wooden carving of a Polynesian god. Traditional with Maori, not Samoans.

Toa. Rooster.

Toāmua (lit. "first rooster"). Village six miles west of Apia, where Aggie was born. Named in honor of Pepe Maiava's fighting cock.

Tōfa my Feleni. "Goodby, My Friend," a song composed by Samoans to bid farewell to American sailors wrecked in the 1889 hurricane.

togafiti (lit. Tonga-Fiji). A trick or prank; also a medical treatment.

tona. Yaws, a disease causing skin sores and deterioration of nose cartilege.

Tua'efu. A village southwest of Apia; also the nearby estate of O.F. Nelson.

Tuamāsaga (pron. Tua-ma-sanga). Traditional central district of Upolu. See Appendix C.

tufuga (pron. too-foo-nga). A traditional Samoan carpenter. An honored position given builders of *fale* and boats.

Tūfui'opa. Section of Apia near the old cemetery which has a natural spring.

Tūgaga. Title of a Safune family to which O.F. Nelson's mother belonged.

Tūimaleali'ifano. A *tamaaiga* title, one of whose elderly imcumbents was active in the Mau uprising against New Zealand.

Tūmua. Top ranking orators of Upolu, who reside in its traditional district seats and have the right to install *papa* titleholders.

Tupua (lit. "idol"). Specifically, a high title whose incumbents are eligible for the *tafaifa* (*tupua* "crown").

umu. Samoan earth oven. Food is spread on heated rocks, covered with leaves and left to steam.

'Upolu. Most populated island of Western Samoa, site of its capital.

Vailima (lit. "water in the hands"). Name of a village above Apia; also Robert Louis Stevenson's estate.

Vaimoso. Village on the western outskirts of Apia which was the headquarters of the Mau rebellion against New Zealand.

Vaiinupō. Birthname of the Malietoa chief converted to Christianity by John Williams in 1830.

APPENDIX B-2.
THE TRADITIONAL HIERARCHY

In traditional Samoan custom, everyone belongs to an extended family or several such families, being eligible to activate membership in as many as appear in his maternal or paternal family tree. Each of these groups of relatives carries a title and usually bestows it on some member of every generation. Henceforth, he is called by that title, his own name being appended only to distinguish him from previous titleholders (e.g., Mataafa Iosefo).

Every title carries with it a role (chief or orator) and a rank in some council *(fono)*. It may also carry special perquisites: a kava-cup name, the right to have a *taupou* or carry important messages. A *faalupega* is a roster of ceremonial greetings used by a village, district, or subdistrict council to indicate what titles (or groups of titles) are included in its meetings and their roles and rankings. In this sense titles thus form a hierarchy different from those recognized by a village to those recognized islandwide.

Even before European times there was a *faalupega* greeting for "All Samoa" *(Samoa Atoa)*. It includes: the *tumua* of Upolu and the *pule* of Savaii, the *tamaaiga* (political family candidates for *tafaifa*), and the ranking titleholders of each district. This *faalupega* is still recited today at important occasions, since by implication it greets everyone. Traditionally, "All Samoa" did not meet to handle lawmaking, public services or disputes as does a modern government. These were matters for village and district councils. The role of top chiefs and orators was to establish and demonstrate what was *faa Samoa* (proper custom). They were the arbiters of acceptable ceremonial procedures, perquisites, and rankings at the highest level. In a society where recognitions are more valued than wealth, such matters can become very tense. Families will fight and die for them. As

335

families wax and wane in strength, however, constant re-adjustments and innovations are essential. It takes strong and imaginative chiefs and orators at the top to determine what is currently *faa Samoa*.

After centuries of jockying, two "crowns" emerged in traditional Samoa. One was the Malietoa "crown," originally bestowed in the thirteenth century on the family who freed the islands from subservience to the Tongans. Today the Malietoa political family still bequeaths this title, though it now has many descent lines with different candidates. The "seat" of Malietoa is in Malie.

The second "crown" is the *tafaifa*, known more recently as the Tupua crown. Its origin is even older. Legend has it that a hero named Pili divided Upolu among his sons: Aana in the west, Atua in the east, Tuamasaga in the middle, and Tolufale in Manono. His twin sons became known as Tui Aana with a seat in Leulumoega and Tui Atua with a seat in Lufilufi. Tuamasaga's title, threatened by aggressive brothers on both sides, disappeared from history. After the Tongan wars, however, Malietoa divided this area between two titles: Gatoaitele to the north, with its seat in Afega, and Tamasoalii in the south, with its seat in Safata. These four titles became known as the *papa* (foundation) titles of Samoa. Unlike most other titles, they were geographic rather than based on kinship. As a result, it did not take ambitious family groups long to realize that they too could get recognition from all Samoa if they could field a candidate who could capture all four *papa* titles.

That, however, was not an easy feat. It took almost four centuries of intermarrige, intrigue, and warfare for one family to finally acquire the necessary bloodlines, allies, and warriors. About 1650, thanks to judicious marriages, canny orators, and the war clubs of the goddess Nafanua, the *papa* titles were all bestowed on one person—of all things, a woman! Her name was Salamasina. The title was called *tafaifa* because of its four sides, and like the Malietoa title was recognized by everyone.

Even after Salamasina provided descendants with all the requisite bloodlines, it was not easy to get the district *tumua* to give their precious titles to the same person. Over the next three centuries, only five such *tafaifa* were universally recognized. It was far more frequent for *tumua* to bless different applicants or withhold their titles completely. With no warriors of their own, they had to wait for a consensus of powerful families to insure acceptance. Fine mats presented at ceremonial occasions are like ballots indicating recognition and support for the person honored. Samoan families collect and reinvest them as judiciously and avidly as westerners do money, accumulating wider recognition rather than wealth.

The *faa Samoa* game has never lost its fascination. Anyone with Samoan blood can find some title or other in his genealogy. Even those who never take a title can get in on the excitement as family members, pig raisers, mat weavers, or reciters of genealogy. The glory falls on the whole group and the stakes can be high. A winner *(malo)* can collect tribute, mount more lavish ceremonies, and dispense perquisites to their supporters. And they are well advised to be generous since their followers have so many genealogical options.

In the eighteenth century, an interesting innovation was added to this absorbing national pastime. In order to collect sufficient mats, political connections, and warriors to impress the *tumua*, some families and villages began to organize more or less permanent alliances. In this book these are referred to as "political families," since, unlike political parties, they unite around family connections. There are at least eleven political families in Samoa, some of those currently active being Salevalasi, Safenunuivao, and Aiga Mavaega.

When Willie Swann first arrived in Samoa, the rival *tamaaiga* for the Tupua "crown" *(tafaifa)* were Tamasese and Mataafa. Malietoa is not technically a *tamaaiga* (though Europeans often call him that), since he does not need to collect titles from *tumua* in order to get his "crown." The Malietoa family does have rival lineage groups, however, which put up rival contenders for their title. Gatuitasina, Moli, and Talavaou lineages are examples.

About 1830, a Malietoa named Vaiinupo acquired all four *papa* titles, thus uniting both "crowns" on one head. This was the closest Samoa has come to having a single "king." Unfortunately, early missionaries convinced Vaiinupo to disperse his earthly titles in favor of "the kingdom of heaven." This left the island factionalized again, just as the European powers were moving in.

But Europeans had rivalries of their own. Britain, Germany, America, France and once even Hawaii sent warships to the islands. The first three kept consuls in Apia, who jointly governed the European enclave (*Eleele Sa*). Each of them would have preferred a single king they could control but as it was they fell prey to the Samoan game and backed different candidates. Until the 1889 hurricane sank their warships, Germany backed Tamasese and Britain and America supported Malietoa. They provided their favorite sons (*tamaaiga*) with guns, but hesitated to go to war themselves, lest their nationals in the homelands object.

Mataafa had the support of most of the thirty thousand Samoans and would doubtless have received the four "crowns" from the *tumua* except that none of the European consuls liked him. He was too independent. In the battles that ensued, the settlers along Beach Road found themselves on the front line. Governments in Europe finally settled the matter in 1899 by agreeing to a German governor for Samoans and settlers alike. He was replaced in 1914 by New Zealand administrators. None of them, however, were able to convince Samoans that their game was over. When the islands of Western Samoa regained their independence in 1962, the basic institutions of *Samoa Atoa* were still quite visible inside its modern legislature. Safenunuivao and Aiga Mavaega political families soon succeeded in getting the *tumua* of Lufilufi to bestow the Tui Atua title on their *tamaaiga* candidate again, but no one has gone on to become *tafaifa*.

MAP 1. TRADITIONAL DISTRICTS
AND TITLES OF UPOLO

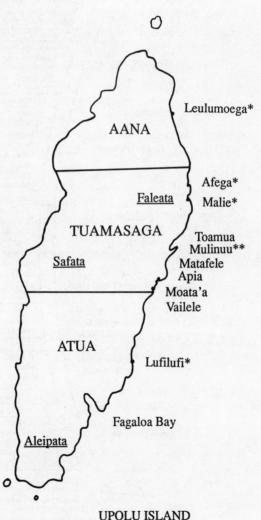

Foundation Titles (Papa Titles)
1. Tafaifa   TuiAana
    (Tupua "Crown")   Tui Atua
                                  Tamasóalii
                                  Catoaitele

2. Malietoa
    (Malietoa "Crown")

Tama Aiga
(Contenders for the Tupua "Crown")
Mataapa
Tamasese
Tuimaleaiipano

Political Families
(Alliances backing candidates for
    Tupua "Crowns")
Safenunuivao
Salevalasi
Satuala
Mavaega
  (and others)

High Orators of " All Samoa"

0   15 miles

Key
Traditional District - (capitalized)
Subdistrict - (underlined)
District Seat - *
"All Samoa" Seat - **

AANA

Leulumoega*

Afega*

Faleata

Malie*

TUAMASAGA

Toamua
Mulinuu**
Matafele
Apia

Safata

Moata'a
Vailele

ATUA

Lufilufi*

Fagaloa Bay

Aleipata

UPOLU ISLAND

339

Map 2 - MAJOR CHANGES ALONG BEACH ROAD
1880 - 1980

Bell - Kruse

Bridge
Vaisigano River

Williamson - Heathrington - British Club - Aggie's Hotel
Brown - Heathrington (Swann Chemist) - Links - Grey's Store
Heathrington - Westbrook - Carruthers
Apia Protestant Church
American Consul - Churchward - Apia Protestant Hall
Westbrook Store - Pouesi Church
Talie tree - LMS Mission - LMS Bookstore

Old Tivoli Wharf
Vacant - Merry-go-round - Alcazar - Oldehaver - vacant
Moors - Tivoli Hotel - BRI - LMS Office Building

APIA VILLAGE

Siumu - Falealili Road

Apia LMS Church
Syddall - Gebauer - Krauss/Preuss - NZ Embassy

Old Public Wharf
British Consul - Apia Hotel - Lands & Survey
MacArthur - Fabricius - Coxon - Government Dept.
St. Foy - Courthouse

Leffiifi Road

APIA HARBOR

Hellesoe - Sase - Immigration Dept.
Meredith - Market Hall - Paul Taxi - Firehouse
Meredith - Old Market
Moors Warehouse - Arcade & Tivoli Theater

Old Moor's Wharf
Moors Store - Tauese Store & Devel. Bank
vacant - Tamasu - Paul Workshop
Coe - DH & PG Hotel - German Hospital - Forsgren
Marist Brothers School

Bridge
Mulivai River

(Current Reclaimed Area)
Catholic Club - Catholic Office Building
Catholic Cathedral
Catholic Residence & Administration
Lighthouse - Johnson - Laubke - Groves - Emilio

MATAPEL

Adler Wreck
Johnson - Mackenzie Store
Methodist Chapel • Bookstore • Office Building
Dean • Maethodist Church

VILLAGE

Raratogan Church - vacant
DH & PG • Butcher • Parker • Keil • Bank West. Sam.

Post Office Road

Parker - vacant
German Consul • DH & PG • Post Office

Bandstand - vacant
Grevsmuhl • Burns Philps

Tattersall - vacant
Gebauer • Burns Philps

MacKenzie - vacant
Vaea Road

Netzler - vacant
Konradt's • Central Hotel • Coolest Spot • NPF

Nelson - Library
Nelson • Klinkmuller • Jackson • Beehive • Peta's
Meredith • Maota Alofa & Chemist Shop
DSG * Rothschild • Union Steam • Bank NZ • Polynesian Air
Swann Chemist • Krauss/Preuss • Nelson Wholesale • Pan Am • Hawaiian Air

International Hotel - RSA
Saleufi Road

Bakery • Hanneman • Gold Star Taxi • Gold Star Office

Customs - Econ. Devel.
Broyer • Hanneman • Nelson's Store
Partsch • Fabricius • Carruthers Store
Riley • Peterson • Apia Pharmacy

SOGI

Sydall • Bartley's Store

DH & PG - Treasury
Caliope Street

DH & PG - Sam. Craft - Agr. St.
Schwesinger • Concordia Club • Morris Hedstrom

Public Wharf
Latapie • Morris Hedstrom

DH & PG - Atoa - New Market
Bishop • Public Works • Morris Hedstrom • Sisters Convent School
Orange Grove • Public Works • Burns Philp

Fugalei Street

Meredith • MacDonald

Old DH & PG
DH & PG shops • Public Works

Wharves
DH & PG Warehouse • NZRE • WESTEC
DH & PG Barracks • Casino • Tusitala Hotel

340

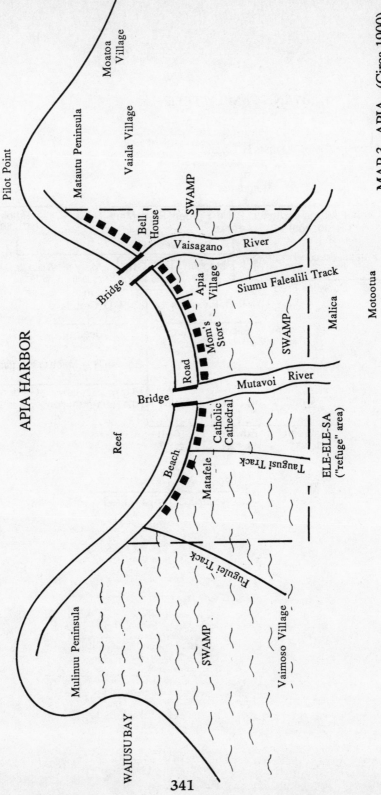

MAP 3. APIA (Circa 1900)

Pilot Point

Moatoa Village

Vaiala Village

Matautu Peninsula

SWAMP

Bell House

Vaisagano River

Bridge

Apia Village

Siumu Falealili Track

Mom's Store

Road

SWAMP

Malica

Motootua

APIA HARBOR

Bridge

Mutavoi River

Reef

Catholic Cathedral

ELE-ELE-SA ("refuge" area)

Taugusi Track

Beach

Matafele

Mulinuu Peninsula

Fugulei Track

SWAMP

Vaimoso Village

WAIUSU BAY

341

4. SWANN FAMILY TREE

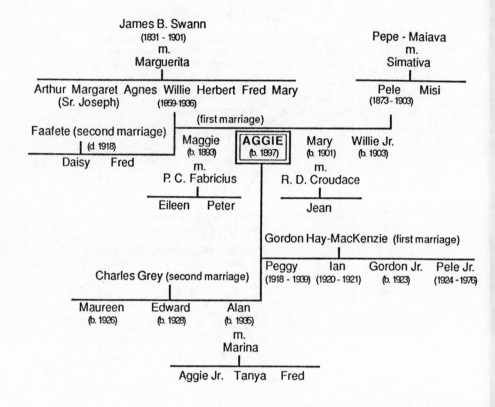

James B. Swann
(1831 - 1901)
m.
Marguerita

Pepe - Maiava
m.
Simativa

Arthur Margaret Agnes Willie Herbert Fred Mary
(Sr. Joseph)   (1889-1936)

Pele   Misi
(1873 - 1903)

Faafete (second marriage)   (first marriage)
        (d 1918)

Maggie   **AGGIE**   Mary   Willie Jr.
(b. 1893)   (b. 1897)   (b. 1901) (b. 1903)

Daisy   Fred

m.
P. C. Fabricius

m.
R. D. Croudace

Eileen   Peter

Jean

Gordon Hay-MacKenzie (first marriage)

Charles Grey (second marriage)

Peggy   Ian   Gordon Jr.   Pele Jr.
(1918 - 1939) (1920 - 1921) (b. 1923)   (1924 - 1976)

Maureen   Edward   Alan
(b. 1926)   (b. 1928)   (b. 1935)

m.
Marina

Aggie Jr.   Tanya   Fred

342

"Tales of the Pacific"

Journey into the watery world of atolls, roaring surf on coral reefs, blue lagoons, volcanoes and hurricanes, Polynesian kingdoms, and exotic brown women. Watch a cast of characters of beachcombers, whalers, missionaries, adventurers, traders, pearl hunters, mutineers, native chiefs, scientists, sun-hungry artists, and American G.I.'s. Read the best of the literature—fiction and nonfiction—from the earthly Paradises of the Pacific — the archipelagoes of Polynesia, Melanesia, and Micronesia. Enjoy dramatic narratives, short stories, and vignettes from a gallery of authors including Herman Melville, Mark Twain, Robert Louis Stevenson, Louis Becke, Jack London, W. Somerset Maugham, James Norman Hall, James Jones, Eugene Burdick, James A. Michener, and others that should be better known. Recall stirring adventures from the days of Captain James Cook and other early explorers through those of Pearl Harbor and the island-hopping campaigns of World War II!

These volumes of reprinted classics from Hawaii and the South Pacific are yours for only $3.95 each (unless otherwise noted). Editor of the series is Dr. A. Grove Day, Senior Professor, Emeritus, University of Hawaii, and author of histories and anthologies of the Pacific region.

To obtain a full description of "Tales of the Pacific" titles, write to Mutual Publishing, 2055 North King Street, Suite 201, Honolulu, Hawaii 96819. To order send $3.95 per book (add $1.00 handling fee for the first book, 50 cents thereafter). For further information or trade inquiries, call (808) 924-7732.

JACK LONDON
Stories of Hawaii
South Sea Tales
Captain David Grief (originally A Son of the Sun)
The Mutiny of the "Elsinore" ($4.95)

HAWAII
Remember Pearl Harbor by Blake Clark
Kona by Marjorie Sinclair
The Spell of Hawaii, ed. by A. Grove Day and Carl
   Stroven
A Hawaiian Reader, ed. by A. Grove Day and Carl
   Stroven ($4.95)
The Golden Cloak by Antoinette Withington
Russian Flag Over Hawaii by Darwin Teilhet
The Wild Wind by Marjorie Sinclair
Teller of Tales by Eric Knudsen
Myths and Legends of Hawaii by W.D. Westervelt, ed.
   by A. Grove Day

SOUTH SEAS LITERATURE
The Trembling of a Leaf by W. Somerset Maugham
Rogues of the South Seas by A. Grove Day
The Book of Puka-Puka by Robert Dean Frisbie
The Lure of Tahiti, ed. by A. Grove Day
The Blue of Capricorn by Eugene Burdick
Horror in Paradise: Grim and Uncanny Tales from
   Hawaii and The South Seas, ed. by A. Grove Day
   and Bacil F. Kirtley
Best South Sea Stories, ed. by A. Grove Day
The Forgotten One by James Norman Hall

TRAVEL, BIOGRAPHY, ANTHROPOLOGY
Manga Reva by Robert Lee Eskridge
Coronado's Quest: The Discovery of the American
   Southwest by A. Grove Day
Love in the South Seas by Bengt Danielsson
Road My Body Goes by Clifford Gessler
The House in the Rain Forest by Charis Crockett
My Tahiti by Robert Dean Frisbie
Home from the Sea: Robert Louis Stevenson in Samoa
   by Richard A. Bermann
The Nordhoff-Hall Story: In Search of Paradise by
   Paul L. Briand, Jr. ($4.95)
The Fatal Impact: Captain Cook in the South Pacific by
   Alan Moorehead
Claus Spreckels: The Sugar King in Hawaii by Jacob Adler